REVIEWS FOR PARTY TIME!

I can't tell you how much I appreciated *Party Time!* This is a substantial book filled with fascinating information. I especially appreciated your look at "war-mongering" traits and what you found out in terms of the breakdown in our society – 70% would go to war if country needed to be defended, 25% would prefer the UN to handle this, and 5% are those war-mongers, similar to what Paul Chappell talks about in terms of "Is humanity naturally violent or naturally peaceful?"

Quite amazing info here – from humiliation studies to the five worldviews that might underlie international conflict to the study of the pensions given out to retired college professors! And so much more. Impressive!

And I really resonate with the thought of the "Common Good Party." When I worked at the New York State Legislature, we had some local people who would go around and study government programs – they called themselves the "goo-goos" for good government. Oh for a team of goo-goos! I can tell that you are one of them!

Party Time provides a fascinating and crucial study into people's psychological traits that shape their political beliefs. Such new knowledge can give us special insight to help restore good government. This is a much needed primary text for Civics 101, American political science classes, and all concerned citizens.

—Jo Ann Deck, former legislative staffer/New York State Assembly, and human rights activist.

As one reviewer said, Dr. McConochie's research findings are provocative. I'm not a typical reader of books about politics. I've found most of them to be inflammatory and based solely in opinion. The thing that makes this book extremely unique within politics is its research-based exploration. It explores dozens of psychological traits and attitudes that define the liberal and conservative world views. I found myself throughout this book learning a lot about my own viewpoints and why I believe the things I do. Some of them, I realized, were genetic, some were environmental with the family I grew up in, and some were in place due to my own experiences as a small business owner. The first section of the book discusses the underlying psychological traits in politics. The second section offers a detailed view (based on research) of the liberal and conservative world views. The third section is all about how to create a new political party that is NOT focused on special interest groups but on common good democracy. I read this book while on vacation with my husband and it sparked three days of debates between us as we discussed, analyzed and applied to our political understanding the research that Dr. McConochie presented in the book. The conclusions are controversial and in some cases eyebrow-raising. Dr. McConochie's fascinating book sheds light on human nature, our politics and a dream for the future.

—Jennifer Revoal

"Party Time!" is a work of depth, great thought and research. This book effectively questions much of our current political system. Such questioning is more relevant than ever in our present political landscape! Yet, while critical, the message of "Party Time!" is one of hope and guidance. The author is a straight-forward, logical thinker with a plethora of creative solutions. His many suggestions and ideas provide rich fodder for consideration and practical implementation. Republicans, Democrats, and Libertarians (and, thus, our whole country) would benefit greatly from a thoughtful reading of this book!

"Party Time!" considers the implications and application of dozens of surveys, which appear to correlate closely with large randomized statistical surveys found in the public domain. I am particularly impressed by the methodologies, scales and survey instruments, which the author suggests for identifying violence proneness in kids and political leaders. Perhaps our society will take note of these instruments as valuable tools for addressing community violence and school shootings. I believe this book provides a cost-effective strategy to restore peace to our communities!

Of course, those at the extremes of our political spectrum will oppose the Common-Good Democracy form of government described in "Party Time!" But moderate thinkers will find much to like with it and the new type of political party proposed to realize it. It may be the very solution needed for our fractious political state of affairs! It can help us reduce the cankerous influence of special interest groups.

Kudos to Dr. McConochie for taking thoughtful and practical steps forward in the quest to improve our system!

—Jeffrey Robinson, MAcc, CPA, CGMA, political conservative.

Dr. McConochie presents a detailed analysis of the psychological roots of our political attitudes, on both the left and right. He makes suggestions for creating a new type of political party that appeals to the majority of citizens and unites the left and right. I met with Bill and we visited for an hour and 40 minutes about his book and my reactions to it.

I told him his book brought to mind many politicians who I told Bill might be interested in his ideas, including Senator Angus King of Maine, former Governor Jesse Ventura of Minnesota, Senator Bernie Sanders of Vermont, Representative Peter DeFazio of Oregon and some other local political leaders in Lane County, Oregon where I have been a Commissioner for many years.

When he asked me if I thought the current Democratic Party might someday morph into this new Common Good Party, I said that I did.

The 2016 Presidential primaries accentuate the need for finding more responsible candidates who we can be confident represent the interests of the majority rather than one or another special interest group, or, God help us, the will of a dictator. This book offers a practical way to do this.

—*Peter Sorenson, Lane County Commissioner*

Party Time!

How You Can Create
Common-Good Democracy
Right Now

William A. McConochie, Ph.D.

A research-based exploration of dozens of psychological traits and attitudes that define liberal and conservative political worldviews and reveal how citizens with these worldviews can unite in a new form of political party to promote common-good democracy that serves citizens as members of the community overall rather than as members of competing special interest groups.

LUMINARE PRESS
EUGENE, OREGON

Party Time! How You Can Create Common-Good Democracy Right Now
© 2014 William A. McConochie

Printed in the United States of America

Cover illustration: William McConochie and Internet Marketing Arts

Luminare Press
467 W 17th Ave
Eugene, OR 97401
www.luminarepress.com

LCCN: 2014949444
ISBN: 978-1-937303-35-8

Section III

Creating a new type of political party to unite conservatives and liberals

PREFACE

Based on his own extensive studies, along with state-wide and national General Social Survey samples, Bill McConochie offers a visionary program for addressing America's political paralysis. The most intriguing research finding is that liberals and conservatives differ far less on major issues than is usually assumed. Correlations with attitudes toward political issues suggest a far larger difference than actually exists. Most Americans, including liberals and conservatives, favor policies that serve the common good rather than special interests. Most favor a positive foreign policy (e.g., "Promote world peace and cooperation without dominating it militarily"), with liberals just slightly more so. There is plenty of room for common ground.

Guided by these results, McConochie proposes the "Common Good Party" and outlines its creation and functioning in considerable detail. While our current political system appears broken, serving special interests more than the general public, the Common Good Party would shape its policies by taking regular polls of both party members and the general public, tapping the collective judgment of citizens. McConochie believes, as his research suggests, that this new approach and party will lead to an agenda that is both progressive and serves the common good. His proposal is bold and challenging, but it just might work!

—Sam McFarland
Professor Emeritus, Western Kentucky University;
International Society of Political Psychology (past president).

Author Notes

Statistics Downplayed

I will downplay statistics in this book. If you are interested in more statistical detail, please see the research papers on my web site, Politicalpsychologyresearch.com.

Urgent Late IQ Data

Since initially writing this book I discovered in the winter of 2015-16 that human intelligence appears to be declining internationally for the first time in many decades. My research report on this appears on my web site, Politicalpsychologyresearch.com, Publications Page, Study #44.

The cause of this decline appears to be air pollution that is affecting the brain. I base this notion on numerous studies such as those reported by the World Health Organization, the U.S. Environmental Protection Agency and the California Environmental Protection Agency. This toxic process underlines the great urgency for governments to quickly eliminate fossil fuel use and release of other toxins from industry and wood burning. It thus also underlines the importance of the guidelines in this book for politically empowering the majority of citizens, who, as research shows, endorse concern for the environment and for the welfare of future generations.

Study Guide Available

Please note the study guide that is available at the end of the book. This is intended for college or university course use, and for use by book clubs.

Psychological Traits That Underlie Politics

Chapter 1

Understanding Our Minds Explains Much About Politics

National columnist Kathleen Parker reviewed a fall 2013 poll of a random sample of 2400 Americans, conducted in a joint effort by firms that had represented left and right politics (1). She concluded that there are more citizens in the middle than on either the left or the right. The country is not as divided as one would think.

She concludes: "The challenge for the moderate middle is to create an organizing principle – all things in moderation? – and produce a centrist, nonideological, pragmatic leader, preferably one unindebted to billionaires or radio babbleheads. A dream perhaps, but wouldn't it be marvy?"

My research in political psychology indicates that citizens want a new form of democracy, a form that serves citizens not as members of competing special interest groups, but as members of the community overall. One gets the impression from history that government evolves over centuries to forms that more and more closely approximate what citizens want. This implies that citizens will push for this new form of democracy.

My research also shows that strong liberals and strong conservatives, while significantly different on dozens of psychological traits or attitudes, are, paradoxically, rather close together on these same traits, and across all major dimensions of political discourse, including religious beliefs, economics and preferred type of government itself. Presumably, the political majority in the middle, as described by Parker, would fall between these two extremes on these dimensions. This book details my research findings and concludes with a detailed model for how to unite liberals and conservatives and the moderates between in cooperative political action, starting at a grass-roots level.

This model eschews central, authoritarian leadership, contrary to Kathleen Parker's longing for a charismatic political leader. Instead the model proposes distributed leadership guided by an empirically based design of a party that empowers common citizens and the candidates they select, groom and fund for leadership positions independent of financial influence from wealthy special interest groups. This distributed leadership depends on leaders from every community, leaders who are elected by fellow citizens who form thousands of active party chapters, ones in every community, every state.

Applied psychologists help clients in schools, private practices and in business and industry, applying scientific information to solve practical problems. The field of applied political psychology is relatively new. It seeks practical applications of scientific information about human nature to political attitudes and behavior.

The field of political science seems to have limited numbers of applied practitioners, based on conversations I've had with political science professors. They focus on what has happened in the past and what is going on at present, but they hesitate to predict the future, perhaps because they're familiar with research by Philip Tetlock that reveals that experts in many fields are very poor at predicting future events (2). Nor do they seem to do much if any research asking citizens what form of government they want or what specific services they want from government.

Public opinion polling companies, such as the Harris and Gallup organizations, ask citizens how they view current issues, and to some extent what they want from government, but leave it at that. They don't use the information gained to design better systems.

In my opinion, one should use science to design systems to take us where we want to go, not just to understand and document where we've been or where we are. We need to ask citizens where they want politics and government to go and then design systems to get us there. This has been my approach, using the science of psychology to explore the human mind and heart. Since 2003 I have done research studies of human traits and attitudes about issues related to politics and government and about what citizens want from government and how this might be realized. I have learned interesting and unexpected things about human political aspirations and potential.

The facts presented in the chapters that follow will challenge several current beliefs and biases of citizens on both the political left and right. Research demonstrates that citizens tend to rather strongly cling to their current political beliefs when presented with contrary information.

I write this book mainly for the general adult public, especially idealistic, energetic young adults and older adults. Young adults have the vision and drive to change systems; older adults have the money, time and concern for their nation to want to improve it for new generations. I do not write for those politicians, scientists or professional practitioners who have too much invested in the present systems of government to risk change.

I believe that only the general public can take politics and government to the new forms that will be necessary to move nations such as the United States beyond partisan conflict and gridlock to quickly and effectively solve the myriad very serious problems that face us all as a species. Small groups of leaders seem too easily corrupted by money to do the job.

Please be patient. Let me build my arguments slowly and carefully. Make notes of your objections, questions and reactions, but don't let them close your mind or this book before you're through it all. There's too much at stake.

The year 2011 was especially memorable politically. It was the tenth anniversary of the 9/11 terrorist destruction of the World Trade Center in New York City. Osama Bin Laden was found and killed. A dizzying array of Republican Presidential candidates rose and fell in popularity with weekly revelations of sexual indiscretions, memory lapses and other gaffes. In several Middle East nations violent internal conflicts and protests toppled dictatorships. The Occupy Wall Street movement erupted and spread internationally. A financial meltdown threatened in Europe, as five nations were dangerously burdened with national debt. Scientists gave increasing warnings of global warming.

How can we make sense of all these poignant events? As social phenomena? Political phenomena? Are they best explained in terms of economics? History? Religion? Philosophy?

Or as mere drama, à la Shakespeare? "All the world's a stage, And all the men and women merely players." Is it comedy à la John Stewart and Steven Colbert? Or tragedy à la fundamentalist preachers, doomsayers, Tea Party members and Occupy protesters? Reflections of public fear? Public anger?

"Much about politics originates in our minds; understanding our minds explains much about politics." This statement appears under my e-mail signature block. It reflects my confidence in the importance of psychology, and specifically in political psychology, for helping us understand and address our mutual community and national problems.

I went to graduate school in psychology and practiced for decades as a clinician. I saw that I could help individuals and even companies, but I could not see how to make an impact on wider community problems or on national and world problems. I could offer no more than just my personal opinions on these matters. Personal opinions are a dime a dozen when it comes to political and community issues. Unless I had some form of scientific credibility, some data of unique significance, my chance of making a meaningful contribution on wider social issues was nil.

In my clinical practice I developed skills for measuring human behavior, initially by building tests to measure traits for screening job applicants. I had learned in graduate school how to program computers. I bought one when I started my private practice and learned how to write programs to create questionnaires, score them, create a typed report and save the data to a file. I learned how to use statistical software to analyze the data saved on samples of 40, 50 and more persons. I wrote a program to score the 566-item Minnesota Multiphasic Personality Inventory, which was tedious to score with templates by hand.

Then I was asked by a trucking company to help them and I clarified and measured more than a dozen traits that define a good heavy truck driver. Use of this test saved that company hundreds of thousands of dollars in reduced accidents. This built my confidence about the value of measuring human traits. I then created questionnaire measures of intelligence, personality traits, knowledge of mathematics, and business management aptitude. I turned to clinical issues and measured traits such as violence-proneness, depression, anxiety and PTSD. I found that I could create very good measures of all these traits, measures that were very reliable and valid. These questionnaires were useful in my clinical work and in providing services to citizens via collaboration with an Internet company, FunEducation.com, which contacted me, asking for tests to measure intelligence for adults and children over the Internet.

In 2003, I read an article in the *American Psychologist*, the flagship journal of the American psychological Association. Roy and Judy Eidelson, Pennsylvania psychologists, presented a theory about five worldviews they believed might underlie international conflict: injustice, vulnerability, helplessness, distrust and superiority (3). They described these worldviews in considerable detail. They had not measured them or tested their theory. Because of the detail they provided I thought I could measure these worldviews. I developed an 80-item questionnaire consisting of statements such as "I am more special and important than other people are" (superiority) and "I belong to at least one group that is often very threatened by other groups" (vulnerability). Research subjects could agree or disagree with these statements on a five-point scale.

I hoped that these items would reliably measure the five worldviews as held by individuals and separately as members of groups. To check the Eidelson theory, I developed a measure of warmongering endorsement, consisting of statements such as "My national government should do what best serves our nation's interests, at the expense of other nations, enforced by military action if necessary." And "Centuries ago, the Spaniards were justified in killing natives in Central and South America to get their silver and gold."

I administered these and related questionnaire items to community college students and church groups. As predicted, the two measures, Social Disenfranchisement (my term for the five Eidelson worldviews) and Warmongering Endorsement, correlated substantially with each other; the higher a person's score on Social Disenfranchisement, the more strongly he endorsed warmongering.

This began a long series of studies. I measured dozens of traits and discovered sobering and encouraging things about human nature and political attitudes. The results suggested to me that there might be a way that reasonable and concerned citizens could empower themselves politically and more effectively than through current competing political processes. Specifically, there appeared to be a way to unite the majority of both liberals and conservatives in a new form of political party, as strange as that may seem.

Problems have been escalating but are ineffectively addressed by polarized parties and factions. Governments in the United States and elsewhere seem to cater to self-concerned special interest groups, liberal as well as conservative. Government spending and policies favoring the agendas of these groups have been taken to extremes, in some cases threatening to bankrupt states and nations.

In this book I will share my research findings, my predictions and my suggestions for empowering you, the common citizen, politically. I can see in my data a strong underlying human desire for a new form of democracy, government that serves citizens not as members of competing special interest groups but as cooperative members of the community overall—government that serves the common good.

I am not an activist, but I can imagine a new form of constructive activism that can appeal to the majority of citizens, conservatives and liberals alike. Indeed, I believe this activism is already alive and restless in the United States and in other nations.

Activism can take two forms, oppositional or promotional. Oppositional activism focuses on blocking, protesting against or fighting existing institutions. Promotional activism strives to create new and improved institutions without first opposing other ones. I believe promotional activism will be much more effective in the long run, in part because it will gain much wider public support and participation. My research suggests how a new promotional activism can constructively transform politics.

I will downplay statistics. The interested reader can get his fill of statistics by reading my research reports and essays on my web site, Politicalpsychologyresearch.com, and other researchers' articles, as referenced. The specific research publications of various researchers that I mention without referencing can be found rather easily by going to Google Scholar or Wikipedia on the Internet. The several questionnaire scales I will discuss are in manuals on my web site, Politicalpsychologyresearch.com. There one can find detailed statistical properties of the scales, including reliability and validity information.

The book is in three sections. The first section (Chapters 2 through 8) presents psychological traits that underlie political attitudes and measures of political attitudes themselves. The second section (Chapters 9 through 15) shows how these many traits and attitude measures cluster together and eventually define the liberal and conservative worldviews. The last section (Chapters 16 and following) presents a model for a new type of political party that can unite liberals and conservatives in constructive political effort that promotes the common good. In the epilogue I report analysis of poll data on large samples of citizens that confirms my findings on smaller, local samples.

Enjoy.

Chapter 2

When is an Opinion not an Opinion?

At the annual dinner show of our business executive club I wandered over to the jewelry booth and admired a large round, milky stone in a sliver clasp, part of a necklace. A young saleslady greeted me and took the necklace out of the case to display its features. I had bought a watch for my wife from her colleague a week before and wasn't in the market for another item but agreed that the stone and its mother of pearl backing were beautiful.

She asked what I did, my business category in the club. I told her I created and marketed psychological screening tests for job applicants but that my favorite current work was research in political psychology, studying psychological traits of liberal and conservative worldviews.

To my surprise she asked if I could tell what her political views were, liberal or conservative, just by looking at her. I looked at her pretty face and gazed into her penetrating brown eyes, hesitating while contemplating a reply. I explained that from my studies I knew that many of us are a mixture of the two, endorsing some conservative views and some liberal ones.

She nodded politely then said "Nobody should tell me I have to buy health insurance. And the less government the better!"

I smiled thoughtfully, and asked her without government who would build her roads.

"Humm", she replied, "I guess you're right".

I added, "Or make sure the water coming out of your tap is safe to drink, or dispose of your sewage?"

She said, "It's my opinion."

I explained that we all tend to think our political opinions are more than just opinions, but rather are facts.

She countered immediately. "But it *is* a fact! I'm right!"

I could see she was locked into her opinions, the very point I was making.

Her comments were similar to some of those in the Letters to the Editor and of columnists in our local newspaper. One citizen may complain that the Occupy Wall Street movement does not represent the 99 percent of citizens or the common good because it hasn't articulated any clear, positive agenda. Another person may be supportive of the movement, arguing that it seems to represent the dissatisfactions of the "99 percent" because virtually all of her friends are similarly dissatisfied with government.

A syndicated columnist might state that because the Occupy movement seems to have violent features in common with the Watts riots of the 1960s that it is doomed to failure. Another might offer contrary ideas, citing the constructive results of other violent public protests, such as those of the French Revolution, which began with violence but ushered in more democratic government in place of monarchy.

If questioned, each of these persons would probably assert that their ideas are likely to be "true", in the sense that they would be good for other intelligent persons to accept as their own. Indeed, they might point out that this is self-evident… they wouldn't have put their ideas in print if they didn't think they were worth other persons' adoption.

If we then pointed out to them that their ideas are contrary to other equally reasonable ideas, they'd probably say that the other ideas are simply wrong. Or, if more generous, they might back off and acknowledge that their ideas are simply their opinions. Still, they'd probably defend them as based on relevant and important information and thus very *good* opinions and maybe even better than others' opinions.

From a scientific point of view, such opinions are just opinions. All opinions are meaningful for the persons who hold them, and as such are "true" for them. But many of us tend to hold our opinions very dear and resist changing them. We tend to seek out information that confirms our current political opinions and avoid information that challenges them. We may assume that anyone who sees things as clearly as we do would agree with us and have the same opinions, or lack wisdom if they don't.

Our opinions are true for us in the sense that we are willing to base our behaviors on them. If, in our opinion, we are obligated by God to obey our leaders, even fighting in wars and dying, and that in return we will go to Heaven and enjoy endless pleasures forever there, then we can be expected to obey our leaders, go off to war and die in battle. If, on the other hand, we believe war and violence are evil, we can be expected to take the stand of a conscientious objector and refuse to fight in wars. In each case, however, the "truth" upon which we base our behaviors is a personal truth, true for us as individuals but not necessarily true for other persons. This is perhaps the "truthiness" coined by comedian Stephen Colbert.

Scientific truth is of a different nature. It is information that tends to be true for all observers who use the same observation techniques, such as those guided by the principles of mathematics, statistics and replication of studies. Scientific truth can include data gathered on human attitudes and opinions.

When it comes to social groups and community affairs, opinions of citizens must somehow be recognized and managed. Some groups live without respecting individual citizen opinions. For example, an authoritarian family can be dominated by a father or mother whose opinions are presented as rules for their children to obey without question. A school classroom can be dominated by a no-nonsense teacher who enforces her will with a switch. A church can be dominated by a pastor who tells parishioners what to believe. A national government can be run by a militant dictator whose personal will is law for all.

In a democratic system, citizens strive to acknowledge and thrive on diverse ideas and opinions, incorporating all in decision-making. In a committee meeting governed by Roberts Rules of Order, a few simple rules of procedure facilitate this openness to all opinions. We solicit ideas, propose plans for action (motions), discuss pros and cons on a motion and eventually "call for the question", putting the motion to vote. For most such issues a simple majority vote carries the matter, determining what the group will do.

Similarly, in community government we solicit public opinion. We vote for candidates for mayor, agreeing ahead of time that the majority vote will win and that we'll all live with the outcome. If the city council puts an issue to us, such as a bond measure for street improvements, we vote and accept the majority opinion to decide the issue. As such, we acknowledge that our beliefs about the bond issue aren't "facts", really, but just our personal opinions. As long as our opinions are heard and respected, as long as our vote is counted, we seem comfortable. We accept majority opinion as a statement about what is good for us all, "the common good".

For either of the two main political parties of the United States to embrace a sophisticated, detailed public polling approach to defining its party platform or setting its government agenda would require a shift of its implicit current mission, which is serving special interest groups. A party basing its agenda on public opinion would have to serve the common good.

This may expect too much of current political parties, as special interest groups, through Political Action Committees, individuals and lobbyists, are the primary source of campaign funds for their candidates. Thus, a new political party that is independent of special interest group money may be necessary.

This is especially important in light of the fact that political parties do not even have control over who runs for office under their banner. An official of the local Democratic Party in my community explained. She said that current law permits anyone to run for elective office. A person can register as a Democrat, declare their candidacy and get on a soap box, soliciting public support. If the candidate garners enough support, special interest groups will start providing him/her money. If this money is used successfully to gain more public recognition, as via mailings, billboards, radio and television ads, they can gain more special interest group support and money.

The party can choose to endorse or not endorse this candidate, but the candidate can get on the ballot in any case. Thus, persons who can "sell" themselves well enough to access the special interest group funding mechanism can rise to political power, independently of political party endorsement per se. The three key ingredients to political power then seem to be a catchy public message and image, access to special interest group money, and willingness, once in office, to promote and endorse legislation that supports the interests of the special interest groups that provide the money. This system is independent of carefully measured public opinion on policy issues of importance to the community.

The candidate's catchy public message and image can be based on "fluff"—good looks, convincing public speaking ability, messages of fear and blame against imagined foes, and other qualities peripheral to important community and political issues. The money can be from highly selfish interests, such as those of the mortgage and financial industries leading to the economic collapse in 2008, or of defense industry contractors who profit from making war materiel, whether needed or not for national defense. Politician willingness to be "bought", to support government legislation that favors campaign donors, is, unfortunately a rather wide-spread human trait, found in all too many elected officials.

Indeed, research data suggests that a new form of political party will be necessary to realize what citizens in general want from government instead of what narrow special interest groups want. This data also reveals much about human nature, good and bad, hopeful and foreboding. A thorough understanding of the psychological underpinnings of political opinions, attitudes and behavior may be necessary to assure successful species adaptation to evolving issues.

We face very serious problems, including environmental degradation, especially global warming from heavy use of fossil fuels. We are also threatened by a burgeoning world population and by escalating wealth differences between rich and poor.

The insights from political psychology and related fields, as from biology, suggest that traits that evolved millions of years ago to assure survival of the species can now threaten the species with extinction if they are not carefully understood and managed. One of these traits, warmongering-proneness, is particularly danger-ous. Fortunately, it can be measured in political leaders from a distance.

There are also interesting insights about the major political worldviews, liberal and conservative. These worldviews seem "worlds" apart when measured in one way, by correlations, but, they are actually very close together across these same dimensions of political discourse when measured another way, in terms of the average scores of strong liberals and strong conservatives.

As an introduction to these broader issues, consider data from one of my studies.(1)This study used two questionnaires total-ing 169 items measuring many psychological traits. In addition to measuring what citizens want in terms of government servic-es, the study provided measures of eleven other traits with brief scales. Four of these traits correlated positively with each other: warmongering endorsement, religious fundamentalism, religios-ity and valuing religion comprehensively. Persons who endorse one of these traits tend to endorse the others. They tend to believe that humans are basically competitive rather than cooperative.

The remaining seven scores measured the idea that the United States should end its war in Iraq, a preference for democratic rather than autocratic government, endorsement of citizen participation in government policy formation, endorsement of a positive and helpful foreign policy, endorsement of protection of the environment, kindly religious beliefs (the Golden Rule, etc.) and endorsement of human rights. These seven traits when combined correlate positively and substantially with viewing humans as basically *cooperative* rather than competitive.

The 37 items in the government services section of the study form a reliable measure of what can be termed "desired government services". ["Reliable" in this sense means that scores for people tend to vary considerably such that a given score reflects a meaningful difference from other scores. This is similar to a steel tape measure, which provides a reliable measure of how tall a person is; his height as measured by the tape measure accurately and dependably differentiates him from persons an inch taller or an inch shorter]. People who want improved government services in one area tend to want them in other areas as well. People who don't want government services in one area tend not to want them in other areas.

Scores on this measure of desired government services correlated substantially and positively with the seven-trait score measuring the cooperative, "pro-social" disposition measured by human rights endorsement, kindly religious beliefs, environmentalism, etc. Persons who endorse the seven pro-social traits tend to want improved government services.

The desired government services score correlated substantially but *negatively* with the competitive disposition measured by warmongering, religious fundamentalism, etc., as described above; persons who don't want improved government services are more likely to endorse invasive war and fundamentalist religion. They tend to depend heavily upon religion to guide their daily lives and to see humans as competitive. This disposition is suggestive of the Tea Party philosophy of not wanting government to be pervasive in society. From this study we would expect that persons who score high on "desired government services" would tend *not* to endorse the Tea Party movement.

Another way to analyze data of this sort is to compute the number of persons who endorse each trait. How many citizens endorse warmongering? How many endorse improved government services? How many see humans as cooperative? How many competitive?

In my studies I typically solicit responses in what is called a 5-option Likert scale format, asking people to tell me how strongly they agree or disagree with statements that reflect trait facets. A person's average score on the items in a scale can thus range from 1 (Strongly Disagree) to 5 (Strongly Agree). To determine how many persons endorse a trait, I use a score of 3.5 as the cutoff and compute the number of persons with average scores of 3.5 or higher.

In the present study, this frequency data was fairly typical of many such studies I've done. Two percent endorsed warmongering. 21 percent endorsed religious fundamentalism (in other studies with a longer scale the percentage has been 5 or 6). 28 percent endorsed valuing religion comprehensively to guide their daily lives. 58 percent thought the U.S. should get out of Iraq. 83 percent endorsed democratic forms of government. 75 percent endorsed a kind and positive foreign policy. 92 percent endorsed protecting the environment.

Overall, the data from this study is interesting but in some respects puzzling. Why wouldn't all citizens want improved government services, including sewer and water systems, public transportation, television and radio transmission frequency regulation, roads and military services? And why do some people see humans as basically cooperative while others see them as competitive?

And is it important that 2 percent endorse warmongering? Two percent might seem like a small and insignificant fraction, but there are 310 million people in the United States. Two percent of 310 million is 6.2 million. Some of those would be children and elderly, perhaps 2 thirds. This still leaves 2 million adults. If those two million formed a political party that advocated warmongering, as the Nazi party eventually did in Germany seventy-five years ago, what consequences might that have for the United States?

We wouldn't want our local police department to hire police officers who are violence-prone. We wouldn't want our military to promote to general rank officers who are warmongers. We wouldn't want to elect to the Presidency a warmongering politician who would deliberately engineer aggressive war against friendly nations. Can we identify such persons by questionnaires? In the next chapter we will begin to explore these psychological traits in more detail, beginning with violence-proneness and warmongering endorsement.

Chapter 3

The killer mind: Violence-proneness and warmongering endorsement

At a Rotary Club luncheon meeting I sat down next to Doug, our recently retired District Attorney. He was talking to his table mate about Kip Kinkel. I asked Doug, "Kip is serving something like 112 years?"

"Something like that", he replied.

Kinkel had murdered his parents and shot several of his high school classmates about a dozen years before in the town next to ours. My daughter was a junior in high school at the time. If she had been in his school she could have been shot and killed. I happened to know a psychologist who had counseled Kip a year prior to his homicides. He told me he couldn't see the homicides coming.

I wondered if I could help with this. I had helped heavy trucking companies reduce accidents, which can easily be fatal. For truckers, I built a battery of ten tests, including three aspects of intelligence and five personality dimensions, including safety habits, work ethic, communication habits and personal life management. The remaining were factual knowledge, one for Federal driving regulations and the other for load-handling skills, e.g. for flatbeds, refrigerated trailers or dry vans.

The company for which I first built this battery of tests was having so many accidents they were at risk for losing their insurance coverage, which would have put them out of business. Their worker compensation costs had been over $800,000 the year before we started using the battery. While we couldn't see any statistically significant correlations initially between test scores and in-house accident records for 107 current drivers, when we used the battery to screen newly-hired drivers the following year, the worker comp costs dropped to only $100,000. They dropped to $50 thousand and $25 thousand in the next two years. The company subsequently won state and national safety awards for their division. Other trucking companies that used the battery enjoyed similar benefits, one getting a million dollars back on their insurance premium in one year because their accidents dropped so much.

Because psychological traits seemed directly related to preventing *unintentional* accidents and deaths on the highway, I wondered if a questionnaire of psychological traits could measure whatever it was that underlay *intentional* deaths, homicides by teenagers. If they did, then counselors could screen teens for homicide-proneness and be especially careful to provide services to teens with high scores.

At a professional meeting I had heard a talk by a psychiatrist who had studied Kip for the court. He thought Kip was schizophrenic. I remember having my doubts at the time. From the information available, it didn't seem to me that Kip was crazy.

I asked Doug, "Did Kip plead innocent because of mental illness?"

"No", Doug replied. "His attorneys tried that but they couldn't make it stick." Doug couldn't recall just what the plea was, but it wasn't insanity.

Kip wasn't crazy, the court had determined, but he was guilty of unacceptable violence. In essence, he was violence-prone, as I had assumed when the case unfolded in the papers years before. To build a test measuring violence-proneness I had studied what psychologists had learned from interviewing several teens who had committed mass murder at their schools. They reported several traits in common, including little, if any, prior criminal behavior. Thus, they weren't criminally-inclined. The psychologists had noted academic problems and, as a precipitating event, social rejection, as by peers or parents. I wrote questionnaire items to measure these and a few other traits that seemed logically related to homicidal behavior, including unresolved anger and enjoying hostile behaviors, such as hitting others and watching movies that include killing.

This questionnaire (the At Risk for Violence test, ARFV) asked persons to indicate how strongly they agree or disagree with each statement by marking one of four options ranging from 1 to 4. One version is for teens, the other for adults. Most of the traits were measured with six items, such as these:

- School failure feelings: The grades I got in school were much lower than I could have gotten.

- Rigid thinking: When I have a problem with another person, there is just one best way to solve it.

- Impulsivity: I often make decisions so quickly that I get in trouble.

- Social rejection: I have been rejected by several persons about my age by whom I wanted to be accepted.

- Low guilt: I feel very ashamed when I lose my temper. (This item is reverse-scored, meaning that *dis*agreeing with it increases your score for "Low guilt".)

- Unresolved anger: I often fall asleep feeling mad or angry.

- Hostility pleasure: I like to play video games where I get to shoot at people, planes, etc.

- Gun skill and access: It would be very easy to get my hands on a gun and bullets during the next week without anyone else knowing about it.

- Closed to help: If I often wanted to hurt other people, I would want to talk to a professional counselor about it.

To provide an initial validation of the test I included eight items designed to directly measure endorsement of homicide as a way to solve personal problems, using these items:

- I can think of at least one person I know that I would like to kill if I was sure I would get away with it.
- I enjoy daydreaming about killing other people.
- It is wrong to kill other people for any reason (reverse-scored).
- I would enjoy shooting someone I feel angry with.
- I think a lot of teenagers these days think about killing someone they're mad at.
- I would enjoy making a plan to kill someone.
- Students who have shot others at their schools probably had good reasons to do so.
- With just a little more stress I think I could lose control and hurt someone right now.

Some fellow professionals to whom I showed these items doubted that people would actually agree with such statements. I administered the questionnaire to many groups of teens and analyzed the data. All of the items and all of the scales in the questionnaire had good test characteristics. For example all of the scales (social rejection, unresolved anger, low guilt, etc.) correlated significantly and positively with the homicide endorsement scale; persons with higher scores on the scales tend also to get higher scores on the homicide endorsement scale. And some persons agreed with each of the 58 questionnaire statements, including those in the homicide endorsement scale.

I have a friend, Dr. Lew Goldberg at the Oregon Research Institute, a nationally renowned psychology research organization. Lew was also a professor at the University of Oregon in our town. I showed him my data for this test. He wasn't surprised that some people agreed with even the homicide endorsement items. He had been commissioned by the American Psychological Association to review the data for commercially used psychological measures of lying, theft and other job problem behaviors, so called "validity" tests. He found that these tests do work as claimed. Job applicants with higher scores tend to have more workplace problems. Lew explained that people will admit to having stolen from prior employers and having committed other misbehaviors because we all tend to think we are normal. We see nothing wrong with the way we are and we're willing to admit how we behave on questionnaires.

Thus, even most people who feel like killing others will openly admit to this on the violence-proneness questionnaire. I conducted a number of studies. Teenagers incarcerated in the local county detention facility had higher scores than non-incarcerated teens on all of the scales except Closed to Help. Incarcerated teens were still open to help. Incarcerated adult male inmates in the State prison were higher than non-incarcerated male job applicants on all of the scales. And the more crimes they had committed, the higher their scores on various scales. A group of several adults who I evaluated in my private practice who had records of past criminal behavior had higher scores than clients without criminal records.

Thus, it seemed that the items and scales were measuring not just a predisposition to commit homicide but a predisposition to all sorts of antisocial behaviors of a criminal nature. And the traits measured by this instrument seemed consistent with what we knew about Kip. He had guns and much ammunition in his bedroom. He had been in trouble for throwing rocks down on cars from highway overpasses. He had a history of school coursework difficulties. He had been rejected and teased by school mates.

I took my violence-proneness test to the vice principal of a local high school, hoping to interest him in making it available to his counselors. He said they couldn't use it because they were broke and because they had too few counselors. The counselors they did have had time only to counsel students on their course planning to get into college. I asked what they did with students who made threats or gave other warnings of potentially dangerous behavior. They kicked them out, forcing them to attend "alternative" high schools. I didn't think he'd be open to hearing that social rejection, such as being kicked out of school, had been a precipitating event for several school shootings.

A school in the town next door referred to me a high school freshman for a violence-proneness evaluation. He had made a drawing with comments that suggested very hostile thoughts. His father brought him to the appointment. I had them both take versions of the violence-proneness questionnaire. I interviewed the boy about his scores. He had elevations on Feelings of School Failure, Unresolved Anger and Social Rejection.

He explained that he was in an Algebra class he couldn't understand. His father was a blue-collar worker but wanted the boy to aim for college. The boy told me he was angry at the judge. His parents were divorced but the judge made the boy and his younger sister have visitation with their mother. She was a very hostile person, the boy revealed. He had to protect his sister from her rages. The mother had tried to run their father over in the driveway. Regarding social rejection, he said that several boys that he had known since first grade didn't seem to want to be his friends any more.

The father's scores were in the normal range. He impressed me as a gentle and kind person. He had custody of the children. I gave him my suggestions, which he had asked for. I urged him to have his attorney negotiate with the judge about the visitation situation, and talk to the school counselor about finding a less challenging math class. The boy was already in counseling privately. I told the father to have the counselor read my report and help the boy make some new friends to replace the ones he felt he was losing. This all happened in the spring. In the fall I called the father out of curiosity to get an update. He said his son was back in regular school, taking an easier math class and passing it, making new friends, and feeling better about the revised supervised visitation schedule with the mother, which had been arranged with the judge.

When I sent my written report to the referring school district the prior spring, they didn't like it. They were going to have to let the boy's mother read it and they feared repercussions from her because the report exposed her seamy side. I stood by my report because I thought the counselor and judge needed the information to do justice to the case and effectively address key issues.

The school district personnel didn't seem to want to accept the violence-proneness in some students. They didn't refer any more students to me.

I'm reminded of a common psychological reaction to unpleasant news: denial. A psychiatrist, Elizabeth Kubler-Ross, decades ago, was asked to study how patients who were dying in hospitals were handling the experience. She went to hospitals but had much difficulty getting their staff to admit that their patients died, though many did as a matter of course. The psychiatrist studied the reactions to dying in detail and found that both dying patients and medical staff serving them tended to go through five stages, the first of which is denial. "Oh, I can't be dying. There must be some mistake. Were the diagnostic signs misinterpreted? Let's get a second opinion."

I remember how I reacted in fourth grade when learning of a classmate's death. I was at the boat house taking off my ice skates one winter Saturday. A friend, Peter, came up to me to ask if I had heard that Marilla Swatek had been killed with her sister and father when their car slid through the gate at the railroad tracks into the path of an oncoming freight train on their way to music lessons that morning. Shocked, I said he was kidding.

He wasn't.

Marilla was a beautiful, gentle, lovely girl. I couldn't believe she'd been killed. Only her mother was left.

Our entire fourth grade class attended the funeral.

The other stages of reaction to impending death are anger, bargaining with God or fate, Depression and, finally, after working through the first four stages, Acceptance.

I'm not sure I've accepted Marilla's death even now, 60 years later. The memory still saddens me.

WARMONGERING ENDORSEMENT

Local violence by individual citizens, like high school shooters, is tragic. International violence perpetrated by individual leaders, such as Hitler, is even more so. One of the first politically relevant scales I developed was a measure of warmongering endorsement, which I needed to test the hypothesis posed by Roy and Judy Eidelson in their article about the five traits that they believed might underlie international conflicts (injustice, vulnerability, etc.).

My first measure had been with only ten statements, as presented in Figure 1. Persons respond to these items by circling one number, 1 through 5, to indicate how strongly they disagree or agree with each statement, as in the scales presented in earlier chapters. A person's score on the trait is the mean of his answers to the individual items. Thus, scores can range from 1.0 to 5.0.

A score of 3 is neutral. 4 means "agree" and 5 means "strongly agree". Thus, persons with a mean score of 3.5 or higher are considered to be "high" on this trait. In several studies of community college students, church members and other groups, I have found that about 6 percent of citizens have scores at or above 3.5, on average, on this scale.

To explore what else might be involved with warmongering, I made scales with more items measuring other things that I thought might be involved in warmongering endorsement. I tried to imagine what known warmongers would have thought, what

> My national government should do what best serves our nation's interests, at the expense of other nations, enforced by military action if necessary.
>
> U.S. President Bush was justified in attacking Iraq and tracking down Saddam Hussein.
>
> It is more reasonable to spend money for a stronger military force than for a national health care program.
>
> It is wiser to spend more money for a strong military than for non-military peace-promoting foreign aid, trade, student exchanges and tourism.
>
> It is more honorable to serve one's nation as a warrior in combat than as an anti-war protester.
>
> The United States should have stuck it out in South Vietnam until it won the war.
>
> The United States was justified in killing off Native American Indians and taking control of their land.
>
> Centuries ago, the Spaniards were justified in killing natives in Central and South America to get their silver and gold.
>
> A good reason for our nation going to war is to kill enemy soldiers and civilians in order to reduce population numbers so there are more resources for the people of our nation.
>
> A good reason for our nation going to war is to assure access to whatever raw materials, such as oil, we need from other nations.

they would have said to their henchmen, what they would have said under their breath and thought to themselves. In retrospect, I think I had Hitler in mind as the epitome of the warmonger, a person who openly and vigorously advocated unprovoked invasion of other nations to kill soldiers and civilians alike. Not just defensive war to protect his nation against invading enemies but starting wars, offensively and without compunction. If other items correlated strongly with the original ones and if they have "face validity", looking right just from their content alone in terms of the concept as defined, then we'd have a more comprehensive and detailed understanding of this trait.

In my most comprehensive study I included 44 items.(1) Statistical analysis showed that they formed eleven different clusters, which I labeled by their content. I list them with the essence of a sample item for each:

- General warmongering endorsement: Preemptive war to prevent weapons buildups is okay.
- Nationalistic warmongering: The Roman Empire was justified in warmongering.
- Selfish cruelty: Killing enemy civilians in war to lower morale of the enemy is a good strategy.
- Vicarious warmongering pleasure: Liking to play war video games.
- Killing helpless and weak persons: Military killing of prisoners is endorsed.
- Love of weapons: Interest in bombs and weapons.
- Vengeance: Imprisonment and execution of traitors is endorsed.
- Battle planning: Would like to design battle plans.
- Nationalism: Would like to be a powerful national leader.
- Cruel self-aggrandizement: Slave labor okay in time of war.
- Survival of the fittest ethic: Ethnic cleansing (liquidation of "foreign" groups) is endorsed.

These are the items in their direct form. I compared this form with another version of the scale in which half the items were written in a reverse-score format. For example, an item in the direct form format that reads "War is a noble and glorious activity" can be presented in a reverse-scored format as "War is not a noble and glorious activity".

This reverse-form version was used to check a controversy in psychology about the importance of including some reverse-scored items in any questionnaire, to guard against what is called "response bias". I didn't think response bias would be an important issue based on opinions of researchers on the other side of the controversy.

To check the possibility of response bias, I computed correlations between the two versions of the warmongering scale with other traits included in the study. The results showed that it didn't matter which version one used. They both correlated with other traits in the same manner. And, as I anticipated, persons completing the questionnaires found the direct version more user-friendly and easier to understand and complete; to endorse the trait they didn't have to reverse their thinking on reverse-scored items. Endorsing items in the direct version always meant endorsing the trait.

When measuring dozens of traits with questionnaires up to 200 items long, as is typical in many of my studies, it's important to make the process as user friendly as practical, to maximize conscientious effort by study participants.

Thus, this expanded scale provides evidence for the complexity of the trait of warmongering endorsement. It has many facets. A warmongering type of person, psychologically-speaking, seems willing to engage in a complex of several behaviors to promote invasive war, just as Hitler did in masterminding his six years of extremely destructive aggression.

Hitler's destructiveness is especially interesting because it included hostility toward even his own people, his own nation. In the end, he believed Germans deserved to die because they had not been successful in achieving all of his grandiose visions of conquest. Such behavior is challenging to explain in terms of its value to a people specifically or to the human species in general. Perhaps it was behavior gone wild, like a cancer. Cancer is unchecked, unlimited cell growth. Some cell growth is necessary for maturing from infancy to adulthood, but unchecked growth destroys the organism.

As another example of the difficulty that people seem to have with information that demonstrates nastiness in humans, many persons, both lay and professional, have balked at my use of the term "warmongering". Some discourage me from using it because they fear others will dislike it and won't take my research seriously as a result.

I have explained that I am not measuring the more benign trait of militarism, a trait that other researchers have measured and studied. Militarism is the endorsement of military force, but without distinguishing between defensive and offensive war policy.

Holly Arrow of the University of Oregon psychology department and I did a study of 244 university students, using questionnaire items to measure how strongly they would endorse various ways to participate in war. 70 percent were willing to fight in a war to protect their country from an attacking enemy. 5 percent were willing to fight in a war to invade other nations to expand our nation's influence and power. 25 percent didn't want to actively participate in either type of war. Thus, in a sense, 75 percent were "militaristic", endorsing military activity.

The 5 percent that were willing to participate in invasive, aggressive, war, was virtually the same as the 6 percent of persons who have endorsed warmongering in many of my studies.

Warmongering is the tendency of this 5 or 6 percent of "normal" citizens to endorse war to invade other countries to expand national power and take what one wants without apology. This was the type of war I thought the Eidelsons were trying to explain with their theory. So this was the type of war I intended to study. I needed to measure the tendency to endorse offensive, not defensive war.

To gain a broader understanding of the warmongering endorsement scale and to determine its validity as a measure of this concept I ran correlations between warmongering-endorsement and other traits as presented in Table 1. The higher the number, the stronger the relationship between the traits. If the number is positive, the higher that people are on warmongering endorsement, the higher they tend to be on the other trait. A negative number means that the higher people are on warmongering, the *lower* they tend to be on the other trait. * means the statistic could have occurred only 5 times out of 100 simply by chance. ** means that it could have occurred only once in 100 studies by chance. Scientists use these levels of "significance" to indicate how confident they can be that a given study result is meaningful.

"Validity" is the scientific term for *meaning*. We speak of various forms of validity. Face or content validity refers to the content of the items in a scale. If the items "look" like we'd expect them to as measures of the concept we're trying to measure, we say they have face or content validity. Another form of validity is "concurrent" validity. If the scale correlates significantly with measures of other traits administered at about the same time, then the scale is considered to have concurrent validity.

Trait	Pearson product-moment correlation coefficient.
Political conservatism	.61**
Violence-proneness (Note 1)	.67**
Social disenfranchisement, group	.70**
Social disenfranchisement, total	.74**
Anarchy endorsement	.46**
Military dictatorship endorsement	.57**
Tribal democracy endorsement	.37**
Religious Fundamentalism	.53**, 60**
Religiousness	.44*, .53**
Anti-Muslim	.80**
Fear of terrorism	.54**
Xenophobic	.39*
Overall clinical anxiety	.54**
Claustrophobia	.40*
Fear of Heights	.60**
Anxious unless busy	.39*
Unspecified anxiety	.41*
Fear of small creatures	.37*
Fear of evil spirits	.40*
Political lying & conniving	.53**
Messianic self-image	.18**
Propaganda endorsement	.45**
Right Wing Authoritarianism (Note 2)	.59**

Social Dominance Orientation (Note 3)	.46**
Political Liberalism	-.46**
Positive foreign policy endorsement	-.74**
Sustainability endorsement	-.69**
Ecology concerns endorsement	-.60**
Human Rights endorsement	-.51**
Kindly Religious Beliefs	-.51**
Public democracy endorsement	-.36**
Big 5 Agreeableness	-.34**
Big 5 Emotional stability	-.26**

NOTES:

1. Measured by the author's At Risk for Violence scale.
2. Measured by Altemeyer's RWA scale.
3. A measure of Sidanius and Prato's SDO scale.

I'll explain the meaning of some of these traits in more detail in subsequent chapters. For the moment, note that warmongering endorsement is significantly related to many other traits. Taking these figures in order, persons higher on warmongering endorsement are rather likely to be higher on political conservatism, measured by the single questionnaire item asking how strongly a person considers himself to be a conservative. Warmongering endorsement is also substantially related to violence-proneness, as measured by the 58-item questionnaire described earlier in this chapter. Recall that this violence-proneness scale differentiates incarcerated from non-incarcerated teens and adults.

Warmongering endorsement also correlates substantially with social disenfranchisement, my term for the Eidelson worldviews, seeing the world from a perspective of injustice, vulnerability, helplessness, distrust and superiority, as will be discussed in Chapter 6. Warmongering also correlates moderately strongly with endorsement of government types that have been associated with militarism: anarchy, military dictatorship and tribal or special interest group democracy (government that serves special interest groups). Warmongering is also significantly and positively associated with the Religious Fundamentalism trait, which will be presented in detail in Chapter 5.

Warmongering endorsement is also robustly associated with many types of fearfulness, and especially for Americans, fear of Muslims and terrorists. Those high on warmongering tend to be fearful of foreigners (xenophobic), and anxious in general (clinical anxiety). "Warmongers" tend to be fearful even of closed places (claustrophobic) and of heights, and of "small creatures" and "evil spirits".

Persons who are high on warmongering endorsement tend to like authoritarianism (following commanding leaders), propaganda to sell unpopular political ideas, social dominance of powerful groups over weaker ones and political lying and conniving to win and maintain control politically. They are slightly more likely than others to endorse messianic nationalism, which is leadership inspired by religious fervor. If you are familiar with the history of World War II you may have noticed how these several traits seem to fit together, as manifested especially in the philosophy of Hitler and Nazi Germany.

Persons higher on warmongering tend to *disavow* another substantial cluster of traits or attitudes. They tend not to endorse political liberalism or a peaceful, helpful foreign policy and are indifferent to protecting the environment. They tend to disavow human rights and kindly religious beliefs, as will be described in Chapters 8 and 5 respectively. They tend to disavow government of the Public Democracy or Common Good type and tend to be lower on the Big Five traits of Agreeableness and Emotional Stability. Violence-proneness (the 58-item scale) also is positively associated with low Agreeableness. Emotional stability in this context refers to anxiety and depression tendencies, not psychosis.

As I accumulated this data I was fascinated, as over the years I had read a fair amount about Hitler's dictatorship and attitudes. I kept seeing his personality reflected in the relationships between warmongering endorsement and these other traits. Also, I was doing these studies in the early years of U.S. warring activities in Iraq and Afghanistan in response to the 9/11 attack on the World Trade Center in New York. Some Americans had expressed criticism of President Bush's motives, implying that they saw him as a warmonger.

In the next chapter, we'll explore terrorism endorsement and warmongering-proneness. Can we use questionnaires to detect citizens who endorse terrorism? Can we determine which political leaders and candidates for political office might be prone to starting wars?

Chapter 4

Terrorism endorsement and warmongering-proneness

A COUPLE OF YEARS AGO, A VERY NICE NEIGHBOR LADY HAD me and my wife and three other families over for Christmas Eve dinner. She told us that she was fascinated with a new television series, "Twenty-four Hours", which had a violent theme. I found this strangely out of character for her.

Three of the four families present belonged to my church. We all went to the 10 p.m. service that night. The assistant minister read from the book of Isaiah 9: 6, which implied the coming of a savior, "The Prince of Peace". Isaiah was a prophet who lived seven hundred years before Jesus. Jesus is believed by Christians to have filled this savior role. He preached non-violence, turning the other cheek and forgiving one's enemies.

The next day, Christmas, I read an article by Jim Salter of The Associated Press in the local newspaper about a new fad of violence among American youth, titled "Unprovoked attacks at heart of 'Knockout King'". This was described as a "game" in which a group of youths select a relatively helpless stranger as a victim who they then beat to unconsciousness and sometimes to death.

My attorney's daughter, when in high school, did a research project under my supervision. She developed a brief questionnaire measure of interest in popular music with violent lyrics. She administered this questionnaire and the Violence-proneness questionnaire to a group of her classmates. The two measures correlated positively and significantly; the more these teens liked music with violent lyrics, the higher their score on violence-proneness traits.

Some of us have violent aspirations on a much larger scale, even endorsing warmongering. To find out how violence-proneness and warmongering endorsement might be related I created a research questionnaire that included both measures and had 48 community college students complete it. I computed the correlation between the two traits. It was positive and quite substantial, as reported in Chapter 3, above. Students who had higher scores on violence-proneness also tended to have higher scores on the questionnaire measure of warmongering endorsement.

For a while I subscribed to a government service, receiving solicitations for research proposals from the Department of Defense. One of these suggested that the military might be interested in studies of terrorism-endorsement. I knew from my studies of warmongering and violence-proneness that even ordinary citizens tend to vary on their responses to questions about gristly, hostile tendencies. I also knew that we have had terrorists even among our fellow citizens here in the United States, such as Timothy McVeigh, who set off a giant home-made truck bomb in Oklahoma City, destroying much of a government building and killing dozens of citizens.

I wrote a dozen questionnaire items to see if they would form a reliable measure of terrorism endorsement. People could indicate on a five-point scale how strongly they agreed or disagreed with these items:

1. If people refused to help you with your problems, you might be justified in killing them.

2. If you are mad at the whole world, then it makes sense to destroy the whole world.

3. The United States deserved the September 11, 2001 destruction of the World Trade Center buildings in New York City.

4. I have the courage to die in committing an act of terrorism.

5. I would be willing to join a terrorist organization.

6. A good way to bring down a corrupt government is to kill its civilians in terrorist acts.

7. People who feel very mistreated by a country have the right to commit terrorist acts against that country.

8. I would enjoy steering a big plane into the Pentagon building to destroy it.

9. If I were wealthy, I would be willing to donate money to a terrorist organization.

10. I would feel honored if I were invited to join a terrorist group.

11. I want to learn more about how to become a terrorist.

12. I admire terrorists who die for their cause.

I included this group of items in several research studies that included other measures. All 12 of the items had good scale statistics and the overall scale was very reliable. The scale correlated positively with Violence-proneness overall and with facets of violence-proneness. Persons with higher scores on terrorism endorsement tended to have higher scores on Rigid Thinking, Hostile Pleasure, Homicide Endorsement, being Closed to Help, being Unwilling to Help Stop Violence and being Dishonest.

Terrorism endorsement also correlated very strongly and positively with endorsement of anarchy (no government at all) and also quite strongly with endorsement of military dictatorship forms of government. It also correlated positively with social disenfranchisement at the group level. It correlated *negatively* with endorsement of government that serves citizens as members of the community overall. Thus persons who endorse the idea of terrorism seem to be prone to violence and endorse forms of government characterized by violence. They seem to feel socially disenfranchised.

Thus, scales that measure violence-proneness, warmongering endorsement and terrorism endorsement seem to have something in common. Persons high on one of these scales tend to be high on the others. For example, the fact that terrorism endorsement correlates positively with anarchy endorsement (no government at all), means that persons who advocate no government (Tea Party members?) also are likely to endorse terrorism. This should give Republicans pause for listening to those who advocate no government.

It seems impractical to think that teaching people conflict resolution skills or anger management skills is a realistic way to protect nations from persons who endorse terrorism, violence or warmongering. The correlation between the trait of warmongering-endorsement and years of general education is virtually zero. Years of education are unrelated to how strongly one endorses warmongering. And persons who are high on these traits are unlikely to be interested in taking classes on conflict resolution. They thrive on conflict and enjoy being violent.

This is not to say that teaching conflict resolution and anger management skills isn't worthwhile. It's only to say that it is unrealistic to think that this is an effective way to change all citizens to assure that no one or a few of them will become dangerous warmongers who can get control of a nation and wreak havoc, as did Hitler.

To protect nations from war then, the trick seems to be figuring out some way to identify warmongering-prone persons and keep them out of high political and military office. As we saw in the previous chapter, there is a very rich and robust complex of traits that are associated with the endorsement of warmongering. Because warmongering as a *behavior* is very important to the welfare of nations, I wondered if there might be a way that citizens could predict whether a given political leader was *prone to warmongering*, a psychological trait or predisposition.

We couldn't expect a candidate for political office to fill out a questionnaire measure of this trait or of other traits measuring potentially embarrassing characteristics. But, to the extent that traits associated with warmongering are publicly observable, as by analyzing writings, public speeches or a politician's voting record on policy issues, I thought we might be able to rate a candidate on his "warmongering-proneness".

I created a 50-item rating scale to measure many of the traits that correlate significantly with warmongering endorsement.(1) A pastor friend of mine in my Rotary club was willing to help validate this scale. Twenty adult members of his church rated two prior candidates for President, George W. Bush and John Kerry. They did this in about 2004 or 2005, several years after these men had run for office.

Here are a few of the items in this scale. Rating options range from Strong evidence *against* the trait (rated 1) to Strong evidence *for* the trait (rated 5).

- Does the person belong to a group, organization or social class that feels distrust of other groups?

- Does the person tend to think rigidly, inflexibly, unable to consider alternative points of view, alternative courses of action?

- Does the person seem to have a reservoir of unresolved anger? For example, does he/she bear grudges?

- Does the person maintain an authoritarian stance vis a vis other persons or groups?

- Does the person hold fundamentalist religious beliefs, e.g. that there is only one true God and that anyone that disagrees with this belief is wrong?

- Does the person disavow international arms control treaties?

- Does the person have a disagreeable personality, being oppositional, irritable, contrary, argumentative or unsupportive of others?

Frankly, I had my doubts about whether citizens would be able to rate political leaders on such traits. However, the ratings for Kerry and Bush were very interesting. For each rater I computed the mean item score across all fifty items for Kerry and then for Bush. All twenty of the scores for Bush were higher than those for Kerry.

Keep in mind that the church members were not asked by me or in the questionnaire instructions to rate these two leaders on warmongering-proneness per se. They were only asked to rate them on each of the specific fifty personality trait items in the questionnaire.

I then invited more ratings by adult friends of mine who felt confident that they knew political or historical leaders very well, as from reading biographies or autobiographies. I gathered many ratings on many leaders, including scores for Gandhi, Mandela, Lincoln, Eisenhower, Churchill, Hitler and Stalin. I then computed the average score across raters for each leader.

The score for two raters of Mandela was 1.16. For five raters of Gandhi the score was 1.71. Jimmy Carter's average score was 1.73. Other scores were George Washington 1.82, Truman 1.84, Lincoln 1.92, F.D.R. 1.98, Bill Clinton 2.09, J.F.K. 2.10, Teddy Roosevelt 2.12, Churchill 2.20, Eisenhower 2.29, Woodrow Wilson 2.47, Lyndon Johnson 2.56, George H. Bush 2.60, George Patton 3.11, Napoleon Bonaparte 3.64, Alexander the Great 3.73, Genghis Khan 3.98, Attila the Hun 4.04, Stalin 4.21, Hitler 4.50 and Saddam Hussein 4.68. John Kerry's score was 2.12. George W. Bush's was 4.00.

To validate the new scale as a measure of warmongering-proneness as a rated psychological *trait* I needed scores for the leaders on their rated warmongering *behavior*. To get this I had another group of church members rate the various leaders on a separate single item measure of their actual warmongering behavior, or lack thereof, as military or political leaders.

I then computed the correlation between this score and the scale scores. The correlation was positive and very high, consistent with the hypothesis that the scale would measure warmongering tendencies, "warmongering-proneness".

I found it interesting that some military leaders, notably George Washington and Dwight Eisenhower, were *not* high on warmongering-proneness. This seems to reflect my intention of the scale to measure not the general trait of "militarism", the endorsement of military strength in general, but the trait of initiating aggressive, destructive wars.

By this scale, then, G. W. Bush appears to have psychological traits that may have predisposed him to look for opportunities to send troops into battle, not just to defend but to aggress. This seems consistent with some critics' views of his invasion of Iraq as unjustified because there was no confirmed evidence that Saddam Hussein and Iraq had any direct connection with Osama Bin Laden and his attack on the World Trade Center in New York.

And Bush seemed to think his mission was accomplished once the war in Iraq appeared to be won. In this he seemed indifferent to the fact that Osama Bin Laden was still at large and thus still posed a threat to the United States as a terrorist. Was he more interested in waging war than in tracking down a single terrorist?

His high score on the warmongering-proneness scale is consistent with the possibility that President Bush used the 9/11 attack as an excuse to invade a Middle East nation, perhaps to increase U.S. military presence there to assure access to oil or perhaps simply to exercise a personal proneness to wage war as a national leader.

As I was writing this chapter in December of 2011, our local newspaper announced that Rod Blagojevich, ex-governor of Illinois, had been sentenced to 14 years in Federal prison. And that two of his four predecessors in that office had been sent to prison as well. I grew up in Illinois and felt ashamed learning of such leadership. Could the warmongering-proneness scale warn of such criminal tendencies? The violence-proneness test seems to signal all sorts of criminal behavior, not just violence-proneness. I expect the warmongering proneness scale will too. If it does, it may warrant another name, perhaps the Wayward Leadership Behavior Proneness Scale. Or perhaps we should develop a separate rating scale that measures white-collar-crime-proneness.

The warmongering-proneness scale could be used to assess candidates for top Federal offices, especially the Presidency. If you're interested in doing this, go to page 244 and copy the Warmongering Proneness scale with its rating options, 1 through 5. Find 6 or 8 persons who feel familiar with the leaders you'd like to rate, e.g. perhaps Trump, Rubio, Cruz, Sanders and Hillary Clinton. Have them independently rate those candidates. Score the test using the instructions that accompany the scale, finding the average for each rater and then the average across the raters for each person rated. Discuss the results. Do they make sense to you?

With practice and care this process could be used by journalists. For example, in the Parade insert of major newspapers every January a group of journalists report on what they consider to be the world's worst dictators. The report is also available online at Parade.com/dictators. The top five for 2011 included Kim Jong-Il of Korea and Bashar al-Assad of Syria. These choices are based on information from several organizations, including Georgetown University, Human Rights Watch and the U.S. State Department. Journalists, university students or State Department personnel could use the warmongering-proneness scale to facilitate these rankings of national leaders.

Citizens could use the scale to score candidates for high political office, including Governors, Congressional Senators and Representatives, and the President. Military organizations could use it to assess candidates for high military office. Political parties could use it to screen their party leaders and their candidates for elective office.

Now you might wonder if a rating scale could also be developed for measuring the opposite of warmongering-proneness. I think it can. My Constructive Leadership Attitudes scale is designed to do just this. It too is based on the same trait research but asks if the person to be rated has evidence of the traits that correlate negatively with warmongering-endorsement, such as Human Rights Endorsement, endorsement of a Positive Foreign Policy, and endorsement of Common Good Democracy, government that serves citizens a members of the community overall rather than as members of special interest groups. I have only a little data on leaders rated with this scale. Obama seems higher than John McCain. You can help create more data by carefully rating leaders with whom you are well familiar. You can do this also at my web site, Politicalpsychologyresearch.com, Help Do Research Page, Study #7.

Criminal behavior can surface in unexpected places, in unexpected people, including elected officials and other presumably trustworthy, admirable folks. In 2010 Cliff Harris was an All-American defensive back for our Oregon Ducks football team, which finished second in the nation behind Auburn. In December of the next year he was kicked off the team for repeated criminal behavior in the community.

A classmate of mine from Carleton College in Minnesota was sent to Federal prison. He was fascinated with firearms in college 50 years ago and became a national expert on American antique firearms after graduation. But as a businessman dealing in them he went astray.

Warmongering-endorsement correlates substantially with religious beliefs, correlating positively with fundamentalism and negatively with kindly religious beliefs. How is it that frequently the Old Testament of the Bible presents tales of war promoted by God but in the New Testament the emphasis is largely on kindness, turning the other cheek and peace? Why does the Koran, the Muslim holy book, speak of both peace and of religiously righteous missions of war? In the next chapter we'll find clues, examining the details of fundamentalism and kindly religious beliefs.

Chapter 5

The cozy relationship between religious beliefs and politics

In January, 2010, one of my best high school buddies died alone in his apartment in a suburb of San Francisco, apparently of a heart attack. I'd last seen him a couple of summers before when I attended the Stanford Summer Institute in Political Psychology. Hunter had very kindly entertained me one full weekend, showing me the countryside, visiting over lunch in an eatery near one of his former advertising job offices and taking me to a little country tavern that Jack London had frequented in the early part of the century.

As we drove around on the expressways he asked about my research in political psychology but seemed to enjoy more telling me about his opinions on politics, waxing wise on one theme after another, a habit he had shown even back in our high school days. He'd majored in philosophy in college and had read on many topics since.

His brother, daughters and friends planned a service for him in March. I made plans to attend but then misjudged the airline schedule and missed my early morning flight. I called the folks hosting the service and apologized. I felt guilty and disappointed. To play on my violin at the service I had made up a little tune that was based on the theme of Taps. Hunter and I were both Scouts as kids. We'd sung Taps in the evenings at Boy Scout camp.

I'd also written a few words about what a wonderful friend he had been to me, teaching me to hunt pheasants and to play the guitar. His dad had let me use their table saw to cut hard birch boards to build a couch/bed for my first apartment after college.

Hunter had sent me a metal box of brass boat hardware, bits of which I'd used in building a sailboat many years ago. I called his daughter, who forgave my snafu and graciously offered to read my comments at the service.

I felt guilty for letting Hunter down. I hadn't attended a church service except for a few funerals for several decades…probably not since my college years. But I decided to go to a church the next day out of respect for my friend. It didn't make much sense, because I didn't believe in supernatural beings, but I still felt an obligation to go.

I called the local Congregational church near the university and attended a class at 9 a.m. the next morning and then the service at 10 a.m. The class caught my attention, being on violence and the Bible. The pastor led the discussion. The parishioners voiced all kinds of opinions on the wide range of philosophies reflected in the Old and New Testaments, ranging from violent, almost genocidal, warring in the Old Testament to turning the cheek and forgiving enemies in Jesus' sermons. The pastor encouraged and respected any and all opinions.

I shared some of my research findings of two different factors or clusters of religious beliefs, one that seems to dovetail with the warmongering endorsed by many of the Old Testament writings and another that seems to dovetail well with Jesus' teachings of kindness, cooperation and forgiveness. These ideas were also taken in stride by the class.

I was hooked. Within a couple of months I had joined the church. While I had to agree that Jesus was my route to God to join, it was made clear that I could define both Jesus and God in my own terms; there was no church definition to which one had to ascribe. That made it easy. For me, God is the universal spirit of human goodness and kindness. I knew from my research that something like 43 percent of citizens, even churchgoers, are comfortable with this definition of God, so I didn't feel like an oddball.

I had created this definition of God from my experience as a member of Rotary International during the prior 21 years. In our weekly lunch meetings we begin with an invocation, but we're careful not to refer specifically to the Christian God, for there are Rotarians all over the world of many different religious orientations. Rotary is also careful to avoid political partisanship.

Rotarians are remarkably compatible with each other, even though they vary from soup to nuts on political opinions and religious beliefs. They are friendly, kind, helpful to a fault and generally fun to be around. They get a lot done in their local communities and internationally, raising money and providing community service ranging from picking up trash along highways to eradicating polio through a worldwide immunization program. They promote peace by sponsoring 70 or so students to master's degree programs in peace studies every year. I could see God at work through Rotarians, God defined in my mind as the universal spirit of human goodness and kindness.

In December, 2011 I received an e-mail weekly update from the Pew Forum with a reference to ten religion news stories of the week. Obama rejected a request to let anyone of any age buy the controversial morning-after pill under Plan B of Medicare. Another headline read "Europe's radical right focuses on fighting Islam". Another was "Fearful of Egypt's Islamist surge, Israelis see mainly disaster in the Arab's world's elections." Another story asked "Who will replace the faith-based donors?"

I mulled over religion. The United States was founded on an interesting mix of attitudes about religion and authority. The founding fathers were careful to avoid creating government that gave overpowering authority to a leader, such as the authority of monarchy, as exercised by English kings. On the other hand, while they declared themselves obligated to form a new nation, separating from England, they justified separating from England by reference to inalienable rights given to humans by none other than

God himself, their ultimate authority. But, they were careful to design the new national government with checks and balances so the top leader, in the form of President, could not exercise excessive authoritarian power.

The Bill of Rights soon followed, clarifying respect for any and all religious beliefs. However, the leaders implicitly separated church from state, giving no one religion or religious authority per se a seat in government. They perhaps remembered vividly the bloody religious history of England and wanted to avoid a repeat. In spite of this arms-length policy regarding religion, religion has permeated U.S. national government in various ways. A newly elected president is sworn into office with hand on the Bible and a pledge under God to serve well. And government declares "In God we trust" on our money, ironic, considering Jesus' anger toward the money lenders in his day doing business at church.

Psychiatrists and psychologists for many decades have theorized about the possible presence of two different types of human religious thinking. They describe one form of religious thinking that as literal, rigid and associated with conflict, and another that is more humanistic and accepting of differences between peoples. The initial theories were based on observation of religious writings and practices. William James, Sigmund Freud early in the 20th Century and Eric Fromm later have theorized about the nature and meaning of human religious beliefs.

Psychologists and psychiatrists have by various methods hypothesized or documented with research two or sometimes more types of religious and spiritual belief systems as basic human traits. For example, psychoanalyst and psychologist Eric Fromm postulated theoretically two types of religion, which he defined as authoritarian and humanistic. Psychologist Bob Altemeyer developed a reliable questionnaire measure of what he called religious fundamentalism by simply brain-storming with a colleague to write questionnaire items. This fundamentalist orientation has been found in studies to be associated with authoritarianism and prejudice; persons higher on fundamentalism tend to be higher also on the other two traits. Psychologist Gerard Saucier has analyzed the English language, specifically words ending with the suffix "ism". Statistical analysis of these words has revealed four basic clusters. One of these seems to be the fundamentalist religious orientation, as measured by Altemeyer and others.

I studied religion by taking a sample of basic beliefs from several major world religions and asking in a questionnaire how strongly people agreed with each of the beliefs (1). In repeated samples of church members, college and university students, and others I found via statistical analysis that these beliefs fell into two main clusters. One matched the fundamentalism type of religion.

The second cluster I labeled "kindly religious beliefs", based on the content of its items, which included endorsement of the Golden Rule, treating others as you would like to be treated, seeing God as forgiving of wrongdoers and eschewing violence toward other humans. Over the years I have found other questionnaire statements that fit into these two scales, clarifying the essence of them as human religious orientations.

I have found that there is considerable value in studying human nature not by studying specific types of humans as social groups but by studying a topic as a psychological trait. For example to study religious beliefs, instead of studying groups, e.g. Southern Baptists, Mormons, Sunni Islamists or Orthodox Catholics, I study religious beliefs as psychological traits. While it can indeed be valuable to study specific groups, it is often much more convenient to study traits that are characteristic of those groups.

Gerard Saucier, a psychology professor, used university students to identify the several spiritual belief types embedded in or reflected in words in the English language. A mutual friend of ours, Lew Goldberg, has used a sample of 800 or so local community adults in a decades-long series of studies of human personality traits of wide variety. Similarly, I have used community college students and other groups to identify traits such as warmongering endorsement, violence-proneness, terrorism endorsement and my two types of religious beliefs.

There are two especially valuable sorts of insight one can gain by this trait approach to studying human nature. One is by looking at the content of the items that make up a reliable questionnaire measure of traits. The other is by studying the relationships between traits.

A reliable questionnaire measure, by definition, is made up of items, which often can be referred to as "statements", all of which tend to hang together statistically. This means that they all tend to vary together. That is, a person who endorses one of the statements in the scale is likely to endorse the others. For a measure of fundamentalism then, we learn from a reliable scale that a person who agrees that "there is only one true God", is also likely to believe that God is a real, supernatural being, not a human concept. If we hear a preacher or lay citizen voicing one of the beliefs measured in a reliable scale, we can guess that he is likely to endorse the others.

Consider, for example these items in my 22-item scale of religious fundamentalism:

1. There is only one true God.

2. Anyone who doesn't believe that there is only one true God is wrong.

3. There is only one source of absolute truth, the holy religious scriptures or writings of my religion.

4. The scientists of my religious faith discover more accurate truths by their methods than do the scientists of other faiths.

5. If a scientist of my religious faith discovered a fact that appeared to contradict the teachings of my faith, that sci-

entist should seek advice from our religious leaders about publishing the findings.

6. The stronger I believe in my religious faith, the more that all of my other beliefs, choices and opinions will be the right and truthful ones.

7. If people of other religious faiths have beliefs, choices and opinions that are different from mine, they are probably wrong.

8. God is a real, supernatural being, not a human concept.

9. Everything in my preferred holy religious scriptures or texts is true as written.

10. There are fundamental, unchanging religious truths that are more important than any other realities.

11. There are eternal religious truths that should be conserved, kept sacred, believed and obeyed without question.

12. People who believe in my God are God's chosen people.

13. We should give financial help only to the needy of our own religious faith.

14. I depend on the religious leaders of my faith to always know and explain the truth about God's will.

15. Men are the natural leaders of religious groups and families.

16. God punishes wrongdoers.

17. Only the righteous are favored by God.

18. Competition between peoples is a natural part of religious struggles.

19. It is natural that we compete against people of religions different from our own.

20. When people attack us, we should attack them in response.

21. God expects us to help Him destroy His enemies.

22. Armies cannot win without the blessing of my God.

Notice the various themes represented by these items. One is a rigidity of belief, as reflected in items 1, 2, 3, 4 and 9. Another theme is dependence on authority, as reflected in items 5 and 14. Another theme is militarism, as reflected in items 18 through 22. From these themes we could guess that this scale might correlate positively with separate scales of rigid thinking, e.g. from the At Risk for Violence test, and with authoritarianism and warmongering endorsement.

We might also expect this 22-item scale to correlate positively with a questionnaire made up of statements that reflect political attitudes of a fundamentalist religious flavor. And it does. It correlates positively and significantly with a scale made up of the following items, which also form a very reliable scale:

1. In it is quite proper that key religious writings be inscribed on public buildings.

2. Our nation cannot be strong unless it is favored and blessed by my God.

3. Prayer should be a regular part of meetings of government officials.

4. It would be good if all public school children began their school day with a prayer.

5. It would be good if all public school teachers were members of my preferred religion.

6. It would be good if the basic truths of my religion were taught in public schools, e.g. about God and how the world was created by Him.

7. Artificial contraception and abortion are against the will of God.

8. Government should support legislation that promotes my religious faith.

9. Religious values are of paramount importance in politics and government.

10. The truths of my religious faith should strongly guide government in my community, state and nation.

11. The truths of my religious faith, e.g. about how the earth was created, should be taught in public schools.

12. The values of my religious faith, about family and sexual behavior, should be taught in public schools and promoted in public laws.

13. Government laws should permit no abortions except under very special cases as specified by religious leaders of my faith.

14. Our national Pledge of Allegiance must always have in it the phrase "under God".

15. Our money should always have printed on it "In God We Trust".

16. It is entirely appropriate that the United States Declaration of Independence included the phrase "endowed by their Creator with certain unalienable rights".

Again, because this second scale is reliable, we can with confidence predict that if we hear a citizen voicing one of the beliefs in it he or she is likely to agree with the others.

And we can take this a step further. It would be unlikely that we could get fundamentalist religious congregations to complete a questionnaire about their private, secret, "politically incorrect" attitudes about government. But, with a questionnaire administered to a general group, such as community college students, we can explore what these beliefs might be. If a scale of them is reliable and correlates positively and substantially with our first two scales of fundamentalist religious beliefs, then we will have a basis for looking into the "secret" mind of fundamentalists. We can create items, guessing what they might be. If they form a reliable scale that correlates positively with the first two scales, we can be confident that the items are likely to reflect the thinking of persons with fundamentalist religious beliefs.

The following items form a reliable scale that correlates positively and significantly with the two prior scales:

1. The more people there are who believe the principles of my religion, the more secure I feel.

2. The more that people believe in my religion, the truer its principles are.

3. My religion is the best way to explain a confusing and frightening world.

4. The stronger my religious faith is the truer are all my other beliefs.

5. The principles of my religious faith are universal and everlasting and therefore should be the basis of all my nation's government policies and programs.

6. My religious beliefs give me much comfort when I think about death.

7. A simple, clear religious explanation of the world comforts me more than a complex, scientific explanation.

8. I find comfort in imagining a perfect place, like heaven.

9. I feel most safe when I am at religious services and activities,

10. Repeating prayers and religious hymns and songs is a good way for me to block out the worries of the world.

11. If I had enough religious faith, I could be given enough power by God to do a miracle, like walk on water.

12. If I had a vision of an angel or of God, I would feel more happy than scared or concerned.

13. My religious faith comforts me like a spiritual security

blanket.

14. It would be good if the principles of my religious faith influenced all government policies and programs.

15. I am confident that when I die I will see God.

16. I believe I will live forever in heaven.

17. If I were a government official in charge of hiring or awarding contracts, I would give preference to members of my own religious faith.

18. Government should give special privileges to radio and TV talk shows reflecting principles of my preferred religious faith.

19. The First Amendment to the United States Constitution should be repealed because it prohibits the establishment of a national religion or government preference for one religion over another.

These items reveal underlying beliefs that go along with the more overt, public beliefs reflected in the first and second scales. They help explain policies that some politicians, those who want to appeal to fundamentalists, might promote, especially some rather extreme and controversial ones, such as reflected in items 5, 14, 17, 18 and 19.

Thus, we can see in these fundamentalist religious beliefs grounds for pressure on national governments to defer to religious authority. In spite of the aspirations of the authors and signers to the United States Constitution and related documents, there is reason to believe that some U.S. citizens even today prefer that religion and government not be separate but melded in one authority, as is found in some Middle East nations.

Next, consider statements in the other religious beliefs type, Kindly Religious Beliefs. By "types" of religious beliefs is meant that these are two clusters of beliefs that tend to occur independently of each other. That is, a person's score on a measure of one of the two types will generally give no clue as to how he would score on a measure of the other type. It's akin, for example, to the independence of human intelligence and skin color. Knowing a girl's score on an intelligence test gives us no clue as to what her skin color will be. Or, knowing how many years of education a woman has will give us no clue as to how extroverted she is. These are all characteristics of humans, but they vary independently of each other, they are separate "factors", statistically speaking.

Here are items in a basic measure of Kindly Religious Beliefs:

1. God takes many forms for different peoples around the world.

2. God forgives wrongdoers.

3. Violence against fellow humans is inappropriate.

4. The peoples of all civil religions are equal in God's eyes.

5. God can be well defined simply as the universal human spirit of goodness and kindness.

6. There are better ways than war to resolve conflicts between nations.

7. Religious truths come from many sources, not just religious scriptures and texts.

8. There are many worthwhile non-religious sources of spiritual guidance for humans.

9. Kindness toward persons different from us is a primary spiritual virtue.

10. God expects us to forgive our enemies.

11. I can read and understand religious writings even without the help of my preferred religious leaders.

12. Cooperation with people unlike us is an important religious value.

13. We should give financial help equally to the needy, regardless of their religious faith or whether they believe in God.

14. When people first offend us, we should turn the other cheek and forgive them.

15. We should cooperate with people of religions different from our own.

16. We should be kind toward people whose religious beliefs differ from our own.

17. God expects peace on earth.

18. Violence toward people is inappropriate.

19. We should do unto others as we would want them to do unto us.

Notice the themes: forgiveness, turning the other cheek, and promoting peace rather than war. Another is general kindness, even toward persons different from one's own group. Notice item 5, the notion that God can be well defined simply as human goodness and kindness, the author's preferred personal definition of God.

We can also explore the political dimensions of this religious orientation by creating a scale with more political content. If the scale correlates with the first one and is reliable, it will tell us something further about religion and politics. The following scale is reliable and correlates positively with the first one.

1. Different human groups have different and equally valid religions.

2. Basic religious truths change, evolve and improve over the centuries.

3. In general, religion and government should be kept separate.

4. Our government should not favor any one religion over any other.

5. Our government should not favor religiously devout citizens more that citizens who do not believe in religion or

God.

6. Citizens of our nation should be free to worship their preferred religion, such as Christianity, Islam, Buddhism or Shintoism, or no religion at all, as long as long as their faith respects civil laws.

7. Prayers and other religious rituals, including religious songs and music, should not be part of public school activities except as cultural or educational experiences.

8. Specific religious beliefs, such as Creationism, the Christian idea of how the world was created by their God in six days, should be taught in public schools only as part of a formal course on several religions, if at all, and only as a religious belief, not as scientific fact.

9. Whether a woman has an abortion is primarily for her and her doctor to decide and should not be governed by other citizens' religious beliefs.

In this scale we see items with clear government policy import. Some persons agree with these items. Thus, for some citizens, religious beliefs underlie political and government policy attitudes. And, as we saw with fundamentalism, we can take this process of exploration one step further, with more "extreme" scale items, as reflected in the following reliable scale:

1. I am comfortable around people who have religious beliefs very different from my own.

2. I use several sources of information as good as or better than religion to guide myself through life.

3. To handle fears, I depend on non-religious information as much as or more than on religious information.

4. To manage temptation, I often use techniques other than religion.

5. To keep a separation of church from state we should not

print "In God We Trust" or other religious slogans on our money.

6. To help keep religions separate from government, elected government officials should not say "God bless America" or other such religious statements in their public speeches.

7. I prefer patriotic songs that do *not* contain references to God.

8. Religions are created by humans to give them spiritual guidance.

This scale correlates positively with the first two for Kindly Religious Beliefs and thus suggests thoughts of some citizens and their attitudes about ideals for government. In addition to studying reliable scale items, we can gain insights into religious beliefs by studying the relationship between scales of religious beliefs and measures of other beliefs.

The first fundamentalism scale presented above is positively associated with Saucier's measure of a similar trait, Altemeyer's Fundamentalism scale, and with Religiousness (frequently attending church, praying, reading scripture, etc.). It is also positively associated with several fears: fear of heights, travel, being alone, fear of fate, evil spirits, and closed places. Americans higher on this fundamentalism scale tend to fear Muslims. They tend to fear small creatures and even body weight changes. They tend to be higher on warmongering endorsement.

Fundamentalism is negatively associated with endorsement of human rights, sustainable policies and programs, and a scale of friendly foreign policy endorsement. That is, persons higher on this fundamentalism scale tend *not* to endorse these other traits.

Kindly religious beliefs, as measured by the scale above, are positively associated with endorsing human rights, a positive foreign policy and sustainable policies and programs. Kindly religious beliefs are negatively associated with Saucier's measure of what appears to be selfish materialism. It is also negatively associated with warmongering endorsement, and with Altemeyer's fundamentalism scale.

Thus, these two apparently basic religious belief orientations are related to traits that are involved in political attitudes. Like it or not, religious beliefs are intimately related to politics.

CHAPTER 6

ACTIVISM, PROTEST AND HOPE: THE OCCUPY MOVEMENT, SOCIAL DISENFRANCHISEMENT, OPPRESSION, HUMILIATION AND SOCIAL AND POLITICAL ACTIVISM

THE OCCUPY MOVEMENT

She lacked her front teeth. Her face was lined and weathered. Her blue eyes held mine with a steady and determined gaze as she talked with vigor and conviction. The problems of society could all be solved if people simply followed the word of Jesus.

We were sitting on five-gallon buckets on a December day in 2011 surrounded by Occupy Eugene tents in a city park. It was chilly but the sun was out and David and I were having good luck getting Occupy Eugene members in the camp to fill out my questionnaire. David, a friend from church, had invited me to some Occupy meetings and out of that came support for a research project. I'd almost given up on the Occupy group because of their lack of follow-through to my initial overtures a month earlier.

At a friend's invitation I had attended an agenda committee meeting of our local Occupy movement in the fall. About 20 people were in the church, including Tony, a scientist friend of mine from the Oregon Research Institute and Bob, a professor from a nearby university. Bob heads a sustainable community studies program and writes a monthly column for the local newspaper.

The meeting appeared to be one of the first for the committee. All present were asked to introduce ourselves. We debated how to conduct the meeting and agreed to simply take turns going around the circle, stating our personal main concern or agenda item for the movement. The leaders jotted them down, as I did while waiting my turn.

These were the concerns: hold Congress and Wall Street accountable for collapse of the economy, regulate Wall Street, get the money out of politics, promote objectivity of the media, let citizens participate in deciding how government money is spent, provide universal health and dental care, shift the nation from a "me" orientation to a "we" orientation, protect the environment, tax the rich more, reduce big corporation dominance of government policy, audit the Federal Reserve to protect the value of the dollar, empower the people and local communities to protect their styles of living, restore jobs that have been outsourced overseas, take care of homeless citizens, prosecute government corruption (even at the Supreme Court level), prosecute pollution violations, tax surplus wealth, tap the power and wisdom of citizens, focus on positive and selfless change, channel rage constructively, fix the political system, maintain a sustained commitment to social justice, maintain a positive vision, teach children well, respect and empower all citizens politically with actions they can do now, and engage as many citizens as possible to find common ground in decision-making.

When my turn came, I said I was concerned that our government did not give an effective voice to the public on government policy issues. I explained briefly that I did research on citizen attitudes and had initial data that suggested that the public could be trusted to provide a very constructive agenda for government. I concluded by saying that by coincidence I had a new research questionnaire that would soon be online and would measure most, and perhaps all, of the various concerns voiced in the meeting. It will measure how strongly citizens value each of dozens of services that we expect from government, and then how well they think government is providing those services.

I explained that the Occupy movement could have their members complete the questionnaire and thus get a measure of the common good, as they see it. The data would provide scores for about 65 government services at the local, county, state and national levels. We could rank order these to determine issues of highest priority. This would provide a positive agenda for the movement. All members of the Occupy movement with Internet access could participate, from anywhere in the country. There was no time for comments about my ideas from the group; others had yet to share their goals. Then the meeting adjourned.

I attended the next meeting about a week later, but it was out-of-doors in the cold and with such poor acoustics (no amplifiers) that people couldn't hear each other talk. I left after a few minutes and sent an e-mail message to the committee leader, offering a copy of the questionnaire for his consideration. He later replied that he and another leader were interested, even if others weren't. However, they did not contact me in the weeks that followed.

I felt disappointed because this sort of questionnaire can convert individual personal opinions of citizens into group facts of considerable value. For example, consider the results of a study of 60 community college students and 11 church-going adults that I did in 2006 (1). These persons completed online questionnaires to indicate how strongly they desired government services, from "Not at all (1)" to "Very much (5)". The average score for each item can range from 1 to 5. Among the many government services presented, the highest average item score was 4.51 for "Affordable health care services for all citizens".

Here are other scores, highest first. Keep in mind that most of the persons in this study were community college students. 4.33 for "More affordable public higher education", 4.32: More affordable housing, especially for young families seeking to buy their first home. 4.32: Improved public schools at the kindergarten through high school level. 4.28: More full-time jobs that pay enough for one adult to support a family of 4 or 5. 4.26: A local economy that stimulates family wage jobs. 4.23: A reasonable program to protect rivers from pollution. 4.22: A reasonable program to protect wildlife habitat, both on land and in rivers, lakes and the ocean. 4.22: Stable, adequate public school funding. 4.09: An effort to balance the federal budget, paying off the national debt. 4.04: An improved form of State government that is more immune from distortion of the best interests of the community overall by the influence of special interest group money and pressure. 4.04: During election campaigns, candidates for office should not bad-mouth candidates from other parties but just focus on what the party platform proposes to improve government. 4.01: An effort to protect the environment through national programs, such as research on non-fossil fuels. 4.01: Cleaner, less polluted air.

These issues were of top priority for the adult students who participated in this study.

Issues with average scores in the "3" range are of importance but come second in priority. These include a score of 3.99 for Food, housing and job-finding services for poor people. Other scores were 3.94: An improved form of national government that is more immune from the distortion of the best interests of the community overall by the influence of special interest group money or pressure. 3.90: A reduction in specific military activities in foreign lands unless approved by the majority of the voting citizens of the country. 3.90: A reasonable program to protect agricultural land from being built over with housing or commercial projects. 3.90: An effort to improve Social Security benefits to the needy, elderly and disabled. 3.87: An effort to create a fair and affordable tax system to support the national government. 3.86: Adequate, fair tax income to support local and state services (education, highways, parks, job promotion, etc.). 3.64: Improved public safety (police, fire, highway patrol services). 3.51: Improved county and state highways and bridges. 3.33: More recreational facilities (parks, ball fields, swimming pools, etc.). 3.29: An effort to develop a reasonable long-term population control program for the nation.

This sort of data can be simplified by computing the average for items of the same type. For example, the average for the 4 items that measure educational concerns is 4.26, in the high range, as it is for the 6 items for environmental protection (4.10). The average for 4 items measuring satisfaction with current political parties is in the low range (2.53), indicating that these citizens were not satisfied with current political parties in 2006, when this study was done. This 2006 study addressed many of the issues voiced by the Occupy movement in 2011.

This type of public opinion poll could be used by Occupy Wall Street to define its national agenda for improved government. Polls also can be used by a city to help set priorities for budgeting or improving services. Polls could be used by a political party to create its party platform. The specific-government-services questionnaire that I offered to the Occupy group was a much larger one. You can view it by completing it at my web site, questionnaires 17, 18 and 19. I'd love it if you would, to help build a sizable sample of citizens. I can't tell you the resulting data because I haven't been able to find a group to take the questionnaires yet. The professor at the community college whose students often completed questionnaires for me had a stroke and hadn't been teaching.

Some students of government and politics fear the public voice as a determiner of government policy, arguing that the public may be prejudiced against minority interests and the rights of individuals… "tyranny by the majority". However, if you poll the public when they're not under extreme threat or pressure, as from propaganda, war or severe weather damage, I believe that you will see what I have seen, concern for all groups of honorable intentions.

Recall the items cited above that call for services to needy people, for health care for all and for affordable jobs, education and housing. Citizens also prefer political campaigns that exclude badmouthing opponents. They endorse attention to population control issues. Thus, public polling can be expected to provide a positive, constructive, compassionate government agenda, one in line with Lincoln's implicit call to the "higher angels of our nature".

Sitting on my 5-gallon bucket in the Occupy camp that day, I never learned the lady's name, but "Grace" would have fit her well. "I've raised three children; and they're all doing well", she said. "My father was a D.A. in a city near Los Angles."

Then she was talking again of society' problems and how Jesus' word was the key to solutions. I gently tried to focus her attention on the two-page questionnaire she held on her lap, but after a few moments reading and answering items she looked up and said that she couldn't do it. I asked why. She mumbled reasons that I couldn't understand.

"Well, thank you for looking at it", I said, smiling, as she rose and wandered off. She kept the questionnaire, saying she wanted to look at it some more.

David and I were fortunate that day, gathering 52 questionnaires from camp members in return for Hershey bars that I had bought for incentives. One young man asked if he could take the questionnaire again to get another bar. I chuckled.

Another participant referred to himself as "Purple", explaining that he had a conventional name but that folks called him "Purple". He was tall, with a weathered face. Dressed in a tidy black suit, white dress shirt and rounded bowler hat, he reminded me of photos of Abe Lincoln. He'd driven down 40 miles from his town to visit the camp for the day. He happily completed the questionnaire, then engaged David and me in an extended and somewhat disjointed autobiography, including claims that he had been a professional photographer and his works had appeared in publications all over the world.

A couple of days later I entered the data from these first questionnaires into my computer. I was struck by several things. At the end of the questionnaire I had left a space for "Comments". Most participants had written thoughts, ranging from simply "Help" to lengthy commentaries on the ills of society and how to fix them. I was also struck by how intelligent some respondents apparently were. The questionnaire asked for high school grade point average, years of education, marital status and other demographic data, in addition to how strongly one agreed with 24 statements based on the social goals expressed by the members of the first committee meeting I had attended some weeks earlier. We had to have a brief questionnaire that persons could do offline, sitting in a public park, as many of the Occupy members were homeless and without Internet access. My much longer research questionnaire was impractical for this situation.

While a few questionnaires were useless, missing an entire page of responses or having responses done mechanically (all "3" or all "5" options marked), by far the majority appeared valid. Among the respondents were many middle-aged, college-educated, divorced or single men who were currently homeless. This surprised me, though in retrospect I recalled visiting with several middle-aged men who seemed clear and focused in their comments.

Other Occupy members who I had heard speak at panel discussions with community leaders in meetings indoors around town were very different from many of the tent camp members. One is a local attorney who represents persons who have had their houses foreclosed abruptly. Another is a Ph.D. candidate in sociology at the university. He held his own very well when debating with a local retired university professor and consultant who holds a Ph.D. in economics from MIT. Others included a social worker with many years of experience in local organizations.

It was clear to me from these subsequent meetings, and with conversations with Occupy members at the University of Oregon with whom I designed a "Census" questionnaire to complement the initial 34-item opinion questionnaire, that tent-campers were only a fraction of the community who identify strongly with the movement.

Another fellow who took the Census questionnaire that we did a couple of weeks later was grey-haired, alert and focused. Informally dressed, he was tidy in appearance and grooming. After completing the questionnaire he handed me a single typed sheet of paper, explaining that he was on an Occupy committee and working on a questionnaire of his own. I asked him to write his name and phone number on the back, so I could contact him.

By coincidence, the following Monday I noticed his letter to the editor in the local newspaper. In it he offered a detailed suggestion about how to change the decision-making process in Congress to force politicians to compromise. He was thinking hard about how to fix government, but his questionnaire form was just a simple check-list of options about how the movement could focus its energies, from anarchic behavior by citizens to things that could be done to promote improvement of existing government.

While names were not on my questionnaire, I could identify his answer sheet. It was one of the first few for the batch and fit his demographic data. He had asked me to add to the questionnaire an item about employment status, specifically the category of "retired", which he was. He was 63 years old, retired, married and buying his own home. His high school grade point average had been only C+, but he reported 9 years of college, implying a Ph.D. I misplaced the sheet he gave me but his name was in the phone book. I called, but the number was disconnected.

I entered the data from our first questionnaire into a file, loaded it onto my statistical program and ran statistics.(2) While I realized that the sample was rather small, on only about 4 dozen citizens, I was curious to see what it might reveal. The 24 core items measured ten meaningful concepts, pleasantly more than I expected. It looked like the questionnaire was providing a rich view into the mind of Occupiers. They had a variegated and generally constructive social agenda.

The primary concept seemed to be a measure of respecting and empowering citizens to promote an overall improvement in government. A central questionnaire item in this concept was: "The Occupy movement and the nation as a whole should maintain respect for all citizens and their needs." The next most meaningful concept reflected a desire that the movement maintain a positive (civil) focus and concern for the homeless and the need for quality public education ("The movement should strive to engage as many citizens as possible, seeking everyone's opinions to find common ground").

The third concept reflected a desire for a variety of money-related services, including improved regulation of financial industries, promoting a fair tax system and promoting family wage jobs ("The government should reinstate and improve regulations of the financial industry to minimize future financial meltdowns"). The fourth concept was a curious combination of three items measuring self-identification as either conservative or liberal politically and a concern for protecting the value of the dollar.

The fifth concept was measured primarily by just two questionnaire items, "It is important that public media (radio, T.V., etc.) be objective and not biased in its reporting", and "As a nation we need to promote more of a focus on 'we', the common good, and less focus on 'me', narrow self-interest."

The next concept simply measured whether a person was an Occupy tent resident, living in the tent community itself. The seventh concept was based on two items having to do with discouraging financial greed and needing to "get the money out of politics" and reversing the notion that corporations are people and have the right to contribute unlimited funds to politician's election campaigns. The eighth concept was sort of a state's rights item, but on a very local, community level: "We should do more to empower local communities to have control over how they protect and promote their local lifestyles."

The ninth concept reflected a tendency to endorse or not endorse independence and green positions politically. The last concept reflected opinions about whether humans are "primarily and naturally" either competitive or cooperative.

I ran correlations between these concepts and the demographic variables. Homeless persons tended to be younger, less educated and had lower high school grades. They tended to be unemployed and not to be students, and more than others want a universal form of health care. The only other relationship of note was the tendency for more educated persons to be less inclined to endorse a universal health care program, perhaps because they already had health insurance themselves.

This questionnaire was followed a week later with another, longer one. One of the movement leaders had asked for a "census" questionnaire. I suggested that it include a variety of additional items, including ones about childhood abuse. He asked some committee members to work on this with me. I heard from one young lady, whom I'll call "Julie", a student at the university.

I sent her a draft of the census questionnaire. She and some of her colleagues objected to the items asking about childhood abuse because she and some of them had been abused. They thought that asking such questions implied that the movement was not legitimate, that people who are abused as children feel abused by society more generally. They didn't want the movement dismissed as just an indirect expression of childhood abuse.

I reassured them in my e-mail reply that this was not my intention. I made adjustments and additions to the expanded questionnaire in line with their suggestions and sent this back to Julie, who was now quite pleased and offered to help me administer questionnaires. She came to my office on her bicycle to discuss plans.

She wore heavy boots, an ankle-length dress and a knitted white hat. Slender, pretty and always smiling and polite, she engaged me enthusiastically and was an extremely helpful assistant, administering questionnaires to Occupy members in the camp, loading the research questionnaire on the Internet at a Google service, entering data into the computer from the paper questionnaires and sending the Internet version out to people in the community via e-mail lists, which she managed for the local movement.

She was fascinated with the whole process and talked of her major in sociology at the University. She was in her senior year and seemed remarkably aware of and focused on social and political issues. She had confidence that we could engage professors from the political science and other departments. She and her husband lived in a small apartment. Her schooling was funded by student loans, it appeared. Her husband helped one day at the camp when I had to leave early for a dental appointment.

We gathered data for 37 persons that day. In addition to all the information in the first questionnaire, this longer one totaled about 55 items measuring traits and eight other items measuring age, education, etc. Factor analysis revealed seven interesting dimensions among the new items added to assess abuse, mental health, incarceration, etc. The primary factor, or item cluster, consisted of 5 items reflecting childhood neglect ("I felt lacking in love and support as a child") and a tendency to feel abused by society in general as an adult ("I feel abused by authority in general", and "It seems to me that government itself is abusive of people like me").

The next dimension reflected mental illness (depression, anxiety and substance abuse). The next reflected incarceration, and hospitalization for psychiatric problems. The next dimension reflected what might be termed "oppositional activism", measured with two items: "I think of myself as a social and political activist" and "I think it is worthwhile to change society by opposing bad institutions and systems." 25 of the 37 persons in the sample agreed or strongly agreed with the first statement and 30 with the second. Thus, the majority of the persons in this sample see themselves as activists willing to be "oppositional".

The next dimension reflected in these items was a religious/spiritual one. The next reflected minority group ethnic status and sexual and other abuse as a victim. The last dimension was a "constructive activism" one reflected primarily in two items "I grew up in a family with parents who were not divorced from each other" and "I think it is worthwhile to change society by creating new and better institutions and systems without first opposing bad ones." 50 percent of the persons agreed with the first item and 64 percent with the second. Thus, half came from intact families and more than half endorsed improving existing institutions to better society, without first having to be "oppositional".

These dimensions were generally independent of age, gender, high school grades and years of education, but Oppositional Activism correlated positively with education, and Religion/Spirituality correlated negatively with high school grades. Oppositional activists tended to have more education. Religious and spiritual persons tended to have lower high school grades.

The sample size of only 37 persons was rather small, so I didn't put too much confidence in these results. I looked forward to analyzing the data again when we had questionnaires from many other groups, both Occupy members and non-occupy citizens.

During the next couple of months I gathered data from groups of homeless persons attending local church welfare programs, including sleeping facilities for two weeks and Sunday breakfasts. I also gathered data from adult church members. I ran more statistics when I had data on almost 200 persons total across all the studies. I compared 64 persons who strongly identified with the Occupy movement with 34 who definitely did not. While the 64 were higher than the 34 on 22 of the 24 items in the questionnaire that measured improvement in government services, both groups, on average, endorsed all 24 items. In effect, both Occupiers and non-occupiers wanted improvement in the wide variety of government services reflected in these items.

Thus, these studies of the Occupy movement members and other citizens show that how we perceive society, including political issues, appears to be colored by our childhood and related experiences. They also suggest that all groups of citizens want improved government services.

Social Disenfranchisement

Our perceptions of society are also colored by other traits, such as those measured by my Social Disenfranchisement scale, the measure of what the Eidelson's thought might underlie international conflict. This scale measures perceptions of the world from a perspective of injustice, distrust, vulnerability, helplessness and superiority. This last perspective, superiority, suggests a desire to compensate for the first four, which reflect a disadvantaged perspective. Superiority suggests fuel for counter-aggression. And, indeed, the Social Disenfranchisement scale correlates positively and substantially with warmongering endorsement.

Social Disenfranchisement also correlates positively with endorsement of anarchy, defined as "no government at all, just roving bands of armed bandits who rob, kill and do whatever they want". It correlates similarly with endorsement of military dictatorship government and with "tribal democracy", defined as government that serves special interest groups. Social Disenfranchisement correlates *negatively* with "public or common-good democracy", defined as government that serves citizens as members of the community overall rather than as members of special interest groups.

Thus, in this measurement instrument we see relationships between views of the world and preferences for different types of government. Persons who feel vulnerable, helpless, distrustful, and unjustly treated also tend to feel superior to other individuals and groups and are attracted to forms of government that involve service to special interest groups, presumably to include their group or especially to serve their own group. They are also inclined to militarism, perhaps to exact revenge or "justice".

Keep in mind that these relationships between traits are "tendencies". They are based on correlations. Correlations that are statistically significant are telling us not that all persons who endorse one notion endorse or don't endorse another but only that persons who endorse one notion, idea or belief are *more likely* also to endorse another. Or, if the correlation is negative, higher scores on the first trait are associated with *lower* scores on the second trait.

Intelligence as measured by a test correlates significantly and positively with school grades. Persons with higher intelligence test scores tend to get higher school grades. Not all intelligent persons by testing get high school grades. An exception to the "rule" does not disprove the correlation between two traits. So, not all persons who feel socially disenfranchised will endorse warmongering or anarchy. It's just that the more socially disenfranchised one feels, the more likely he will endorse warmongering and the less likely he will endorse common good democracy.

Felt Oppression.

The relationship between childhood experiences and adult perceptions of the political world was also revealed to me in a study that compared a group of 14-year-olds living on the Gaza Strip in the Middle East to adult church members in my home town, Eugene, Or. (3)I met a psychiatrist, Jeff Victoroff, at a professional convention. He had developed a questionnaire of felt and perceived oppression and had data for the teenagers in the Middle East. He kindly made this data available to me for analysis and permitted me to use his questionnaire.

I administered it and measures of other traits to a group of local adult church members. Surprisingly, both groups saw the world as equally "oppressive", even though from an objective point of view life on the Gaza Strip was much more threatening due to chronic military conflict with Israel. Equally interesting was the fact that persons in Eugene who had felt unpleasantly and unfairly treated in their childhood families were more likely to see the world as oppressive when adults. Eugene adults who hadn't been mistreated as children did not see the world as unusually oppressive. This is not to say that all adults who weren't mistreated as children see the world as fair and trouble-free.

Again, we're seeing tendencies, not absolutes. But the tendencies are real and of interest.

Felt Humiliation.

In the late fall of 2007 I learned of a conference to be held the next month in New York City on humiliation. It was the annual convention of the Human Dignity and Humiliation Studies organization. In their invitation they expressed special interest in novel ways to measure humiliation as a trait, presumably to facilitate research on the topic.

I sent an e-mail message to the organization, offering to come and share ideas about how to measure this concept, but warned them that they should be open to surprising findings if I did. I was assured in reply that I would be quite welcome, so I called my sister, a retired professor, who lived just a mile from Columbia Teacher's College, the site of the convention. She kindly offered to have me stay with her, so I made plans.

Based on my study with Jeff's Oppression scale, I suspected that persons who feel humiliated as adults would be more likely to report humiliating experiences in their childhood families. I was confident that I could create questionnaire measures of humiliation and childhood and adult manifestations of it.

The founder of the humiliation organization was a woman of

interesting and varied background. She had degrees in both medicine and psychology and had practiced as a clinical psychologist in Egypt. Her family had been displaced from a country in Eastern Europe during the Serb-Croatian conflict and settled in West Germany. Her father was apparently quite stressed by this, spending much of his time in his room, praying. She had a theory that humiliation is a major cause of international conflict and war and spent much of her time in Switzerland writing on this theme. At the convention, she conveyed an attitude of love and caring for all. One of her close assistants had done her college dissertation years before on humiliation, measuring a form of it with a questionnaire.

At the meetings a call for a research coordinator came up. No one offered, so I did, and was accepted. A few members offered to help me. I said my first effort would be to do a study to measure humiliation and related traits to explore the underlying hypothesis that this trait is directly related to endorsement of warmongering and related traits.

Back at my office a week later I drafted a questionnaire and sent it to my committee assistants. One in particular, an engineer by training, took exception to some of the items, questioning my strategy and arguing my explanations virtually indefinitely. I felt puzzled. I felt puzzled further when I sent the questionnaire to the organization leader, asking her to send it out to members to gather data. Several of the members were university professors, one in Rome and another in England. I expected them to have their students fill it out, a common research practice. The leader expressed hesitation for reasons that seemed tangential and puzzling. I began to wonder if she resisted finding out things about humiliation that she didn't want to hear.

Months went by with no one offering to gather data by having people fill out the questionnaire. Finally I was able to get my colleague in the psychology department of the local community college to have his students do it. I analyzed the data and found what I expected. Childhood humiliation in the home was correlated directly with feeling humiliated elsewhere… at school, by peers in the neighborhood and by local police. And childhood humiliation was associated with feeling humiliated as an adult… by governments and even by "unfair fate".

But, in contrast to the leader's primary hypothesis, humiliation did *not* correlate significantly with measures of terrorism or warmongering endorsement. Thus, if there was a relationship between humiliation and international conflict, it was indirect and probably in combination with other stressful experiences, such as exposure to belligerent leadership, or in combination with other traits, such as social disenfranchisement and violence-proneness.

I wrote up the study results(4) and sent them to the committee colleague who had argued so vehemently and to the leader of the humiliation organization. They both thanked me. The committee colleague thanked me for including him in my report distribution. The leader thanked me for doing research that supported her theory. I was puzzled by this, as it seemed to me that the data clearly did *not* directly support her theory. But she is a very gracious lady, so perhaps she was simply grateful for what I had done. She didn't ask me to do any follow-up research, however.

Belligerent Peaceniks.

I've been puzzled also by other experiences with persons who are enthusiastic about understanding and addressing problems of war. My wife invited me to join a peace choir a few years ago. But once involved, we learned that it had been torn asunder by conflict between the members, many of whom left and formed another choir. Some of the troublemakers remained. One was quite opinionated. Another designed militaristic video games for a living.

About this same time I learned of a new peace studies program at the local community college. I attended a couple of their annual conventions. At one, after the guest journalist gave his featured speech and the program was opened to question and answer, members of the audience were soon arguing, yelling and swearing at each other. At another convention a featured speaker had a national reputation for being arrested for protest activities in meetings of the U.S. Congress and other government meetings.

Social and Political Activism.

I couldn't understand why persons who wanted to protest war were themselves so hostile and disruptive. I designed a questionnaire study to measure social and political activism as psychological traits, which is relatively easy to do if one knows how to create questionnaire measures. And it is much easier than studying activists themselves.

Reviewing background research in this field revealed that most activism, at least as traditionally defined, is oppositional in nature, consisting of protesting, destroying or otherwise interfering with current institutions or programs. And such activities tend to be relatively short-lived. Their leadership members are not infrequently in conflict with each other. The organizations often lack funding and depend on volunteers. Some activist organizations are dangerous enough to society and governments to be secretive about their activities. Thus, for many reasons such oppositional activist organizations are difficult to study.

I designed my study questionnaire to measure not only oppositional activism but also what I conceptualized as positive or promotional activism.(5) I defined this type of activism as devoted to developing new programs or organizations for helping society without first opposing or interfering with current ones. Examples I cited were Rotary International, the Red Cross, the United Nations and micro-lending services to poor citizens.

An interesting example of these two types of activism can be found in the National Forests of my state, Oregon. About 15 years ago eco-terrorists burned down the headquarters building of the Willamette National Forest, protesting forest management practices of the administration at that time. In contrast to this oppositional activism, in 2001 a consortium of organizations was formed to manage the Siuslaw National Forest, evolving into a model program of cooperation between previously conflicting interests. The organization successfully promotes the interests of all concerned parties, including preservation of waterways, promoting healthy forests, harvesting timber and creating jobs, an example of promotional activism.

Ninety-one community college and university students completed the research questionnaire that I designed to study activism as a psychological trait. 39 percent of these students considered themselves to be social activists and 23 percent political activists. The questionnaire measured promotional activism with a seven-item scale, including statements such as "I actively support one or more local social service organizations, such as Kiwanis, the 20-30 club, Assistance League or Rotary" and "I feel confident that our current social and political systems can be improved." Oppositional activism was measured with six items, including "I believe in undermining and opposing current social systems" and "I believe in undermining and opposing current political systems."

The correlations between these trait measures and other traits measured in the questionnaire revealed that promotional activists tend to be higher on charitableness, endorsing a positive foreign policy, and the Big Five personality traits of agreeableness, openness and extroversion. Promotional activism was also associated with having a positive worldview and denying having an indifferent worldview.

Oppositional activists tend to be higher on self-reported criminal tendencies and prior humiliating experiences. They tend to be lower on the Big Five trait of conscientiousness. They report having been badly treated in life, feeling socially disenfranchised and having an oppositional worldview.

I sent this article to the editor of a European journal on social and political activism but he rejected it because he did not think I respected the tradition of activism sufficiently. The initial form of my article discussed activism as of two types, "antisocial" and "pro-social". I later sent the article to another editor of an American journal. He liked it but wanted a more detailed review of prior literature. In the process of doing this review, I came across a book edited by the first journal editor. It was on the methodology used to study activism. Reading this book, I understood why he was offended by my initial terms of "antisocial" and "pro-social" to describe activists.

Much of the research in social and political activism has been conducted by researchers who in their younger lives were activists themselves. These researchers define all activism as an oppositional activity, opposing current political and social systems. They consider this activism to be desirable. My term "antisocial" to describe their oppositional activism, thus, was implicitly critical of them. I changed my terms from *antisocial* and *pro-social* to *oppositional* and *promotional* in the revised manuscript. I hoped this would increase the appeal of my article to the second editor. It did. One of his reviewers found the paper very interesting but wanted another study with a refined measure of my terms, which I designed and loaded on my web site.

In addition to homelessness, social disenfranchisement, feelings of oppression and humiliation that motivate activists, there are positive sources of human inspiration, aspiration and idealism that can underlie and motivate political attitudes. These range from the ideals in human rights charters to attitudes about local school funding. And the issues get complicated. The civic ideals of fairness across social groups that are promoted in our educational institutions can be inadvertently betrayed by the institutional leaders themselves, as we'll see in the next chapter.

Chapter 7

Retirement benefits:

an inadvertent evil?

Lew was kindly treating me to dinner at the Chinese restaurant we'd often frequented over our almost 40 years of friendship. I would treat him to the basketball game in Matt Knight Arena across the street in an hour. I had tickets that a fellow Rotarian had given me. Lew has been my friend and statistical guru and research guide for decades. He had been a professor of psychology at the U of Oregon and still worked at Oregon Research Institute down the street.

He summarized findings from his ongoing research on the Big Five personality traits, on which he's a renowned expert. They're finding that Conscientiousness and Extroversion are moderately stable from childhood to adulthood and that Agreeableness and Openness are mildly stable. Emotional Stability can change much; you can't predict from childhood Emotional Stability what the adult level of this trait will be. I summarized my latest research with the Occupy movement and my findings that point to public desire for a new type of democracy depending on public opinion polls for policy decisions.

Gazing past me, Lew frowned as he slowly rubbed his head, then presented a challenge to my notion that a new political party would evolve that depended on polls of the public to define its platform. "But Bill…." He paused as if wanting to assure me that his intention was not to offend. "How can…? The issues are so complicated. How could you expect people to know enough about the issues to…?" The waitress came over with the check. It was time to go to the game.

Our thoughts moved to lighter topics as we crossed the busy boulevard and we never got back to the topic. I had an answer for the question I assumed he would ask, as I'd heard it before: How can the public be trusted to know enough about issues to provide a sound basis for a political agenda? My answer is detailed but when I'd heard the question before I'd often suspected it came from persons who feared losing something. They might lose some special advantage that they currently enjoyed as a special interest group under the present system of government, such as the power to get special benefits for themselves in return for campaign contributions. I wondered if this could be true of Lew. What special benefits did he enjoy as a member of a special interest group? Mulling this over a couple of days later it occurred to me that he might be enjoying a very comfortable retirement from the university. His special interest group was the teachers' union.

By coincidence our Oregon Public Employee Retirement System (PERS) plan had been in the news recently. The benefits to some retired State employees were so generous that the State had had to modify them to prevent bankruptcy of State government. Two newspapers had to sue to get the State to release the details and won after a ten-year battle, forcing release of the PERS payouts to all retired citizens. Why did the papers have to force the issue? Were beneficiaries embarrassed about how much they were getting?

In fairness to Lew as an individual, he later explained to me that while he is a fan of unions now, he had never been a member of the teachers' union and that the Oregon PERS system had been established by the state legislature, apparently with benefits high enough to compensate for the relatively lower salaries at Oregon universities compared to other states.

I went online and learned that Mike Bellotti, our retired University of Oregon football coach, is getting nearly half a million a year, $41,000 per month. A member of the Rotary Club, retired from decades of public service, including service as Attorney General of the State, Dean of the Law School and president of the University of Oregon, is getting $252,000, or $21,000 per month.

A friend of mine from our church, a retired high school math teacher who taught our son, is getting S43,000 per year. Two of my married neighbors, who are retired from the University as psychology department professors, are together getting $200,000. Several retired former public employees, members of my Rotary club, are on the list. Other members of our Rotary Club include a retired public school superintendent ($104,933), the former district attorney ($141,597) and a judge ($209,530). My friend, Lew, is getting $101,000.

In contrast to these public employees, after 40 years of private practice as a Ph.D. psychologist, I was getting Social Security benefits of only $24,000 per year, less than ¼ what my Ph.D. psychologist friends are getting from the Oregon Public Employee Retirement program. I had to pay 15 percent of my annual income into Social Security, sometimes more than I had to pay in Federal income taxes. Some PERS employees, the judges, as I recall, have had to pay *nothing* into the PERS program.

I called a banker friend that I knew from Rotary and my business executive club we'd been in for years. I asked "How much would I have to have in savings at your bank to generate an interest payment of $100,000 per year?" He said he'd have a staff member work on it and get back to me. I saw him at a business club meeting a couple of days later and asked how the calculations were coming. He said his staff member wondered if I wanted the return for just one year or continuously. I said, for ten years. He called a couple of days later and suggested that the three of us meet in person.

I went to his office. His colleague joined us and was friendly and attentive. In addition to work at the bank, he still taught asset management at the university, his specialty for many years.

His face was lined with experience and seemed to say *"I know my field forwards and backwards, almost to the point of boredom. How can I help you?"*

He was very familiar with the public pension issues I raised.

I asked him what it would take to generate 100 thousand per year in payout. He said a ten-year treasury bill would pay about 1 percent. For a yield of 100 thousand I'd need to invest 10 million. He talked further on the topic, confirming my suspicion that the PERS system was not sustainable. He said the contracts the state had signed with the unions required more money eventually than the state could afford.

He said it was sort of a Ponzi scheme. The first folks in were getting their retirement payouts, but down the road there wouldn't be enough funds to cover the obligations to others. He said that retired firemen in the town next door get retirement benefits based on their last three years of employment so they take all the overtime they can muster those last three years to jack up their subsequent payouts. With an air of resignation, he said: "Everyone knows how to work the system".

He said that when the contracts were initially negotiated de-cades ago the stock market was going up steadily year by year. The unions got the state to guarantee an 8 percent minimum gain per year. But over the past 10 years stock gains have been flat. A dollar invested in stocks ten years ago was now worth 91 cents, having *lost* value, he said. But the PERS retirees still got their guaranteed 8 percent *gain* on their retirement nest-egg each year.

Both bankers were frank in admitting it was an unsustainable arrangement and that many states had similar obligations that they weren't going to be able to fund in the end. We drew parallels with the five nations in Europe that were up to their necks in debt from borrowing.

A couple of weeks passed. I noticed in the Wall Street Journal that a 10-year treasury bill paid about 2 percent, not one percent.

So, the nest-egg to generate $100,000 per year wouldn't have to be 10 million, as the banker had said, but only 5 million, still a substantial amount. I phoned my accountant and asked him to calculate the forty-year set-aside necessary to generate a $5 million nest-egg. He said brokers would say the stock market has gone up 10 percent or more on average over the past 40 years, though the past 5 or 10 have been "ugly", paying much less than that. I asked him to use and average gain on investment of 10 percent per year for the calculation.

He called me back a few minutes later and said it would take a set-aside of $9,480 per year over 40 years to generate a $5 million nest-egg. If the rate of gain was not 10 percent but 8, the set-aside would have to be $17,064 per year. If it was the current T-Bill rate of 2 percent, it would require a set-aside of $6,796.62 per month, or $81,559 per year!

So, if the PERS system generated an 8 percent per year gain, the minimum rate demanded by and negotiated with the union, to generate a $100,000 payout to Lew per year, the state would have had to set aside and invest $17,064 per year for the 40 years he had worked as a professor. If the PERS system hadn't set that aside or made 8 percent on the funds set aside, the State was still going to have to pay the retirement benefit under their contract to the retired employees. If they didn't have sufficient funds, the taxpayer would have to make up the difference.

Now in fairness, I learned from making a direct inquiry to the PERS board that this 8 percent guarantee has been done away with. But the same day that I got the PERS board reply I also read in the paper that an attorney in our state is suing the judges of the state to prevent them from hearing PERS cases, as most of the judges, like most of Oregon State legislators, are themselves now members of the PERS system. In his Guest Viewpoint newspaper article this attorney lists years of decisions by the State legislators to increase their own PERS benefits and *reduce* their obligations to the PERS system. Now they don't even have to pay into the system to get benefits; the public pays their way.

The State of Oregon pays out about 3 billion per year in retirement benefits to 110,000 retired state employees. It has a pension fund portfolio of 55 billion. Thus, it must generate a profit of 5.4 percent per year on its investments just to stay even. A current treasury bill would only generate 2 percent. This may help explain why the managers of such portfolios are increasing the percentage of their investments in private equity funds, funds that own shares in companies like Bain Capital, the one that Presidential candidate Mitt Romney made his millions working for.

Bain specializes in buying companies, and then making them more profitable. To do this, sometimes they fire workers. Sometimes they hire them back at lower salaries or replace them with labor overseas at much lower salaries. Then, eventually, they sell the companies for a profit. The public fund portfolio managers justify their investment in funds that cost American workers their jobs by saying their specific obligation is to simply make the most money they can for their portfolio, not be concerned with the morality of job markets.

When I shared my thoughts about all this with my wife, she was annoyed. As a retired private school teacher, she empathized with the teaching profession, even though she didn't get a state retirement benefit and her Social Security benefit after about 30 years of work is only $12,000 per year. She said I seemed to have it in for public employees.

I explained to her that all of the retired persons whose PERS salaries I'd mentioned were very nice people. I knew them personally. The problem isn't that they're bad for getting very generous public retirement benefits. The problem is that they have been inadvertent participants in a system that is good for them personally, as individuals and as members of a special interest group, but potentially bad for the common good.

A professor acquaintance of mine at our church explained this as the "tragedy of the commons"; what an individual does doesn't have much effect but what we do collectively can have catastrophic effects. The Wikipedia statement is: "In economics, the tragedy of the commons is the depletion of a shared resource by individuals, acting independently and rationally according to each one's self-interest, despite their understanding that depleting the common resource is contrary to their long-term best interests."

Another manifestation of this is that the school children of the State suffer because to honor the teacher union contracts the State has had to cut junior teachers, cut school programs and increase class sizes. "Fewer than half of students spend a full day in class", reports the lead story in our local Sunday newspaper, referring to high school students for whom there aren't enough teachers and classes (1). Some bright students want advanced placement classes but can't get into them. They spend their idle time in the school lounge playing cards. What's good for tenured teachers, strong salaries and retirement benefits, is bad for students.

A friend of mine, a professor at an Illinois university, read a draft of this chapter of my manuscript and pointed out that annuities don't need as much money socked away as my rather naïve mathematics assumed. He derided my "blaming the teachers" for school budget crunches and offered the opinion that military budgets were too high and that *that* was the problem, blaming society for having distorted budget priorities.

I countered that our city doesn't have a military force and that just 20 years prior our school budget had provided for a much more comprehensive program for children, with plenty of classes, reasonable class sizes, had happy teachers, etc. I told him I wasn't blaming teachers but the *system*, a system that sucks reasonable citizens into contracts with government that provide benefits to public employees as members of a special interest group but that inadvertently work against the common good in the long run. Evil systems can, in effect, corrupt good people and let others down.

Many private and public pension funds are well-intended but underfunded. Many large corporations and even entire industries periodically fall to corruption, some failing completely and others requiring government bailout to survive, such as several large commercial banks in 2008. Special interest group governments and societies seem quite vulnerable to such corruption, where self-serving individuals and small groups of individuals collude to make great personal profits at the risk of wide segments of the economy, all under the umbrella of free enterprise.

The phenomenon occurs even within modern, advanced forms of government, including democracies. One can cite the system by which wealthy special interest groups buy legislative decisions with campaign contributions, especially prominent at the national level in the United States. In 2011 over 12,000 lobbyists channeled $3.33 billion from these groups to legislators. The will and welfare of the majority of citizens on policy issues can thereby be overridden by special interest group power.

Corporate pension funds have been raided and depleted, even causing bankruptcy of companies and depriving retired employees from collecting promised benefits. In some cases public insurance programs pick up the pieces, paying benefits for failed private pension funds, including those of Bethlehem Steel, Delta Air Lines, Trans World Airlines and Kaiser Aluminum (2).

This problem reminded me of a research study I did many years ago on students in a truck driving school. Most, if not all, of the students were attending the several-week school on a Pell Grant, a Federal loan. I had the class of about 25 students complete my battery of ten tests measuring the traits of heavy truck drivers, both before they started and at the end of their training. At the beginning, the scores on intelligence and personality traits were low compared to employed truck drivers. The factual knowledge (Federal Regulations) score was also low.

At the end of the school program, as expected, the scores on the Federal Regulations test improved, moving up into the average range, similar to scores for experienced drivers. Scores on the three intelligence and five personality trait measures did *not* increase, again as expected, for these are basic traits that generally change little, if at all, with experience.

The low scores on intelligence and personality traits implied that this group of candidates would not make good heavy truck drivers. When I contacted all of the students a month or so after graduation, only one or two were driving. I viewed this at the time as a failure to screen students before they were admitted to the driver school. Intelligence and personality traits don't change much with experience. Student applicants should have been limited only to those with average or above scores on the intelligence and personality traits.

The failure of the government to insist on such admission requirements is an example of a system that is designed to do good but which inadvertently is a waste of public money. This particular Pell Grant program was meant to help train citizens for employment but in reality seemed mainly to just line the pockets of truck driving school administrators and staff. It is another example of good people inadvertently transgressing the common good; driver applicants are attracted in the hope of getting a job but they aren't adequately screened and their grant money is wasted.

What do these failed systems have to do with psychology? They appear to be examples of a moral weakness in human nature clarified by classic studies by psychologists Philip Zimbardo and Stanley Milgram.(3,4,5) Their research demonstrated that normal citizens, specifically university students and local residents in research experiments, can be rather easily persuaded to participate in behavior that is clearly not in the best interests of the common good.

Zimbardo got students to treat fellow students inhumanely in a simulated prison in the basement of a Stanford University building. In fact, they were so cruel that the experiment, which was funded by the U.S. military, had to be terminated early, after only 4 days. Zimbardo himself had to be told by a graduate student to terminate it, as he was so enmeshed himself in the experiment as the "Warden" that he couldn't objectively see the severity of the damage being done. He took the student's advice and terminated the study. He also married her.

Milgram recruited ordinary citizens from New Haven, Conn. to participate in research studies in which they obeyed commands to administer simulated electric shocks to persons. The shockers were led to believe they were inflicting increasing degrees of pain and, at the highest levels, possible death. Forty psychiatrists were asked to predict how many of these ordinary citizens would administer severe (simulated) shocks. They predicted 1 percent. The actual number was 65 percent. Two out of three citizens did as they were told in return for $4.00 for participating.

Public employees, such as school teachers, have not engaged in this sort of *hostile* behavior toward fellow citizens, but if normal persons can be easily persuaded to be directly hostile, would it not be even easier to persuade public employees to participate in generous retirement contracts that seem reasonable at the time they are negotiated with the state but which progressively, over several years, jeopardize the education of children and the solvency of state budgets?

Even my three friends, very experienced retired psychology professors who must have been aware of the classic studies by Milgram and Zimbardo, let themselves participate in a program of benefits that were good for themselves but now jeopardize the common good.

U.S. military prisons recently have been criticized for torturing war prisoners to extract information. This is in violation of the Geneva Convention regarding treatment of prisoners of war. Even professional psychologists, from a profession we would expect to be especially careful *not* to violate human rights, have been involved in the design and implementation of this torture program. Presumably they were offered lucrative contracts for their services.

Many other psychologists have vigorously opposed this activity by fellow psychologists, citing it as a violation of professional ethics. Zimbardo served as an expert witness to a marine who the military blamed for this prison misbehavior. Zimbardo knew from his studies decades before that circumstances, such as orders from authorities, can easily persuade normal citizens to be cruel to fellow humans. In court Zimbardo argued that the soldier's misbehavior was caused not so much by personal flaws in the individual soldier but mainly by circumstances, specifically military prison policies. The military court ignored the circumstances and punished the soldier.

Many psychologically normal German citizens were persuaded under the Nazi regime to participate in inhumane behaviors, including genocide and murder. These citizens weren't prosecuted after the war. They were excused as tools of an evil system. Their leaders were held accountable for designing the evil system. Goering and others, those who designed the evil system, were found guilty of war crimes, crimes against humanity, crimes against the common good.

U.S. citizens are recruited to fight in wars that are sometimes of questionable defensive value to our nation. During WWII the U.S. military and our Presidents Roosevelt and Truman willingly participated in fire-bombing enemy cities in Germany and Japan, deliberately causing the deaths of hundreds of thousands of civilians. Presumably such mass killing of civilians was intended to demoralize the enemy into surrender. But it could be considered the ultimate moral transgression against the common good of civilians. Even allied political leaders were swept into war decisions that in retrospect were clearly in violation of the common good.

Each of the citizens participating in these various activities that violated the common good could have seen themselves at the time as justified in their behavior and acting in the interest of some socially respectable goal. Each could have claimed they were following acceptable social codes, such as playing by the current rules of the game, pursuing their rights as union members, obeying the laws of the land, following the code of their social group, looking out for the needs of their families, or obeying the explicit or implicit orders of their armed forces superiors, or in the case of Presidents, serving the best interests of their nation. But, if they are asked in retrospect if their behavior was moral, ethical, or in the long-term best interests of the human community overall, they might take pause.

Now, in the Twenty-first Century, we tend also to ask if our behaviors are in the best interests of the planet overall. We are learning that indulging our human and national "rights" to life, liberty and the pursuit of happiness can inadvertently destroy habitat, cause the extinction of other species and degrade the environment of the whole world.

Another issue of psychological import in all of this is the fundamental one of how we manage ourselves as a state or a nation. The Oregon teacher union and other public employees have played by the rules. The rules implicitly include the idea that it's a competitive world and you compete for what you want. They've "competed" and negotiated good wages and very good retirement benefits.

At the national level the United States has a debt of over 16 trillion dollars, more than $40,000 per citizen, including the elderly and children. If only one in three citizens is a breadwinner, each breadwinner is burdened with $120,000 of the debt. Several nations in Europe have heavy debt, so heavy that there is fear of default, a form of bankruptcy that can have catastrophic effects on financial systems. Nations seem to have trouble living within their means. They spend for military, retirement, welfare, public health care and industry subsidies…all worthy budget categories, each represented by competing interests. However, if nations spend more than they take in, they can go broke.

One could argue that this is just human nature, people competing against each other, each seeking his own best interests. But systems do not have to be governed by a framework of competition. In competition there are winners and losers.

Humans can be either competitive or cooperative. Systems could be governed by a framework of cooperation, in which there aren't losers. Social systems, including governments and economic systems, can be designed to promote one or the other of these worldviews.

Competition and cooperation can be considered worldview facets. For example, in my studies I have asked persons how strongly they agree with statements that measure these two dimensions, such as in the religion scales discussed in Chapter 5. Four statements from the Religious Fundamentalism and Kindly Religious scales are presented below, with the percent of 189 community college students who agreed or strongly agreed with each:

- Competition between peoples is a natural part of religious struggles. (25 percent)
- It is natural that we compete against people of religions different from our own. (22 percent)
- Cooperation with people unlike us is an important religious value. (67 percent)
- We should cooperate with people of religions different from our own. (91 percent)

This data suggests that the majority of citizens might very well endorse cooperation over competition as basic social policy. The correlations between these items and political orientations show that liberals are more likely to think in terms of cooperation and conservatives in terms of competition, consistent with the general theory of the two differing in-group survival roles these two orientations seem to serve, which we'll explore in a later chapter.

If the majority of citizens want policies and programs designed from a cooperative rather than competitive worldview, how could a state or nation achieve this? Could public employee salaries and benefits be negotiated via a cooperative rather than a competitive procedure? Would special interest groups resist such a change in philosophy?

If we can't trust special interest group government, a system based on a competitive worldview, what is the alternative? Can we trust the common citizen to help decide cooperative government policies? Or to design government with stronger guarantees that it won't go bankrupt in providing services to citizens?

My banker friends had asked me who was going to make the decisions to change government to prevent Ponzi scheme contracts with public employees. I replied that I wasn't sure how it would be done but only that I was confident that it could be done. I added that from my research I was confident that most citizens want something different than government that serves them as members of special interest groups.

In the 15th and 16th centuries political philosophers couldn't yet see the details of how a democratic form of government would work but they could imagine basic features of such a government. And they sensed accurately that citizens would prefer representative democracies over the monarchies that characterized European government at the time.

Albert Einstein has opined: "Imagination is everything; it is the preview of life's coming attractions." We can use our imaginations to create models of government that serves citizens as members of the community overall.

As an example of how imagination can be used to do research about what citizens want, consider an empirical example, this time about citizens' opinions about public school funding. In my studies I've asked citizens how strongly they endorse two types of public school funding. One option is the standard current practice, by contract between teacher unions and public officials, such as school district superintendents and their representatives. The salaries and benefits of tenured, experienced teachers take precedence. Other aspects of the budget must be pared if necessary due to budget limitations.

The other option is a hypothetical one, one that I imagined and termed the "proportional budgeting system". The proportional system starts with a school system design that includes all desired features, including a wide range of content offerings, manageable class sizes, adequate support services and adequate physical facilities. Each is funded as a proportion of the overall available budget.

The proportional system keeps the proportion of each budget category the same from year to year and class sizes are kept constant. If revenue for schools goes up, all aspects of the budget go up by their proportional share. If revenue goes down, all aspects are reduced by their share. No teachers or other staff members are laid off. Junior teachers are not dismissed to keep senior teachers' salaries and benefits rising with years of service. Class sizes aren't increased and classes aren't eliminated to compensate for dismissed teachers.

What sorts of citizens endorse these two options? I measure this trait with three statements asking how strongly one agrees with each option "as a public school teacher", as a "parent with a child in school" and "as a taxpayer".

Persons who prefer the proportional option over the contract option tend to have higher scores on the Big Five personality traits of Agreeableness, Emotional Stability and Conscientiousness. They tend to endorse more democratic forms of government and sustainable policies and programs. They tend *not* to endorse warmongering and social disenfranchisement. Thus, they seem to be nice people.

Specifically, in a sample of 383 adults, 48 percent endorsed the proportional option. 36 percent were undecided. Only 9 percent preferred the contract-driven option. Thus, the ratio of persons *for* versus *against* the proportional option was 48 to 9 or 5 to 1. More citizens preferred the proportional system. In a class of 40 university students taking an education department class, many who were preparing to become teachers themselves, 80 percent endorsed the proportional option.

But, this is not how things work at present. Teacher salaries and benefits are determined by contracts negotiated between teacher unions and governments. Who in government signs these contracts? Are they government employees, such as school district superintendents, who are also receiving salaries and benefits under contracts negotiated with their state, such as via PERS in Oregon? Are they hoping that their retirement benefits will be as generous as those for teachers? Do they thus empathize with the teachers? Would they be inclined to deny contracts to teachers that are similar to their own contracts? Would Oregon judges, who are also scheduled to receive PERS retirement benefits, be unbiased in hearing a case involving a dispute of PERS benefits?

And who represents the pubic in these negotiations? The public taxpayer is responsible for paying for the resulting obligations. If the obligations outrun revenues, governments have to cut expenditures. In public school systems they cut junior teachers, cut school days, cut classes, cut budgets to other public programs and/ or raise taxes, or borrow money.

At the federal level too, nations borrow if they don't have enough revenue for obligations, e.g. for public employee salaries and benefits, for military bases, for research grants to universities, for medical, welfare and retirement payments to citizens (e.g. Medicare and Social Security). If nations borrow too much, they can go bankrupt, as was near to happening in Portugal, Italy, Ireland, Greece and Spain in 2011. Nations can also go bankrupt if they invest public retirement funds unwisely, as happened recently to Iceland, which went bankrupt when their investment portfolio collapsed with the financial meltdown of 2008.

States have billions of dollars of pension fund money that they invest to have money to make payments to retired public employees. At least one pension fund manager, Robert Price of Bridgewater Associates, fears that heavily indebted nations may go bankrupt in the years ahead, complicating his job of finding predictable financial markets in which to invest institutional funds, such as public employee pension funds. He refers to the economies in the U.S. and Europe as "operating on life-support". He opines "You've got insolvent banks supporting insolvent sovereigns [states and nations] and insolvent sovereigns supporting insolvent banks" (6).

Government policy issues must be decided by someone. Retirement systems have to be designed, managed, interpreted and executed. Who does this and by what rules and worldviews can have an effect on whether it is done fairly, in the best interests of the community overall, or whether it is done unfairly, in the best interests of one or more special interest groups and at the unfair expense of the general public.

My research results suggest that a majority of citizens wants a new form of democracy, one that serves them not as members of special interest groups but as members of the community overall. For research purposes I have imagined that this will be realized through a new form of political party that depends on polls of citizens to form the political party's agenda and eventually the political agenda of communities. And so, if we are to trust citizens with making basic policy decisions on such important matters, we must know what sorts of decisions they would be likely to make.

Would they support amendments to their state and national constitutions that declare that any contract or legislation that is or becomes clearly contrary to the common good then becomes null and void? Such an amendment would empower courts to decide if and when the common good is violated. It would enable the courts to strike down policies and programs that become doomed to bankruptcy or that egregiously favor some special interest groups at the expense of a state or nation, or that seriously tarnish the international reputation of the nation or that seriously jeopardize international environmental protections.

Would citizens make wise choices on such matters, as I hope, or poor ones, as my friend Lew has feared? We can see clues to these questions by measuring their attitudes with questionnaires, as we'll explore in the next chapter.

CHAPTER 8

FOREIGN POLICY, HUMAN RIGHTS AND EXECUTIVE ETHICS

THERE ARE DANGERS TO LETTING GOVERNMENT POLICIES BE dictated by special interest groups. But can we trust the common citizen to make government policy decisions? Thomas Jefferson, one of the founding fathers of the U.S. government, seemed to think we should, as he wrote "A well-educated citizen can be trusted with his own government."

However, political opinions may be more a function of beliefs than of facts or knowledge, as I pointed out to the jewelry store clerk (Chapter 2). So, how much information or knowledge one has about a political or government policy issue may not be the most relevant factor in deciding who should make such decisions. The quality or nature of the attitudes and beliefs of the majority of citizens would be of central importance in a government whose policies were to be determined heavily by public opinion.

This brings us to the crux of the matter. The answer to Lew's question about trusting the public with government policy matters has two parts. I'll explain it briefly here and in more detail in later chapters. Political issues are indeed complex, but what people want from government in *general* terms is rather simple. And what citizens want is determined not so much by facts about the issues but by their beliefs, attitudes and opinions. For example, some U.S. citizens want a national health care program, not because they understand all the facts about this form of health care but because they just want it. Other citizens don't want it, again, not because of facts but simply because of their opinions and desires. We can call services such as a national health care program "*general* government services".

Let's imagine a government that depends heavily on public opinion to set its national agenda. Let's further assume that the majority of citizens, say, 80 percent, want a national health care system and that if put to a public vote public opinion would carry the issue and make it reality. The next step of the process would be to decide what kind of health care system it would be, and here is where the complex facts come in. A government department, or a committee in the case of a political party, would be responsible for researching the issue and coming up with perhaps two or three options based on relevant facts: What works in other nations? What level of funding will be available? Where will funding come from? How will the system be administered? How will medical and administrative personnel be trained? What facilities will they work in? How will their salaries and benefits be determined?

These are all questions for which facts are relevant. Considering all the facts, the committee designs three options, explains them in detail with their pros and cons and then citizens are polled to determine which option they most prefer. At this second stage, the facts *are* relevant to their decisions. Citizens are encouraged to become familiar with the details of the three options before they choose between them. The organization preparing the options is responsible for making the facts clear enough for citizens to understand. These are options for a *specific* government service.

So, in brief, citizen opinions are mainly what count in determining *general* government policies and programs and citizen understanding of facts and details are necessary to inform them in choosing *specific* government policies and programs. "I want a national health care system just because that's my opinion, and I want option B to be how it is delivered because the facts for that option make more sense to me than the facts for options A and C".

Another example: "I want a graduated personal and corporation business tax system to fund the majority of federal government expenses because that's my opinion. And I want option D regarding the specific tax rates for each level of income and the related deductions because the facts about that option make more sense to me than the facts for options A, B and C."

More on this later, but for now, let's focus on the question of whether a community or state or nation can trust the opinions of citizens to provide a reasonable and constructive set of *general* policies and programs.

We have seen that citizens who prefer a hypothetical proportional budgeting system for funding school programs tend to be nice people, in that they also tend to endorse a variety of other pro-social or constructive attitudes, such as agreeableness and sustainable policies, and eschew anti-social traits, such as war-mongering endorsement and social disenfranchisement.

If we are to consider common citizens' beliefs and opinions as a guide to such general policy decisions, it behooves us to explore whether citizens who endorse other policies also have trustworthy and constructive attitudes. Consider, for example, research findings on what I call "positive foreign policy". This scale measures attitudes about national government. The first four asterisked items in the scale below are reverse-scored (endorsing them *lower's* one's score). In questionnaires the Positive Foreign Policy scale is presented as follows:

"Regarding foreign policy, how our nation relates to other nations, how strongly do you agree or disagree with the following foreign policy positions?

In foreign policy our nation should:

1. Get as much natural resources from other countries as we can afford.

2. Buy as much inexpensive products as we can, even if it means some U.S. adults are unemployed as a result.

3. Control the world with military power.

4. Ignore how much pollution of air and water we cause by our use of natural resources such as oil and coal.

5. Set limits on our consumption so resources are available for other nations.

6. Help other countries with peaceful means rather than military ones.

7. Promote prosperity, stability and peace in other nations by student exchanges, cultural and sport exchanges and tourism.

8. Help other countries by medical aid to fight AIDS and other diseases.

9. Help other countries by supporting the United Nations.

10. Fight civil wars in and terrorism from other countries by helping other countries provide opportunities, jobs, education and better standards of living.

11. Help other countries develop and maintain sustainable communities and economies by population control, agricultural development, education, women's rights promotion, etc.

12. Agree to international arms control and pollution control treaties to reduce the dangers from wars, global warming and destruction of forests, ocean fisheries, etc."

These items form a reliable scale; persons who endorse one of the items tend to endorse the others (with items 1-4 reverse-scored). This trait correlates positively with endorsement of human rights, protecting the environment, preference for more democratic forms of government and kindly religious beliefs. It correlates negatively with endorsement of warmongering, anarchy and military dictatorship forms of government. Thus, citizens who endorse this positive foreign policy trait also seem to be "nice" people. This is reason to think that citizens could be trusted to make reasonable general decisions about foreign policy. At least citizens who endorse a peaceful and helpful foreign policy seem to hold a variety of constructive political attitudes and eschew belligerent ones.

In examining this fundamental issue of politics, who should decide what is good for a nation and its citizens, one can explore charters or "declarations" of human rights. For example the United Nations has such a charter, which was inspired and created under the leadership of First Lady Eleanor Roosevelt. Christian church groups united to create a similar charter. Other groups created the Earth Charter, emphasizing concern for the environment.

It is one thing for well-meaning authorities to create such charters, but it would seem important to give citizens the final say, as by polling them, to determine if they agree with the authorities that the items in the charter are indeed desirable.

For my research studies I created a 44-item scale based on the three above-mentioned charters. It included items such as "Everyone has the right to food, clothing and shelter", "We should promote local, regional and global civil society, and promote the meaningful participation of all interested individuals and organizations in decision making at the local, regional and global level" and "everyone has the right *not* to have one's religion denigrated by public media or education professors."

The items in this scale form a reliable measure. Persons who endorse one item tend to endorse the others. And the content of this scale is consonant with what citizens actually think. For example, consider this excerpt from a letter to the editor of our local newspaper:

"Imagine regulation as protection; corporations are not people; sustainable agriculture and real food; unions living up to their moral and social roles; ... protecting and preserving nature; having more funding to end hunger and homelessness;...finding good will through human relations and not through endless wars;

providing health care for all; enjoying moral democracy…There is enough for everyone if we all practice the principle of sharing….”

My 44-item Human Rights Scale correlates positively with kindly religious beliefs, peace endorsement, ecology (environment) endorsement and endorsement of more democratic forms of government. It correlates negatively with warmongering endorsement, religious fundamentalism, anarchy endorsement, military dictatorship and the belief that “The peoples of the world should compete…let the ‘best’ win.” Thus, persons who endorse human rights also seem to be constructively-minded, “nice” people.

Another way to assess the trustworthiness of citizen opinion as a gauge of general government policy is to explore citizen ethical beliefs that are related to political issues. Our society tries to imbue noble ethics in citizens in a wide variety of ways, such as through our religious institutions, youth organizations, and professional and service organizations. Religious groups teach principles such as the Ten Commandments against killing and coveting, and for honoring parents and loving God and our neighbors. Scouting organizations urge us to be trustworthy, loyal, helpful, friendly, kind, brave and reverent. Professional organizations have codes of ethics that direct against violations of patient trust and confidentiality and for doing no harm. The Rotary International organization has a simple code of ethics that members are expected to use to guide their personal and business lives, consisting of four questions, the Four Way Test: Is it the truth? Is it fair to all concerned? Will it build good will and better friendships? Will it be beneficial to all concerned?

Ethical belief systems can be studied with questionnaires. I had puzzled in recent years over what sort of ethics underlie the decisions of top government and business executives whose decisions have seemed indifferent to the common good. Why did the Bush administration invade Iraq in the absence of good evidence that

Iraq was involved in the 9-11 terrorist attack on the World Trade Center? Why does the U.S. Congress not ratify climate change treaties? Why did Congress de-regulate big financial institutions, knowing that those regulations were put in place after the great depression of the 30's to prevent equity market collapses? Why did top executives of big commercial banks then invest in hyper-risky instruments that went bad and caused the financial meltdown of 2008? And why did they give themselves multimillion dollar bonuses after accepting billions in bailout money from the government without which their banks would have failed? And why in recent years did some psychologists participate in designing and overseeing torture methods in U.S. military prisons, in spite of the professional ethics code for psychologists that prohibits transgression of human rights?

What ethical beliefs do such leaders and professionals hold? Because such persons are unlikely to be directly available for study of their ethical motives, another approach is necessary. One approach is to imagine how such leaders might think, and then write statements that express this thinking. These statements can be included in a questionnaire and administered to general citizens, such as adult students. To this end I designed a questionnaire study of 212 items, about 100 of which measured ethical beliefs. I gathered data from 195 students at a local Christian university and the local community college.

The questionnaire yielded many reliable measures of traits, including many used in prior studies (warmongering, violence-proneness, positive foreign policy, religious fundamentalism, kindly religious beliefs, authoritarianism, human rights endorsement, environmentalism, common good democracy endorsement and the Big Five personality traits) (1).

Data analysis revealed several reliable measures of ethical dimensions. I gave them names to fit the content of the questionnaire statements of which they were composed. Their labels and some questionnaire statements in each are these:

In-group elitism. "Corporate executives are more deserving of government favors, such as bailouts and tax deductions, than are citizens who claim physical or mental disabilities. Our government best serves our nation by serving special interest groups. I like the athletic coach slogan: 'Winning isn't everything, it's the only thing'. Government should serve my group primarily. I sometimes enjoy the feeling that I am above the law. I believe in the superiority of my own ethnic group."

An item that correlated *negatively* and very strongly with this trait is: "I like the motto 'Service above self'." This is the motto of Rotary International. Persons with higher scores on In-group Elitism tend to *disagree* with this motto.

Messianic nationalism. "I sometimes feel a divine inspiration to lead. Religion should play the most important part in civic affairs. I have profound respect for historical institutions, laws and traditions. I love and am devoted to my country. Our nation is God's chosen one." An item that correlates *negatively* with this dimension is: "We ought to welcome foreigners to enter and become part of our nation." High scorers tend to disagree with this statement.

Guarded self-protection. "We should have strong regulations of banks to guard against misbehavior by bank executives. We must protect our homes and our possessions. Our citizens should have personal weapons in their homes to protect themselves and their possessions." Items that correlate negatively with this dimension are: "I am opposed to the death penalty (execution) as a punishment for crimes" and "My opinions were respected in my childhood family." This last item is peculiar and interesting. It raises interesting questions to be explored by further research. For example, are persons who felt disrespected by their parents more inclined to protect their physical possessions to compensate?

Common good concern. "Businesses have an obligation to

help nonprofit organizations in their communities. I support the missions of the United Nations. I support government programs promoting heath care and public education for all citizens. The citizens of our nation, by public polls or other voting, should have more direct say in how long we stay in wars. Wealthy people should have a higher tax rate than poor people." Items that correlated negatively with this dimension are: "I like to think of our nation as the best in the world" and "I think of myself as a Conservative, politically."

The traits of persons who endorse these four ethics dimensions give hints as to what types of people they are. The In-group elitism trait correlates positively with warmongering, violence-proneness, religious fundamentalism, authoritarianism and with social and political elitism measured by a separate cluster of questionnaire items. It correlates negatively with positive foreign policy endorsement, kindly religious beliefs, common good democracy, human rights, environmentalism and the Big Five personality traits of Agreeableness and Openness. Thus, persons high on the In-group elitism ethic appear to have potentially dangerous tendencies, higher scores on a cluster of traits related to warmongering and violence.

The Messianic Nationalism ethic is positively correlated with warmongering, valuing religion to manage one's entire life, religious fundamentalism and authoritarianism. It correlates negatively with positive foreign policy, environmentalism and Openness.

The Guarded Self-Protection ethic correlates positively with warmongering, violence-proneness, religious fundamentalism, authoritarianism, and with social and political elitism measured with the separate cluster of items. It correlates negatively with kindly religious beliefs, environmentalism and Agreeableness.

Thus, all three of these ethics dimensions seem to have dangerous potential, as they all correlate with traits such as warmongering endorsement, violence-proneness or authoritarianism.

The Common Good Concern ethic correlates positively with positive-foreign-policy endorsement, kindly religious beliefs, meta-religion endorsement, human rights endorsement, environmentalism, Agreeableness and Openness. It correlates negatively with warmongering, valuing religion to manage one's entire life, religious fundamentalism, authoritarianism, and social and political elitism measured with the brief scale. Thus, persons with higher scores on the Common Good Concern ethic appear to be nice rather than potentially dangerous people.

The percentage of citizens who hold these four ethical belief orientations can be roughly estimated by computing the percentage in the present sample of 195 persons who have high scores. For this purpose, "high" means having an average score on the scale of 3.5 or higher. Recall that a mean item score of 4.0 means that on average the person agrees with the statements in the scale. A mean score of 5.0 would mean the person strongly agreed with every item in the scale. Only one of the 195 persons (½ percent) was high on In-group Elitism. 15 percent were high on Messianic Nationalism. 25 percent were high on Guarded Self-Protection. 50 percent were high on Common Good Concern.

Thus, in this sample of students, the percentage of persons who endorse common good concern outweighed the percentage who endorse the three other potentially more problematic ethical orientations.

While only one half of one percent of citizens may endorse in-group elitism, a trait that we might expect Hitler to have endorsed, one-half percent of a million citizens is 5,000. There are 300 million Americans. Thus, there are probably tens of thousands who endorse in-group elitism, enough, to fill many seats in Congress if they manage to win elections. And there would be enough persons who endorse in-group elitism to fill the boardrooms and executive suites of many corporations.

These last two chapters have been heavy-duty. Special interest groups, including large commercial bank executives and public school teacher unions, have been able to craft very good benefits for themselves. Our society is a competitive system. Many special interest groups have played the current game very well, competing against other groups. They can buy legislators' loyalties by making contributions to their campaigns through lobbyists. They can run big banks to their personal advantage, making millions in salaries for themselves while jeopardizing the stability of world financial markets and the wellbeing of millions of citizens. They can engineer union contracts to yield very good benefits, at least for their members, if not for their whole profession.

In competition, there are winners and losers. The losers tend to fare more poorly than the winners. Special interest groups tend to fare better than the general citizen, who can be on the hook to live with the tab as taxpayers.

Alternatively, we could give citizens more say in making policy decisions, so they will feel served by government as members of the community overall rather than as members of competing special interest groups. The majority of citizens appear to be "nice" enough to trust with this responsibility. But this would take a transition from one type of government to another. What new type of government might this be?

PSYCHOLOGICAL TRAIT CLUSTERS THAT CONSTITUTE THE LIBERAL AND CONSERVATIVE WORLDVIEWS

CHAPTER 9

GOVERNMENT TYPE PREFERENCES AND POLITICAL PHILOSOPHY

BORN IN 1939, I HAVE LIVED THROUGH MANY DECADES OF public opinion about government in the United States. After WW II and during the Korean War it seemed without question that the United States was a nation of honorable principles, defending the world against tyrannical leaders and nations. However, upon leaving office, President Eisenhower warned of a too-cozy relationship between industry and the military, a relationship that he warned would promote excessive militarism in the decades ahead unless the citizens reined it in. During the cold war with the Soviet Union and early in the Vietnam War the U.S. was still thought of by many Americans as on a noble mission.

However, as the Vietnam War progressed, serious doubts arose. Our involvement with South American governments during the Reagan administration also raised questions about hyper-militarism. And over decades the U.S. arranged to develop and maintain military bases in scores of nations around the world. In response to the terrorist attack on the World Trade Center the Bush administration invaded Iraq, even though justification for doing so proved to be unfounded; Iraq was not a sponsor of the attack. Then our warring spread to Afghanistan.

Early in my studies of the Eidelson worldviews, beginning in 2003, and then of warmongering, I wondered how these two traits related to types of government. For example, I assumed that persons who endorsed warmongering would also tend to endorse military dictatorship as a form of government. As the United States had seemed to be involved in excessive preoccupation with militarism, consonant with Eisenhower's warning, I thought it might be fruitful to see if some Americans endorsed not just defensive war, as characterized U.S. involvement in WW II, but aggressive militarism, unprovoked meddling in other nations' affairs.

So, I included in my questionnaire study the following:

"For each of the following items, indicate how strongly you agree that it is a desirable form of government by circling one number, using this code:

1	2	3	4	5
Strongly disagree	Disagree	Neutral	Agree	Strongly agree

1 2 3 4 5 1. Anarchy. No government at all, just roving bands of armed bandits who rob, kill and do whatever they want.

1 2 3 4 5 2. Military dictatorship, headed by a powerful military leader who controls everything and everyone in the country and prevents anyone else from replacing him.

1 2 3 4 5 3. Monarchy, headed by a king or queen, with a supportive parliament of elected representatives. They run the country as they "benevolently" see fit.

1 2 3 4 5 4. Tribal democracy. Elected officials run the govern-

ment to serve the short-term economic interests of the special interest groups ("economic tribes") which helped them get elected.

1 2 3 4 5   5. Public democracy. Elected officials run the government to serve the current and long-term best interests of the community overall, including sustainable programs such as conservation of resources and control of pollution and global warming. No special interest groups are favored.

Each of the first four of these types of government *could* be defined differently and the difference might influence research results. But I felt I had justification to use these definitions based on my familiarity with governments. I wanted to span the whole continuum of government types and do so parsimoniously. As I measure many traits in each study, I try to measure each expediently. I learned that often one can measure a trait reliably with just a few items, as turned out to be the case with these five.

I found that some Americans do indeed endorse even military dictatorships. For example, in the ethics study reported in an earlier chapter, data was obtained on 196 students from a Christian university and the local community college. The five government type questionnaire items as a cluster were moderately reliable, reverse-scoring the first four and combining them with the fifth. The first four items tend to correlate negatively with the fifth item. Persons who endorse the fifth item, Public Democracy, tend not to endorse the first four items (anarchy, etc).

In this study 6 percent of the 196 student subjects endorsed anarchy, 4.5 percent military dictatorship, 22 percent monarchy, 27 percent special interest group democracy ("tribal democracy") and 92 percent public democracy. A person responds to each item separately, so the total percent endorsing can be greater than 100. For example, a person can endorse both public democracy and special interest group democracy.

What type of person tends to endorse public democracy? Correlations between the five-item measure of public democracy endorsement and other traits measured in the ethics study provide clues. In this study, persons who endorse public democracy tend to be higher on positive foreign policy, kindly religious beliefs, human rights, environmentalism and on the common good democracy ethic. This 90 percent of citizens thus appears to be pro-social, pro-society, "nice" people. They tend to be lower on warmongering, violence-proneness, authoritarianism and in-group elitism.

Stated conversely, persons who endorse anarchy, monarchy, military dictatorships and special interest group democracy tend to endorse warmongering, violence proneness, authoritarianism and in-group elitism.

You will recall that I expected persons who endorse warmongering would also endorse military dictatorship government. In this ethics study the correlation between these traits is positive and statistically significant, in line with this prediction; persons who endorse military dictatorships do tend to endorse warmongering.

What other traits characterize persons who endorse special interest group democracy, government that serves citizens as members of special interest groups? This information is very important if one is puzzled with U.S. Government in recent decades. How can we explain the presence of more than 11 *thousand* lobbyists in Washington (1)?

These lobbyists court legislators with special interest group campaign money in return for favors to special interest groups. In 2010 the U.S. Supreme Court Citizens United decision gave corporations 'personhood', giving them unlimited campaign funding privileges. Government funds much public education and research and thus teacher salaries and benefits.

Presumably lobbyist money promoted legislative decisions in

Congress that undid the banking industry regulations that let big investment banks run wild, leading to the financial crisis in 2008.

In the ethics study, persons who endorsed special interest group democracy (a one-item measure) tended also to endorse warmongering, violence-proneness, authoritarianism, in-group elitism (quite strongly), messianic nationalism and guarded self-protection. They tended *not* to endorse a positive foreign policy, human rights, environmental protection, and the Big Five trait of Openness. They rather strongly tended not to endorse the common good ethic. They very strongly tended *not* to endorse public democracy government, measured with the five-item scale.

These results suggest that recent concerns about U.S. Government reflect not just quirks of a particular Congress or President or Administration. The results suggest that U.S. Government in recent years, and perhaps for decades, seems to reflect the interests and ethics of persons with a specific cluster of measurable psychological attitudes. U.S. Government seems to cater to special interest groups and is staffed with elected and appointed officials willing to promote this form of government, "special interest group democracy".

In the ethics study, only 27 percent of the 196 students endorsed special interest group government. In contrast 92 percent endorsed public democracy, (and 90 percent on average in my many studies). Thus, it appears that a minority of citizens have control of U.S. government, a minority that maintains special interest group democracy.

It seems likely that the majority of citizens would favor a new form of democracy, government that serves them as members of the community overall. This may help explain why citizens have been so vocal about their unhappiness with lobbyists, big corporation control of Congress, militarism in foreign lands, budget deficits and big corporations being declared "persons" with unlimited campaign contribution rights.

While I conducted my studies on the psychology of politics and saw evidence for roots of an unflattering presence of public opinion sufficiently robust to underlie and support a warmongering mind set in U.S. government, I reflected on the general history of human political systems, which have been fraught with war for millennia.

Political systems have seemed to progress gradually over the thousands of years documented by written history. Early groups of humans seemed to be led by single leaders, such as the chiefs that led the essentially stone-age tribes of Native Americans when first encountered by Europeans. As groups increased in size, such leaders took on the status of royalty: kings, queens and emperors, often justifying their roles as leaders with religious claims to divine authority. With increases in military technology, some nation leaders became dictators who justified their right to lead not with divine power but simply with an iron fist, police and military power enforced by weaponry.

These elite leader forms of government have tended to evolve gradually into more broadly based authority, as in Great Britain, where monarchy has been complemented with a parliament of elected representatives. These representatives are elected by the citizens of the nation. Many variations on these government types exist, with some dictatorships paying lip service to democracy, having elections in which the only option is to endorse the current dictator for another term or with elections rigged so that the incumbent dictator is assured victory over challengers.

Karl Marx interpreted the history of human politics as evolving in such a manner that Capitalism would be replaced with rule by the laboring class. However, efforts to create governments based on this theory have often turned into military dictatorships, as in Russia and China, with dictatorial leaders merely using communist philosophy as a propaganda tool to confiscate private property in the name of the state and enforce conformity of the masses to dictatorial mandates.

More successful manifestations of socialism exist in nations such as Norway, where policies prevent large corporations from controlling governments too completely and substantial taxation assures financial security and benefits to all citizens, as in the form of higher education, health care and welfare services.

It seemed that my public opinion research data roughly paralleled the evolutionary stages of human government, with the least favored type of government, anarchy, characteristic of pre-government groups, the next most favored type, military dictatorships, characteristic of governments ruled simply by military might, monarchies the next most favored type, typical of monarchies that tended to replace militant governments, and democracies more favored than any of the other types.

In all of these types, the more favored ones are characterized by more citizen input, greater citizen say in government policies. In the most favored form of government, government that would serve citizens as members of the community overall, I imagine that citizens would all have a vote not just on representatives to government but a vote on national government policies and programs as well.

Giving citizens a vote on policies and programs is a relatively recent feature of governments. In the United States, for example, at local and state levels citizens now vote on referenda, citizen initiatives, bond measures and other policy matters. For example, citizens may vote on whether public bonds will be sold to fund the construction of a sports arena or new public schools, or whether a new grocery store 5-cent refund for cans and bottles will be instituted.

The rough parallel between how strongly citizens endorse various types of government and the evolutionary stages of human government types over the centuries seemed to reinforce the notion that humans prefer government that gives them a relatively direct say in determining policies and programs. The more say they have, the more they like it.

I also wondered what the history of political philosophy might have to offer that would help put my political psychology findings in perspective. I studied a couple of comprehensive texts on political philosophy, finding interesting highlights.(2,3) For example, some political philosophers as early as the 17th century recommended dependence on science rather than on theology or philosophy for basic principles upon which to design ideal governments.

Some philosophers have advocated representative government as superior to authoritarian government. Some have gone ever further, advocating dependence on public opinion for determining government policies. And there are recommendations for repeated assessments of such opinion, attention to the dangers of special interests groups usurping government power at the expense of the common good and recommendations for flexible design of governments to be sensitive to the needs and desires of peoples in different regions of the world.

It seemed that the thinking of political philosophers of prior centuries, and increasingly so of more recent thinkers, is quite consonant with data from recent scientific studies of citizen attitudes about political issues. I found this reassuring, as even scientific data can be interpreted differently by different scientists. It seemed that philosophers, especially many from the past few centuries, accurately sensed the evolving trends of human government and foresaw what I have interpreted scientific data of psychological traits to be revealing: the majority of humans prefer an increasingly direct voice in government policies.

There are several implications of the two types of democracy I have studied: special interest group democracy and common good democracy. One way to diagnose the presence or degree of special-interest group democracy in a nation would seem to be calculating the percentage of a nation's peace-time budget that is dedicated to military activity. The higher that portion, the more likely that government would fall into the special-interest group form, implicitly, as this form of government is associated psychologically with endorsement of warmongering.

Another way to diagnose special-interest group democracy is to measure the amount of money that flows directly from special interest groups to election campaigns of government leaders (Presidents and Congress persons in the U.S., for example). This money can also flow through lobbyists to government leaders. The greater the portion of campaign financing that is provided by special interest groups, the more suggestive this is of special interest group rather than common good democracy.

There are also implications for foreign-policy. The G.W. Bush administration argued that the invasion of Iraq to depose Saddam Hussein and install a democratic government was in the best interests of the Middle East. If the U.S. feels entitled to exporting democracy to other nations, we should be careful to clarify which form of democracy is under consideration, that which supports special interest groups or that which would support the common good. In the Middle East the United States also supports Israel as a democratic nation surrounded by nations governed by monarchies and dictatorships. Much of this support is in military aid, suggesting an interest in supporting Israel as a special interest group democracy.

Current estimates of the number of U.S. military bases around the world run as high as 662 in 38 nations (4). In how many nations does the United States have a Peace Corps presence? Seventy-six, according to the Peace Corps web site. Comparing these figures can inform judgments about what sort of democratic institutions the United States government tends to promote in its foreign policy activities.

Many nations in the Middle East have been rebelling against long-standing dictatorships, presumably in the hopes of establishing more democratic forms of government. If other democratic nations intend to offer help in such transitions then it would again be relevant to explore which kind of democracy they are promoting. If efforts to help such nations in transition are characterized primarily by forming power alliances reinforced with military equipment and training, then promotion of special-interest group democracy would be implied.

If, on the other hand, assistance to nations in transition from dictatorships is intended to promote common good democracies, we would expect the emphasis to be on building institutions focusing on human rights. Also, we would expect promotion of open and fair elections of leaders, women's rights, public education, public health services, trials by jury, and international exchange of cultural activities such as music, athletic events and student exchanges. From the United States we would expect offers of Peace Corps assistance.

Another implication of these two kinds of democracy, from a psychological traits perspective, is that we would expect to see evidence of these two kinds of government in civilian institutions. Because the percentage of citizens who endorse public or common good democracy is apparently more than three times higher than the percent who endorse special interest group democracy, we would expect most civilian activities to be of a peaceful, friendly and kind nature. Evidence of this friendly and kind disposition seems readily apparent in organizations such as Rotary International and other nonprofit charitable organizations which provide billions of dollars and a wide range of services to citizens in need. This friendly and kind disposition also appears to be reflected in the policies and activities of most religious organizations, in the United States at least.

Charitable giving in the U.S. by individuals and groups in some years is as much as 166 billion dollars, 3 percent of income(5). And this kindly disposition seems in many cases to be international in scope. For example, Rotarians of all ethnic and religious groups in scores of nations are nice people, get along very well with each other and do good in their communities and around the world. They trust each other. They believe in service above self. They guide themselves by a code of ethics characterized by good will and fairness. They are not xenophobic.

However in the United States, we also see signs of civilian behavior consistent with special interest group democracy, as in fascination with violence and aggressive competition. Examples include interest in violent video games, violent movies and television programs, aggressive competition and violence in team sports and a fascination with civilian gun ownership, including guns and personal motor vehicles of military style. Even the competitive interactions between trade unions and employers, both private and public, seem to reflect the special-interest group focus. These two tendencies, kind and violent, seem very prominent in human nature. We'll explore this dichotomy further in the next chapter.

CHAPTER 10

GOOD GUYS VERSUS BAD GUYS

IMPORTANT INSIGHTS INTO HUMAN BEHAVIOR CAN BE GAINED by looking at the relationships between traits. For example, intelligence is related to school grades and job performance, as is conscientiousness. Indeed, intelligence is the best of all predictors of job performance. This information can be used by colleges and universities to select students for admission and by employers to select among job applicants. Low agreeableness is associated with violence-proneness, as are feelings of social rejection and enjoyment of hostile music lyrics and violent video games. This information can be used by counselors to steer troubled youth away from lives of crime.

Warmongering endorsement correlates positively with violence-proneness, religious fundamentalism, social disenfranchisement, military dictatorship endorsement and endorsement of special interest group democracy. It also correlates positively with three ethical orientations: in-group elitism, messianic nationalism and guarded self-protection. It correlates *negatively* with human rights, kindly religious beliefs, environmentalism, positive foreign policy endorsement and endorsement of environmental concern. As explained in chapter 3, information such as this can be used to create a rating scale for measuring warmongering-proneness in political leaders.

These relationships between traits are computed one at a time. But there is another, more advanced way to study the relationships between traits. Briefly, the statistical procedure used is called *factor analysis*. It is a procedure for asking how several traits are related to each other and, more specifically if there are clusters of traits. For example, when studying the traits of heavy truck drivers

I first interviewed several drivers, asking them to describe what they did hour by hour on the job. Then I sorted the behaviors into groups of similar behaviors and developed questionnaire measures of these groups, of which there were ten. We administered these questionnaires to about 100 present drivers.

For each driver we had ten scores, one for each of the questionnaire measures. I then used factor analysis to explore whether the ten trait measures fell into clusters. The resulting answer was "yes", three factors. Three of the questionnaires clustered together: Mental skills (math problems and other problem-solving skills, such as logic problems), map reading skills, and memory. These were forms of what are considered basic aspects of intelligence: verbal aptitude, spatial aptitude and memory.

Another five of the questionnaire measures clustered together, meaning they correlated positively with each other. These were measures of personality traits: work ethic, safety habits, communication skills, personal life (relations with family and personal habits related to exercise, etc.), and loyalty. These five roughly parallel the Big Five personality traits of Conscientiousness, Openness, Agreeableness, Emotional Stability and Extroversion. The final cluster consisted of two traits, which I termed "factual knowledge specific to trucking" traits. One was Federal Regulations. The other was Load-handling skills for flatbeds, the type of trailer these drivers mainly handled. Hiring only driver applicants with scores in the average range or above helped companies eliminate accidents dramatically.

In my role as an industrial psychologist building this test battery, I wondered why the work skills of humans seemed to be of three different types…intelligence, personality traits and knowledge specific to a given job. I theorized that all of these types of traits or aptitudes or knowledge equip humans to succeed in doing work of various sorts.

These three general traits: intelligence, personality characteristics and factual knowledge have interesting properties. Intelligence is largely inherited and can be reliably measured from about age 5 on. The Big Five personality traits are about 50 percent inherited and 50 percent shaped by environment, by some estimates. Factual knowledge can be learned throughout one's life. Thus, some traits are stable early in one's life; some are flexible throughout life.

Intelligence gives humans the capacity to solve problems, figure things out and create. Personality traits help them persist and attend to details (Conscientiousness), get along with other people (Agreeableness), lead and persuade others to follow them (Extroversion), learn new and unusual facts (Openness) and handle stress (Emotional Stability). Factual knowledge, e.g. of business management, writing, arithmetic, geology, music, or banking, gives humans specific information needed to perform tasks in a specific field of activity.

As I accumulated trait measures while studying political attitudes, I eventually wondered whether they too might cluster, so I created a study involving 16 of these and did factor analysis. The traits fell into four clusters. The first had positive loadings (correlations with the factor) for sustainable policies and programs endorsement, positive foreign policy endorsement, improved government services endorsement and human rights endorsement. I called this factor a *pro-civilization* factor. A person with a high score on this factor would be one who strongly supports government policies that promote sustainable living, a friendly foreign policy, gradual improvement of all government services and endorsement of human rights.

The second factor I called a *pro-constructive government* factor. It had positive loadings on citizen participation in government, public democracy endorsement and kindly religious beliefs endorsement. It had negative loadings on violence-proneness and terrorism endorsement. Thus, a person with a high score on this factor would advocate for direct citizen participation in government policymaking, and would endorse public democracy serving the common good and kindly religious beliefs. The person would tend to disavow violence-proneness and terrorism endorsement.

The third factor I termed a *valuing religion* factor, as it had positive loadings on personal valuing of religion (using religion to guide one's personal life comprehensively), religiousness (a tendency to engage in religious activities such as church services and prayer on a regular basis), and meta-religion endorsement (endorsement of religious practices that periodically honor and promote constructive relationships across different world religions).

The fourth factor I termed *authoritarian selfishness*. It had positive loadings on authoritarianism and religious fundamentalism and a negative loading on proportional public school budgeting endorsement. Thus, a person high on this factor would tend to endorse authoritarian leadership, fundamentalist religious beliefs and would tend to disapprove of a proportional budgeting system for public schools.

I computed the proportion of the community college students in this study who endorsed each of these four orientations: 100 percent endorsed pro-civilization, 90 percent the pro-government orientation, 25 percent valuing religion and only 1 percent the authoritarian/selfishness orientation.

How confident can we be that these proportions hold true for the population of the nation? This wasn't a random sample or an especially large one. However, I feel fairly confident that these proportions might be fairly typical of citizens in part because I once administered the BFI (Big Five Inventory) test to students at this community college. The BFI is a 44-item measure of the Big Five personality traits. This test has been taken by tens of thousands of persons over the Internet. The average scores and other statistics for this very large sample are available. The community college students' scores were virtually identical to those of the large sample.

Traits such as those I measure are personality measures, like the Big Five traits. Therefore, it seems to me that data for these personality traits are likely to be typical of what we would find if we measured them on much larger samples of citizens. It seems reasonable to assume that most citizens in general are "pro-civilization", endorsing sustainable policies and programs and a positive foreign policy. They want improved government services and respect and endorse human rights. Most citizens are also probably "pro-government", as defined above. About a quarter of citizens, one in four, endorse active participation in religion and the notion of tolerance of religions different from their own. A very small proportion, perhaps only one in 100, endorse authoritarianism and selfishness.

[When you get to the end of this book, the epilogue chapter will show that analysis of poll data for large random samples of Americans is consistent with what my studies on smaller samples of citizens have revealed.]

This data suggests that citizens who vigorously advocate for less government or for eliminating government altogether (Tea Party folks?) are a very small minority. If the value of government as an institution were put to a public vote, we'd expect the "pro-government" voice to carry the day. This data is consistent with the findings reported in earlier chapters, for example that 90 percent of citizens typically endorse the model of government that serves them as members of the community overall rather than as members of special interest groups. It is also consistent with less than 5 percent typically endorsing anarchy defined as no organized government at all.

What value could such trait clusters have for the human species? Government is a different arena than school or employment. What is the value of government to the species and what psychological attitudes would be necessary in humans to promote effective government? Are the above trait clusters relevant to this question?

I ran another factor analysis, asking the software to give me just one factor. It had positive loadings for human rights endorsement, sustainable community endorsement, positive foreign policy, common good democratic government, proportional school budgeting and desire for improved government services. The negative loadings were for warmongering, terrorism endorsement, authoritarianism and religious fundamentalism. This suggests that humans can be grouped into two "types" those who endorse the positively loading traits (human rights, etc.) and those who endorse the negatively loading traits (warmongering, etc.). We've seen from prior data that the majority of citizens endorse the former and only a few endorse the latter. Most seem to be "good guys", only a few "bad guys".

How would this serve the species in terms of evolution? Endorsing the positively loading traits would seem to promote civilization in general, defined as cooperative living together in large groups and getting along peacefully with neighboring groups. Government can be considered by definition to be the formal system by which complex societies are regulated and managed. But what function would be served by endorsing warmongering, terrorism, authoritarianism and religious fundamentalism? These are very uncivil traits.

Or are they? If a neighboring group threatens to attack, wouldn't the home group need to defend itself? And wouldn't persons who like war be better suited to defend the home group than other citizens?

And it isn't too difficult to see how warmongering fits with traits such as authoritarianism and religious fundamentalism. Unquestioned obedience to authority is necessary in military action. And fundamentalist religion is characterized by strong respect for authority and belief in the absolute righteousness of one's actions. It also typically includes belief in an afterlife, a comforting concept for persons engaged in deadly activity in which one's life is in peril.

Thus, these psychological traits and their clustering seem consistent with the notion that characteristics evolve in species because they have given the species a survival advantage over other related species that lacked the traits. A species of primates that has most members with traits suited for cooperative group living and a lesser number with traits suited for military combat, to be ready in case of attack, would have advantage over a species that lacked either or both of these components. And such a species would have advantage over another that had mostly warmongers and only a few peace-oriented citizens, for endless war would destroy neighbors and resources, both of which can be of value to a group.

When I've shared this data and theory with other people, some have raised a question: How can a nation effectively wage war if only a small minority, for example 5 or 6 percent, endorse warmongering? How can the rest of the generally peaceful citizens of a nation be persuaded to change their colors? To explore this issue recall the study I did with psychology professor Holly Arrow at the University of Oregon. We created a brief questionnaire measure of willingness to participate in war, with three options. Our subjects were military age young adults, 200 plus university students. We phrased the options two different ways and got essentially the same results both ways. 5 percent were willing to participate in war of a warmongering nature, aggressively invading other nations to take what we want from them. This figure was similar to the percentage in many other of my studies.

70 percent were willing to participate actively in war but only defensively, to protect our nation and way of life from other aggressive nations, as the United States did in WW II. 25 percent did not want to participate actively in war in either of these ways, preferring to depend on diplomacy and the United Nations for conflict resolution.

This brings to mind a famous quote, or perhaps we should think of it as infamous. Herman Goering, Hitler's second-in-command, while being interviewed by a psychologist, Gustav Gilbert, in prison awaiting trial for war crimes, said that it was easy to get citizens to participate in war (1). He said the common citizen does not want war. Leaders engineer war. "All you have to do is tell [the citizens] they are being attacked and denounce the pacifists for lack of patriotism and exposing the country to danger."

So, to recruit the 70 percent, leaders tell them they are being attacked, framing war as a defensive necessity, whether this is indeed the reality or not. Propaganda can be used to make the case.

My subsequent studies further clarified the nature of these two different human trait clusters, the traits of "good guys" and "bad guys". The next chapter takes us deeper into the fray.

CHAPTER 11

INTO THE POLITICAL FRAY

POLITICAL TRAIT FACETS OF CONSERVATISM AND LIBERALISM.

The lecture auditorium was large enough for us 55 or so students, but the seats were remarkably hard and uncomfortable. I was surprised, considering that we were at Stanford University in Palo Alto, California. I'd heard good things about this private university. I bought a Stanford sweat shirt in the book store that I rolled up for a pad behind my back during the several hours of lecture each day. Jogging for 30 minutes around campus each morning with a fellow student also helped me endure the long hours indoors.

I was attending the Summer Institute in Political Psychology in July, 2007, a three-week program sponsored by the International Society of Political Psychologists (ISPP), as there are few academic programs at universities focusing on political psychology. We listened to lectures by several professors, usually for half a day to a full day each. Some professors were in their 80's, like Albert Bandura, whose theory of personal agency (feeling effective in accomplishing things in one's personal life) decades prior had helped to inspire a successful television sitcom in Africa to increase use of condoms to stem the spread of AIDS there.

We'd been sent a foot-high stack of journal article reprints as reading material, which I'd read before flying down. Some I found interesting, some not so relevant to my research topics. My fellow students were all younger than I, ranging from undergraduates to middle-aged employees of the CIA. Ten of these CIA "analysts" were attending to broaden their understanding of leadership traits, as their jobs consisted of developing dossiers on foreign leaders to help inform top government officials, including the President, on foreign policy.

In conversations with some of them I described my rating scale for leadership warmongering-proneness. They didn't show much interest, explaining, for example, that they couldn't use their skills for analyzing U.S. leaders. G. W. Bush was still President at the time. In an article published in the flagship journal of the ISPP he had been rated by other researchers as the lowest of all Presidents on Openness (1). But the atmosphere in the Stanford Institute did not invite discussion of this or of other information that would embarrass current politicians.Indeed, during occasional small-group workshops led by graduate students, when I mentioned my research I was sometimes challenged rudely by a student from Harvard. He seemed a peculiar fellow in general, but I was surprised that the workshop leaders were not more supportive of my ideas. Frankly, I was surprised at the intolerant atmosphere. The Hoover Institute across campus is of conservative focus, I was told. Perhaps the topic of political psychology could be tolerated on campus only within limits. University professors depend heavily on Federal grants for research. Too much controversy could have jeopardized funding. I sensed that there could very well be a politics of political psychology itself, a politics that I had not appreciated, being in private practice and dependent on no grant money to support my research.

For the first several years of my studies in political psychology I had not asked research subjects about their political orientations, e.g. liberal or conservative, perhaps because I didn't want them to think I was siding with one political party or another. It was clear in my own mind that I was interested in fundamental, basic human traits that might underlie war and other important issues, not traits that were specific to transient United States politics or culture or any other culture.

To this end, I conducted studies of foreign students at the University of Oregon and occasionally of other foreign groups, including English, Nigerian and Chinese citizens. Generally, the results were consistent across these groups, as had been the findings of many other researchers in the field, with the exception that about 50 percent of the Chinese students (studying in America) were high on warmongering endorsement.

Then, about a year after I'd been at Stanford I ran across a very interesting series of journal articles in Political Psychology, the flagship journal of the International Society of Political Psychology. These articles by John Jost and his colleagues presented a review of research showing that literally dozens of personality traits are associated with the conservative and liberal worldviews (2,3,4). Conservatism has been related to a wide range of usually rather unflattering traits: uncertainty avoidance, pro-death penalty attitudes, anti-abortion attitudes and Right Wing Authoritarianism (RWA). RWA in turn is correlated with endorsement of social privilege or elitism, a preference for a hierarchical social community, social dominance, endorsement of large financial differences between social classes, desires for certainty, fear of change, fear of radicalism, harsh punishment of deviants, endorsement of aggression, promotion of war, opposition to civil rights, idealization of authority figures, focus on authoritarian religious values, religious orthodoxy, intolerance of ambiguity, rule-following, need for closure and cognitive structure, pro-capitalist attitudes, racial prejudice, homophobia, victim blaming, endorsement of covert government activities, opposition to environmentalism, opposition to abortion rights and opposition to ethnic diversity on university campuses. RWA is also associated with opposition to civilian gun control laws and desires for reducing freedom of speech and of the press. Other traits associated with conservatism include mental rigidity, dogmatism, close-mindedness and cognitive simplicity versus "cognitive complexity". These relationships appear on several different continents, suggesting that they are universal human characteristics, not a function of culture.

Theories have been offered to explain the various clusters of conservative traits. One theory hypothesizes that conservatism is a mechanism for handling environmental uncertainty, "uncertainty avoidance", with activities including militarism. Another theory focuses on closed-mindedness as opposed to open-mindedness to characterize conservative thinking. Another is a theory of left-wing versus right-wing polarity, assuming that ideological predilections permeate nearly every domain of a person's life.

Another theory has a regulatory focus and proposes two goals. The "promotion" goal is focused on individual citizen hopes and aspirations and is associated with the liberal political orientation. The "prevention" goal is associated with the conservative orientation and is focused on safety, avoidance of threat and change.

Social Dominance theory is grounded partially in biological theory. It reflects beliefs that men should dominate over women, whites over blacks, upper social classes over lower ones, etc. Canadian psychologist Bob Altemeyer sees the Social Dominance Orientation (SDO) as reflecting an "alpha animal" (alpha male) orientation. System justification theories explain conservative political beliefs as seeking to justify underlying systems of attitudes such as prejudice, superiority and dominance of out-groups.

Jost and his colleagues posit fear as the central underlying element of conservatism. They point out that while threat in many instances increases a move of citizen attitudes to the right, this is not universally so, suggesting that factors other than social or cultural influence predispose citizens to their conservative or liberal orientations. If liberals do not move to the right when threatened, their attitudes would appear to be grounded in something more fundamental than current circumstances.

Jost et al more generally postulate that human beliefs, such as political philosophies, are deduced from sets of underlying, more basic, beliefs or premises and are related to psychological needs, values and motivations.

Jost discusses the history of the study of political ideology. He points out that the left-right, liberal-conservative distinction between political attitudes has been a useful concept for more than 200 years and has been used constructively in many cultural contexts.

Liberalism is associated with concerns for social equality, aid to the disadvantaged, promotion of change for improvement in society and tolerance of dissent. Liberals tend to be higher on the Big Five personality trait of Openness.

Conservatism is associated with the belief that people are unequal, due unequal rewards, and that order and authority are important to a stable society. Conservatives also tend to be more rigid in their thinking and more close-minded (lower on Openness). They prefer relatively simple, unambiguous and familiar art, poems and songs. They tend to see the world as a dangerous place and fear crime, terrorism and death. They tend to condemn others, for example persons they consider sexually unconventional. They tend to be more dogmatic than liberals. They are higher on the Big Five trait of Conscientiousness.

Jost posits that a citizen can shift in liberal or conservative attitudes, for example more toward conservative ones under fears of death or threat, a phenomenon that has been empirically demonstrated and is referred to as "mortality salience". On the other hand, he also cites studies that document the considerable stability of conservative and liberal ideologies in citizens and that these ideologies clearly underlie voting for liberal and conservative candidates for national leadership. Differences between liberals and conservatives on the basic personality traits of Openness and Conscientiousness also appear to reflect fundamental, perhaps biological differences.

Conservatives tend to have more organizing supplies, such as laundry baskets, in their bedrooms, while liberals have more maps and travel documents. Even early childhood traits tend to predict later political ideologies. Expressiveness, self-restraint, resiliency and impulsiveness are associated with liberalism in adulthood. Inhibition, indecisiveness, fearfulness and rigidity are associated with adult conservatism. Twin studies show greater similarity in political attitudes of identical versus fraternal twins, further suggesting biological origins of these political ideologies.

Jost with others further review research on political ideologies and offer their theory that the key element of ideological differences is liberals tending to advocate social change toward greater equality among people versus resistance to such change in conservatives (5).

They point out that there has been resistance to psychological explanations of political ideologies, perhaps because of a fear of implicit challenge to the rationality of political beliefs, just as persons of religious faiths might resist psychological explanations or studies of religion. Undeterred, the authors aver that psychological traits of many sorts underlie political ideologies.

Specifically, the evidence by 2008 documented liberal ideologies as associated with preferences for flexibility, rebelliousness, chaos, feminism, welfare, social security, universal health care, remedying social injustices, equal rights, egalitarian attitudes, environmentalism, creativity, novel and different experiences, diversity, poetry, Asian food (by Americans), jazz music, travel and foreign films.

Conservative ideology is associated with preferences for order, adherence to tradition, conformity, stability, justification of current economic systems, convention, exclusive in-groups such as fraternities and sororities, prayer, religious people, sport utility vehicles, big corporations, rich people, the military and promotion of economic inequality between groups.

As mentioned above, data such as this has been found consistently across many countries and continents, further suggesting that the basic "left-right" dichotomy may be a fundamental characteristic of the human species in general.

The authors note that death anxiety and concern for system threat are among the most characteristic psychological traits or issues associated with conservatism.

In 2009 Jost, Federico and Napier again reviewed the field of political ideology, reviewing data on the traits of liberals and conservatives and various theoretical efforts to explain facets of political ideology (6). They point out that political scientists tend to explain ideologies from a "top down" perspective, while psychologists take a "bottom up" perspective. Political scientists tend to explain ideologies as the products of political elites who supposedly craft ideologies and present them competitively to electorates in the interest of getting votes.

In contrast, psychologists document that many psychological traits correlate with political ideologies. This implies that citizens tend toward one or another political ideology for psychological trait reasons independent of persuasive messages from elites.

In reviewing the traditional left-right ideological positions, Jost et al note that the conservative view has been associated by research studies with several broad orientations, including maintaining the status quo, order, capitalism, nationalism and fascism. The liberal view has been associated with progressiveness, system change, equality, protest, socialism and communism.

They also cite evidence that these two orientations are not simply opposite ends of a bi-polar dimension but to some extent represent independent factors. It is possible for people to be socially liberal and economically conservative. Universality of the conservative/liberal dimension of human political worldviews is suggested by consistent research findings across as many as 41 of 44 countries in one study.

The authors raise the question why some citizens are predisposed to side with left ideologies and some with right. They then cite research that suggests biological substrates for some political attitudes in the form of twin studies and traits of children that predict adult political preferences. The twin studies yield an estimate that 40 to 50 percent of these attitudes are genetically based.

Research by Skitka and others is cited by Jost et al that leads Skitka to opine that it is easier for liberals to temporarily move to the right than it is for conservatives to move to the left, suggesting that conservatives tend to hold their political views more rigidly. Conservatives are especially concerned with in-group status, prejudice and discrimination against out-groups, authority, racism and "purity". Research has shown that reminders of death can induce both liberals and conservatives to move more to the right, characterized by greater stereotyping, hostility, aggression and clinging to religious beliefs.

The authors note that death anxiety and concern for system threat are among the most characteristic psychological traits or issues associated with conservatism and cite opinion that the left/right political ideology model exists in all societies.

Jost et al call for psychologists to seek further scientific explanations for political ideology differences, reminding that political behavior has extremely important consequences for nations and the world in general.

This information reassured me that psychological traits such as the ones I had been studying, including Altemeyer's religious fundamentalism and authoritarian measures and Sidanius and Prato's Social Dominance Orientation, as well as the Big Five traits, were indeed considered by many researchers around the world to be intimately related to politically relevant issues.

However, I was puzzled that the bulk of the evidence reported seemed to be on the relationships between traits and conservative political orientation. I expected that the majority of researchers, probably mostly academics, are of liberal orientation. Had they

inadvertently or deliberately focused primarily on traits of conservatives?

I was also puzzled that many of the traits associated with conservatism were so unflattering. Citizens are sensitive to unfairness
in politics. Researchers are expected to be objective.

Then, I heard a very interesting talk at the University of Oregon. The conference was on the anthropology of war. One of the
last presenters was Randy Thornhill, a biologist from the University of New Mexico. He and his colleagues have a theory about the
evolutionary origins of conservatism, which we'll explore next.

Chapter 12

Jungle Politics: Biological and Evolutionary Origins of Conservative and Liberal Worldviews

THE ABOVE LITERATURE REVIEW OFFERS EXPLANATIONS OF political behavior via "bottom up" approaches. Possible biological origins of human political behavior are hinted at by various data: the universality of conservative and liberal orientations across many nations and continents (common findings across many cultures on traits associated with these two orientations) and differences on psychological traits that are as much as 50 percent genetically based, twin studies and childhood/adulthood trait consistencies.

Psychological theories, based on concepts such as those of Jost et al that liberals tend to advocate social change toward greater equality among people versus resistance to such change in conservatives, still leave unanswered the question of why some humans advocate social change and some resist such change. Or why some humans have a penchant for militarism as a response to threat while others do not. Or why some humans tend to promote hopes and aspirations while others focus on preventing change, threat and danger.

It is reasonable to ask what functions these two basic political orientations serve, not just for current groups of humans but for humans as a species. One answer is provided in theory by biologist Randy Thornhill and colleagues. They have a theory based on the frequency of various human behaviors and institutions around the world (1). The closer communities are to the equator, the higher the frequency of conservative governments, different religions, different languages and war.

In addition, the closer one gets to the equator the more disease pathogens there are. These biologists offer the theory that the conservative political worldview, a cluster of psychological traits, evolved in the human species as a mechanism to promote protection of in-groups. Specifically, it protects an in-group from disease pathogens in neighboring groups against which the in-group does not yet have immunity.

Presumably, primate groups that had members who were fearful of neighbors and kept them at a distance by united militant activity were less likely to be overwhelmed by their neighbors' diseases. Other primate types that were less fearful were more easily invaded by or otherwise exposed to neighbors and their disease pathogens too quickly to build immunities to their diseases and were killed by illness. These early primate groups did not have to understand disease or disease pathogens per se to benefit from the fearful/militarism/in-group elitism mechanism. They were protected by it indirectly by its tendency to keep them away from foreigners and their diseases.

More specifically, it can be reasoned that groups that tended to bow to authoritarian leaders of fearful, bellicose disposition were better isolationists than groups that did not. So, a cluster of leadership preference, religious and other complementary traits evolved to serve this in-group protection mechanism. These included preserving the in-group's own language and culture as sacred and unique, and their religion as unique and favoring them as their god's chosen people. They crafted their religion to support a bellicose foreign policy, reinforced by blind obedience to authority.

Thornhill's conservative mechanism of protecting the in-group from disease pathogens is perhaps most dramatically evident in the history of Native American peoples, who were diminished by European diseases more than by European military might per se. They lacked the military technology to adequately defend themselves against the incursion of Europeans and thus were rapidly exposed to their diseases.

This theory was particularly interesting to me because it seemed to dovetail with one of the human trait factors or clusters revealed in my studies, the one that included endorsement of war-mongering, violence-proneness, authoritarianism, fundamentalist religious thinking, competition and favoring government that serves one's special interest group.

I broadened Thornhill's theory. I considered the conservative worldview as a mechanism for protecting in-groups not just from the threat of disease pathogens, but from threats in general from outside groups, such as attempts to overwhelm with war to gain land, females or natural resources.

I further broadened Thornhill's theory to explain the presence of my other cluster of psychological traits, the one that includes kindly religious beliefs and endorsement of a peaceful foreign policy, human rights and sustainable policies and programs. It includes endorsement of government serving not special interest groups but citizens as members of the community overall. This factor represents a type of humans who tend to be cooperative, kind, and comfortable with differences in ideas and traditions, such as those in different religious traditions. In light of the data reviewed by Jost and colleagues, this cluster of traits seemed to reflect the liberal political worldview.

I theorized that the liberal worldview also serves the in-group, but by a different mechanism. It serves not by distancing from neighboring groups but by promoting gradual peaceful interaction with neighboring groups to benefit from the opportunities of trade, including trade in goods and services, trade in technologies and trade in genetic materials that eventually will impart immunities to one's in-group against the disease pathogens of neighboring groups.

This broadened theory then sees both the liberal and conservative worldviews has having had complementary survival value for human groups specifically and for the species in general.

More precisely I proposed that there are two psychological trait clusters, "conservative" and "liberal". These correspond to two species survival functions, an in-group protection function and an in-group promotion function respectively, as follows:

1. Protection from threats function. Protection is provided by defending the status quo in language, religious beliefs and social hierarchy and by keeping neighboring groups at a distance by military activity. Powerful groups promote this system by establishing a social hierarchy that enables them to dominate less powerful groups. This dominance hierarchy is promoted not only between local and neighboring groups (tribes, nations) but also within one's own local group (family, clan, tribe or nation). Powerful groups demand blind obedience to their authoritarian political and religious leadership, justifying this with various arguments, including a divine right to lead, devotion to the "Motherland", male dominance arguments, fear propaganda, etc.

2. Promotion or taking advantage of opportunities function. The in-group's interests are promoted via dialogue, trade, and cooperative interaction with neighboring groups, and discovery of new information and modes for doing things in general, as by promoting and respecting creative innovation by any members of a relatively well-educated, healthy and politically empowered citizenry.

General hypotheses generated by this theory are:

1. Human groups that had members of both of the two above dispositions were more likely to survive than groups that did not.

2. The dozens of psychological traits found by prior researchers to correspond to liberal and conservative political orientations represent several identifiable dimensions of common political discourse (economic policy, preferred

government types, foreign policy, attitudes toward disadvantaged citizens, etc.). It is possible to create reliable and valid measures of these psychological traits with a comprehensive range of politically relevant content. These traits will cluster into two factors or groups statistically, one representing the conservative worldview and another representing the liberal worldview. These clusters will be consonant in content with what have been referred to by observers such as sociologists and psychologists as "political ideologies".

3. These clusters will relate statistically to preferences for conservative and liberal political orientation specifically in a manner consistent with prior research (as summarized above by Jost, et al).

4. These clusters will be anchored by traits in two clusters found by prior researchers and by the present author such as authoritarianism, religious fundamentalism Social Disenfranchisement (the Eidelson dimensions), Social Dominance Orientation and militarism. Specifically, trait measures developed and used by the present author in several prior studies will include measures of violence-proneness, warmongering endorsement, and endorsement of religious fundamentalism, authoritarianism and authoritarian governments on the "protective" side. On the "promotional" side will be measures of human rights endorsement, and endorsement of kindly religious beliefs, public democracy, sustainability and a positive and helpful foreign policy. These two clusters will be found to correspond to the conservative and liberal dimensions of political discourse respectively.

5. Additional "miscellaneous" questionnaire measures will correlate as expected with conservative and liberal political

orientation. Those items related to fear of disease pathogens and other elements of the protective/promotional
evolutionary theory of political worldviews will correlate
with liberal and conservative orientations as predicted,
with fearful items correlating with the conservative worldview and travel, trust and interaction items correlating
with the liberal worldview.

6. Research data that reflects biological and primitive tribal
    culture worldviews will correlate in such a manner as to
    support theory that the conservative trait factor evolved in
    the species to serve an in-group *protection* mechanism and
    the liberal/pro-social trait factor an in-group *promotion*
    mechanism. Specifically, the data will support "protection"
    as protecting against disease pathogens from neighboring
    human groups and "promotion" as promoting peaceful
    and cooperative interactions with neighboring groups.

To test this theory with data, I designed studies to measure
traits that I expected would represent the conservative and liberal
political worldviews across ten basic dimensions of political discourse (2,3,4,5).

These dimensions, representing the conservative and liberal
worldviews respectively, are:

1. Religious beliefs. Fundamentalism versus kindly religious
    beliefs.

2. Group belongingness preferences. Social disenfranchise-
    ment versus feeling accepted.

3. Gender attitudes. Male superiority versus female egalitari-
    anism.

4. Foreign policy. Militarism/competition/dominance versus
    peacefulness, cooperation/equality.

5. Government type preferences: In-group services versus all
    group services.

6. Economics: Self-serving versus sharing.

7. Civilian violence management: Violence and self-protection versus civility promotion.

8. Social group relations: Dominance versus social egalitarianism.

9. Locus of government authority: Authoritarian elite versus citizen authority.

10. Environment policy: Consumption versus conservation.

For each of the ten dimensions I created six questionnaire trait measures, three on the hypothesized conservative side and three on the liberal side. Within each cluster of three were imagined levels: *a* through *c* and *d* through *f*. The "*a*" level is a basic underlying psychological trait, such as religious fundamentalism on the conservative side. The "*b*" cell is the overt political manifestation of the "*a*" level trait. This is the overt political attitudes, policies, and preferences of citizens on the content of the dimension, conservative political religious policies, in this first example. These are beliefs that are openly discussed in the media. The "*c*" cell represents corresponding covert religious attitudes, ones that are extreme enough to be kept private, e.g. to avoid criticism, especially from political opponents, perhaps as "politically incorrect". I gave a detailed example of this in Chapter 5, above.

The corresponding cells on the liberal side of the first dimension are: *d*. Kindly Religious Beliefs, *e*. their overt political manifestations, and *f*. their covert beliefs.

Many scales were based on ones I had created for prior studies. These included scales for Religious Fundamentalism, Kindly Religious Beliefs, Social Disenfranchisement (the Eidelson worldviews), Warmongering Endorsement, Positive Foreign Policy Endorsement, Violence Proneness, Human Rights Endorsement, Authoritarianism Endorsement, and Sustainability Endorsement.

The remaining scales were written specifically for this study.

I tried to create measures that were independent of each other in content but true to the level of the dimension of which they were a part (basic trait, overt political content, covert underlying content).

This was a big study, in that I needed over 800 questionnaire items to measure all the traits, including extra ones for disease phobia, hypothetical tribal beliefs and miscellaneous items. I put about 200 items in each of four questionnaires and had them loaded on my web site. My community college psychology professor colleague gave his students extra credit, along with some students from a New York university. The sample totaled from 150 to about 190 for the four questionnaires.

I ran the statistics. All of the trait measures were reliable and all correlated positively with the conservative or liberal worldview they were expected to represent. 94 percent of the correlations were statistically significant. This seemed to confirm the basic hypothesis that there are many facets to these worldviews, and that they specifically include the ten dimensions for which the questionnaire measures were written.

In addition, seven items provided a reliable measure of disease phobia. This scale correlated positively with conservatism and negatively with liberalism, as predicted. Persons who self-identify as conservatives are more likely to fear diseases. The items in this scale are presented in Table 1.

The first item in this Disease Phobia scale is from a five-item scale written for this study to measure hypothetical primitive tribal attitudes characteristic of the hypothesized conservative worldview. This five-item primitive tribal attitudes scale was reliable and correlated positively with conservatism, as predicted. The corresponding five-item scale measuring hypothetical primitive tribal attitudes of the liberal worldview correlated positively with liberalism. The items in these scales and the introduction to them in the questionnaire are presented in Table 2. Items are

1. There may be times when we may need to take military action to keep groups of diseased people from invading our country.

2. We must be very concerned about keeping diseased people from other nearby tribes from coming into our territory.

3. I worry about diseases coming into our area from foreign places.

4. People of different language, skin color or nationality are more likely to carry disease than people like me.

5. People living in foreign lands are more likely to carry infectious diseases that people in our nation.

6. People in other states are more likely to carry infectious diseases than people in my state.

7. People in other towns or cities are more likely to carry infectious diseases that people in my town or city.

identified for your convenience as C for conservative and L for Liberal (these identifiers were not in the questionnaire). Persons responded to each item by indicating how strongly they disagreed or agreed with it.

This data was consistent with the theory that the conservative and liberal worldviews evolved with our species. Primitive tribal attitudes cluster together as we'd expect if the theory was correct. One cluster represents attitudes about fear of diseases, fear of neighbors, a bellicose stance vis a vis neighbors to keep them out of one's territory and protection of the in-group's ways, religion and language from change.

The other cluster represents attitudes of friendliness toward neighboring groups and corresponding interest in traveling to visit them, trade with them, learn from them and intermarry co-

Primitive society model.

Imagine there is a primitive human community, perhaps in the Amazon river basin in South America or in the forests of New Guinea. Imagine that in a certain tribe there are a few basic beliefs and attitudes that are held by a few different types of citizens. Please try to imagine which of these beliefs and attitudes you would agree with if you were one of these citizens:

1. We must be very concerned about keeping diseased people from other nearby tribes from coming into our territory. (C)

2. We should look for ways to trade goods with neighboring tribes. (L)

3. We should protect and preserve our own unique religious beliefs and practices from change. (C)

4. We should consider new religious beliefs and ideas from time to time. (L)

5. I would strongly support efforts to train our young men in use of war weapons.(C)

6. I would strongly support a group that wanted to go exploring into foreign territories to make new friends. (L)

7. We should preserve our own unique language, keeping it pure and special. (C)

8. We should occasionally incorporate new words into our language, adopting words from other neighboring languages. (L)

9. We should fight neighboring tribes to kill their men and take their women captive.(C)

10. We should have occasional friendly meetings with neighboring tribes to dance, sing and arrange marriages between our young people. (L)

operatively with them. Adopting new words for the in-group's language and new concepts and beliefs that can improve the in-group's religious beliefs makes good sense from this worldview orientation.

Table 3 presents all of the 60 scales measuring the ten facets with sample questionnaire items. Scales *a-c* correlate positively with self-identified conservatism and scales *d-f* correlate positively with liberalism. Keep in mind that scales a and d are basic traits. Scales b and e are the overt, publically acceptable applications of the basic beliefs in politics and government. Scales c and f are the "far-out", extreme, perhaps ideal extensions of the beliefs.

TABLE 3. SCALE NAMES AND SAMPLE ITEMS.

1a. Religious fundamentalism. There is only one true God. There is only one source of absolute truth, the holy religious scriptures or writings of my religion.
1b. Religious conservatism. Our nation cannot be strong unless it is favored and blessed by my God. The truths about my religious faith, e.g. how the earth was created, should be taught in public schools.
1c. Security-oriented religion. My religion is the best way to explain a confusing and frightening world. I find comfort in imagining a perfect place, like heaven.
1d. Kindly religious beliefs. God takes many forms for different peoples around the world. Violence against fellow humans is inappropriate.
1e. Religious liberalism. Our government should not favor any one religion over any other. Whether a woman has an abortion is primarily for her and her doctor to decide and should not be governed by other citizens' religious beliefs.
1f. Spiritual eclecticism. I am comfortable around people who have religious beliefs very different from my own. To keep a separation of church from state we should not print "In God We Trust" or other religious slogans on our money.

2a. Social disenfranchisement/compensatory superiority. I am more special and important than other people are. I prefer to be a member of a group that is entitled to special rights that we will fight for, if necessary.
2b. Cultural conservatism. Our nation is the best and should strive to keep its status. My preferred political group's judgment on important political matters is virtually always correct.
2c. In-group elitism. I prefer to be a member of an elite, special group. Large, powerful corporations are more important to our nation than are individual citizens.
2d. Social enfranchisement/all group respect. I identify with all humanity. I generally trust people and groups that I do not yet know very well.
2e. Cultural Egalitarianism. "All men are created equal" means to me that all humans should have the same basic rights to life, liberty and the pursuit of happiness, jobs, educational opportunities and health care. We should support research on stem cells and other technologies that hold promise for improved medical treatments.
2f. Egalitarian Philosophy. I believe that all individual persons have equal value, regardless of nationality, race, color or religious beliefs. Our nation should design effective birth control programs to offer nations that need and want such help.
3a. Male dominance preference. It gives me a sense of security to know that males are strong and powerful. I would rather be a member of a lion pride, where the most important member is the strongest male, than a member of a beehive, where the most important member is the queen bee.
3b. Masculine politics. In general, males make better leaders than do females. With few, if any, exceptions, there should be no birth control measures or abortions for the women of our group.

3c. Alpha male-ism. Male humans are superior to females in almost all ways. Our group should increase in numbers relative to other groups.

3d. Female respect. I think women deserve just as much basic respect as men in all matters. I am comfortable with scientific reports that girls mature more rapidly than boys.

3e. Female politics. Women should have equal say with men on legislation that directly affects women per se, such as abortion laws. Women should have full government support in getting jobs, promotions and pay equal to that of men.

3f. Female dignity. Women should be honored for their exceptional contributions to human culture. For every public statue of a famous man, a community deserves one of an equally famous or honorable woman.

4a. Warmongering endorsement. My national government should do what best serves our nation's interests, at the expense of other nations, enforced by military action if necessary. It is more honorable to serve one's nation as a warrior in combat than as an anti-war protester.

4b. National militarism. Our nation should maintain the strongest possible military strength, even in times of peace. We should have a unilateral military foreign policy, going it alone, if we can find no allies among other nations.

4c. Militaristic Philosophy. I believe in survival of the fittest... that the strongest are destined to survive while weaker individuals don't. I think that civilian vehicles that look like military ones, like the Jeep or Humvee, are really neat.

4d. Positive foreign policy endorsement. In foreign policy, our nation should...share our natural resources with other nations via trade programs.....and...set limits on our consumption of world resources so resources are available for other nations.

4e. Peace politics. In the U.S., only Congress, not the President, should declare war. We should support United Nations programs to quickly stop civil wars and genocides.

4f. Peace promotion. Citizens via referendum vote should be able to terminate war that their nation is waging. The U.S. National Peace Institute should have free reign to promote research on warmongering and other inappropriate war-related behavior by U.S. leaders.

5a. Special interest group government. Government should serve primarily the most powerful segment of a nation. I can imagine belonging to a special interest group that would feel justified in overthrowing an existing government by military coup.

5b. Power politics government. Government should serve the special interest groups that have the most money. Elected officials should vote on legislation the way their biggest campaign contributors want them to.

5c. Elitist government philosophy. Government should be controlled by the wealthiest citizens. Government should be willing to make its own policies as it sees fit, even imprisoning and eliminating opposition citizens.

5d. Common good democracy endorsement. Elected officials should run government to serve the current and long-term best interests of the community overall...no one special interest group should be favored. Government should have policies that promote a world safe for lower species.

5e. Majority opinion government. Majority opinion of all citizens and their fairly chosen representatives should drive government decisions. Big money should be kept out of campaign contributions, so that elected officials aren't indebted primarily to their biggest contributors.

5f. All citizen government. Government should serve the interests of all citizens. Government should carefully assess and heed public opinion in setting policies and programs.

6a. Profit economics. It is more important that we use natural resources to make money now than to conserve resources for the future. It is more important that big corporations be free to make money than to protect the environment from air pollution and greenhouse gasses.

6b. Conservative economics. Taxes on wealthy people should be kept as low as possible. Military budgets should be increased.

6c. Self-wealth economics. Ideally, no citizen should have to pay any taxes. I do not worry about future generations having to pay for our nation's current borrowing and spending.

6d. Balanced economics. The national budget should be balanced, not spending more than we take in. I prefer a reduction in our government's military spending.

6e. Liberal economics. Progressive income taxes are reasonable, with the wealthy paying more than the less wealthy. Government should promote programs to assure adequate jobs for all able-bodied citizens who can work.

6f. Share economics. Citizens who have above-average income should share it (via taxes) with citizens who make less. Citizens should have a direct vote on how much of the national budget is allocated to each major category: military, foreign aid, health, national parks, etc.

7a. Violence-proneness. I often fall asleep feeling mad or angry. It would be very easy to get my hands on a gun and bullets during the next week without anyone else knowing much about it.

7b. Violence enabling. Citizens should be allowed to own rifles and shotguns. We should put more money into police forces than into school counseling for violence prone-children.

7c. In-group self-defense. I feel safer in my country than I would in any other country. One important reason our citizens must have rights to own handguns is for self-defense in their own homes.

7d. Social agreeableness. I seldom lose sleep over angry feelings. I think cooperation with people from other lands is better than competition against them.

7e. Violence prevention. I think it is shameful that citizens of our country have lynched minority group members in times past. We should do more to prevent child abuse in our families.

7f. Civility promotion. We should encourage the Catholic church to do research to understand and prevent priests from sexually abusing parishioners. We should have an amendment to the Constitution that mandates diplomacy, conflict mediation and other sophisticated, peaceful techniques be used by our national leaders before they resort to war.

8a. Social Dominance Orientation. Some groups of people are simply inferior to other groups. Inferior groups should stay in their place.

8b. In-group favoritism. The platform of my favored political party should be determined by an elite group of party leaders. It doesn't matter much that some workers lose their jobs in hard times, as long as employers can keep their businesses going.

8c. Power oligarchy. Our party should do whatever is necessary to win elections for party members. Lower class people failing to get to the polls to vote for national leaders is not that bad, because they often vote for the less appropriate candidates.

8d. Human rights endorsement. All people of all nations
   should have the same basic human rights, such as life and
   liberty. We should affirm the right of indigenous (native)
   peoples to their spirituality, knowledge, lands and resources
   and to their related practices of sustainable livelihoods.

8e. Anti-oligarchy policy. Government should not be controlled or run by families and relatives of leaders just
   because they are related. We should <u>dis</u>courage political
   power maintained by economic favoritism given to political
   party loyal supporters.

8f. Social Egalitarianism. All groups of civil citizens should be
   respected for their unique place in society. A nation should
   not assign nasty, dangerous jobs, such as foot soldiering
   in war, primarily to underprivileged minority groups or
   classes of citizens.

9a. Authoritarianism. Persons should learn to depend on rules
   given by authorities more than trust their own judgments.
   We should not question persons in positions of authority
   but rather take them at their word.

9b. Nationalism. Our nation is entitled to more of the benefits
   of the world than are other nations. My preferred political
   party always has the best ideas and policies for our nation.

9c. Leader Devotion. In general, the leaders of a group are
   more important than are the group members, Without
   powerful leaders, there would be immediate chaos in society. I would be comfortable with a political leader who was
   almost Godlike in power and wisdom.

9d. Progressive government. Government should do more to
   assure affordable housing. Government should do more to
   improve government itself.

9e. Liberal Political Agenda. Government should provide sufficient regulation of major financial institutions to assure the
security of their savers and funding for qualified personal
and business borrowers. Government should reduce the
"earmarks" system of entitlements based on deal-making
among politicians instead of what is fair overall and truly
needed by citizens.

9f. Citizen authority. Our government should conduct carefully designed polls to determine how citizens want government to run and incorporate the findings into government
policy. Our government should fund research on the development and maintenance of sustainable communities, to
include the carrying capacity of each county and state (the
number of people that can be supported by the available
energy, fresh water, jobs and resources in the area).

10a. Personal resource use. I am not concerned about global
warming. I see nothing wrong with burning coal in electrical generating plants.

10b. Government resource use. Our government should support oil drilling even at the risk of harm to the environment. Government should not require that farmers plant
crops or plow their fields in ways to reduce topsoil erosion.

10c. Human natural resource use. Humans are destined to
dominate all lower forms of life on earth. Maintaining our
nation's power with much use of oil is too important to
worry about global warming.

10d. Sustainable community endorsement. My national government should support ... international treaties and
efforts to reduce greenhouse gasses and global warming.
...and a national health care system that provides basic,
affordable care and protects communities from disease
epidemics.

10e. Green/clean/safe politics. Our national forests should
be protected from excessive cutting so there is an endless
crop of harvestable trees. Government should establish and
enforce adequate standards to minimize harmful discharge
of sewer and industrial waste products into our streams and
rivers.

10f. Ideal sustainability. Our government should fund and encourage research on the design of sustainable communities.
Our government should support research on how communities can provide adequate jobs for all employable citizens
without constant growth of land area covered by houses
and commercial buildings.

11a. Miscellaneous conservative values. I tend not to worry
about poor or unfortunate people unrelated to me. There
may be times when we may need to take military action to
keep groups of diseased people from invading our country.
It is smart for my preferred political leaders to lie and cheat
if necessary to win elections and hang onto political power.
If scientists come up with facts that are contrary to my religious beliefs, I expect my religious leaders to explain why
the claims of the scientists are false.

11d. Miscellaneous liberal values. I feel deep concern for the
less fortunate citizens of my own nation. I value friendships and experiences more than physical possessions. I
like abstract beauty in art and music such as blues, jazz
and symphonies. Candidates for political office should not
degrade their opponents to make them look bad.

The 120 plus items presented in Table three are but a fraction
of the 800 items in the scales. The complete scales are included in
a manual on my web site (3). They give a detailed picture of the
conservative and liberal worldviews.

You may recognize among the items in Table 3 some of the
ideas expressed by politicians in campaign speeches, by partisan
news media commentators and by citizens in their letters to the

editor of your local newspaper. Knowing which worldview a given political idea is correlated with can help you identify whether a given speaker tends to be liberal or conservative, at least in the expression of that idea.

There were additional interesting insights in the data from this study and the one that followed it, which we'll explore in the next chapter.

Chapter 13

The Psychological Anatomy of Liberal and Conservative Worldviews; the Secret to Making Harmonious Political Music

I POURED OVER THE DATA FROM THE TEN-FACETS STUDY DE-scribed in Chapter 12 and learned several interesting details. While the correlation data confirmed that the conservative traits overall tend to be positively associated one with the other, and the same is true for liberal traits, there seemed to be individual person exceptions. Some persons who described themselves as strong conservatives by agreeing or strongly agreeing with this questionnaire statement: "Politically, I consider myself a conservative" had low scores on some of the conservative traits and high scores on the corresponding liberal traits. For example, a strong conservative might eschew warmongering and strongly endorse peace promotion, and strongly disavow indifference to the environment and strongly endorse environmental protection.

Conversely, a person who self-identified as liberal, strongly agreeing with "Politically, I consider myself a liberal", might favor conservative economic policies over liberal economic policies, or conservative religious beliefs (fundamentalism) over liberal beliefs (kindly religious beliefs). When I shared this finding with my wife she nodded in agreement and could immediately voice preference for some conservative government policies though she thinks of herself as primarily in the liberal camp.

Thus, it seemed to be an oversimplification to label a given person as "liberal" or "conservative" without knowing details about their political attitudes on all of the dimensions or facets that differentiate these two worldviews. Most of us are probably a mixture of the two, though leaning more strongly one way or the other overall.

Knowing that a woman is a fundamentalist religiously (dimensions 1a, b and c) won't be a guarantee that she is a conservative on foreign policy (dimension 4a, b and c) or preferred government type (dimensions 5a, b and c). Or, knowing that a man endorses liberal foreign policy (dimensions 4d, e and f) won't guarantee that he also endorses liberal civilian violence-management policy (dimensions 7d, e and f).

Factor analysis revealed the same clustering of traits seen in prior studies. All the conservative traits clustered together and all of the liberal traits clustered together, consistent with the notion that there are two fundamental political worldviews for humans. Specifically, for each dimension I combined the three traits (a-c) to create a summary score on the conservative side and three traits (d-f) on the liberal side. A two factor solution showed the first factor, or cluster, with positive loadings on all of the ten liberal traits and negative loadings on the corresponding conservative traits, as might be expected from the correlations between the separate traits and the liberal and conservative political orientations.

The second factor had positive loadings on all of the conservative traits and negative loadings on the corresponding liberal traits. The measures of the primitive tribal beliefs were included in this analysis and showed the same relationships with the conservative and liberal worldviews as they did in the correlation study. This factor data supported the theory that the many political attitudes or traits measured by these questionnaire scales are consistently tapping these two worldviews, liberal and conservative.

I also calculated frequency data. The frequency or prevalence of traits was calculated as the number of persons with mean item scores of 3.5 or higher on the scales, indicating greater than neutral endorsement of the items that measure the trait (Agree or Strongly Agree responses). I calculated the percentage for each of the three facets of each division, conservative and liberal. The data was generally similar to data obtained in prior studies for variables previously used, such as religious beliefs, foreign policy attitudes and environment attitudes. For example, in prior studies 6 percent typically have endorsed religious fundamentalism and 89 percent have endorsed kindly religious beliefs. In the present study the figures are 3.6 percent and 71 percent.

There were some exceptions. For example, in government type preferences (dimension 5), in prior studies as many as 20 percent have endorsed government serving citizens as members of special interest groups and 90 percent as members of the community overall. For the present study the corresponding figures are 0 percent and 79 percent. This difference might be due in part to the fact that in prior studies I used only one questionnaire measure for each of the government types. In the present study these two types were measured with longer scales.

24 percent of this sample endorsed conservatism. 46 percent endorsed liberalism. 54 percent endorsed green politics, while 50 percent endorsed independent politics. Each of these political orientations is measured with a separate questionnaire item, so a person responds to each of them independently.

The percent of persons who endorsed each of the dimension traits is presented in Table 1.

TABLE 1. PERCENT OF PERSONS FALLING IN POLITICAL DISCOURSE DIMENSIONS.

160 William McConochie

Political discourse dimension:	Traits a + b + c (Conservative) Percent with mean item score of 3.5 or higher	Traits d + e + f (Liberal) Percent with mean item score of 3.5 or higher
1. Religious beliefs: (fundamentalism… traits a, b and c) versus (kindly… traits d, e and f).	3.6%	71%
2. Belongingness (social disenfranchisement vs. social enfranchisement).	0%	79%
3. Gender attitudes (pro male, female egalitarianism).	0%	86%
4. Foreign policy (militarism/peace).	0%	76%
5. Government type preferences (special interest group vs. community overall).	0%	79%
6. Economics (restricted vs. share).	1.7%	79%
7. Civilian violence management (self-protection via guns vs. civility).	1.9%	83%
8. Social group relationships (social dominance vs. all group respect)	1.9%	91%
9. Locus of authority (leaders vs. the people).	0%	79%
10. Environment philosophy (consumption vs. protection).	2%	80%

11. Miscellaneous cluster of items ("conservative" items vs. "liberal items").	0%	78%
12. Tribal attitudes (conservative, liberal)	12%	71%
Mean (average) of all 12 scores:	1.9%	79%

The implication of these percentages was not immediately clear. In prior studies the ratio of similar traits tended to be in the order of 13 to 1 in favor of the "pro-social" traits, as I initially termed them. The present data ratio is much higher, 41 to 1, liberal to conservative.

These percentages were puzzling, especially because the percentage of self-identified liberals was 46 and conservatives 24, a ratio of about 2 to 1. Why were so many persons endorsing the "liberal" traits and so few endorsing the "conservative" ones? Were some conservatives endorsing the liberal traits?

Seeking an answer I separated out the strong conservatives and strong liberals, persons who Agreed or Strongly Agreed with the political orientation items. There were 151 to 189 persons total in the study (different totals for the 4 separate questionnaires), of which 35 were strong conservatives and 80 strong liberals.

I computed the average (mean) score for these two groups on all of the dimensions, as presented in Table 2.

Table 2. Mean items scores for Strong Liberals (L) and Strong Conservatives (C) on Dimensions of Political Discourse.

Political discourse area:	1 Strongly disagree	2 Disagree	3 Neutral	4 Agree	5 Strongly agree
1. Religion					
A. Fundamentalism	1.8 L	2.8 C			
B. Kindly Religious Beliefs			3.9 C	4.1 L	
2. Social group belonging:					
A. Social Disenfranchisement		2.2 L, 2.4 C			
B. Social enfranchisement			3.56 C, 3.58 L		
3. Government type pref.:					
A. Spec. interest group govt.	1.7 L	2.0 C			
B. Common good govt.			3.9 C	4.5 L	
4. Gender attitudes					
A. Male dominance		2.45 L	3.0 C		
B. Female respect				4.2C, 4.4L	
5. Foreign Policy:					
A. Warmongering	1.6 L	2.5 C			

B. Positive Foreign Policy			3.8 C	4.4 L	
6. Economics:					
A. Profit economics	1.7 L	2.4 C			
B. Balanced economics			3.8 C	4.3 L	
7. Violence management:					
A. Violence enabling		2.4 L, 2.9 C			
B. Citizen civility			3.7 C, 3.9 L		
8. Social group relations:					
A. Social dominance orientation	1.8 L	2.5 C			
B. Human Rights Endorse.				4.0 C, 4.6 L	
9. Leadership type pref.					
A. Authoritarianism		2.2 L, 2.9 C			
B. Citizen government			3.7 C	4.3 L.	
10. Environment policy					
A. Personal consumption	1.5 L	2.4 C			

B. Sustainable community endorsement			3.8 C	4.4 L	
11. Miscellaneous traits:					
A. Conservative traits		2.0 L 2.6 C			
B. Liberal traits			3.8 C	4.2 L	
12. Tribal beliefs:					
A. Conservative		2.6 L	3.1 C		
B. Liberal			3.6 C	4.2 L	
13. A. Lying and conniving		2.0 L, 2.4C			
14. A. Disease phobia		2.0 L, 2.4C			
15. A. Groupthink	1.8 L	2.3 C			

The scores for the strong liberals and strong conservatives were remarkably close together on every dimension, including the measures of tribal beliefs, disease phobia and other scales. Furthermore, consistent with the correlations that documented significant differences between liberals and conservatives on all of these dimensions, the liberal mean was higher than the conservative mean on every dimension that correlates positively with liberalism. Conversely, the conservative mean was higher than the liberal mean on every dimension that correlates positively with conservatism.

For example, on Dimension 5, Foreign Policy, they both dis-

*Correlation coefficients, or simply correlations, are a statistic that indicates the degree of relationship between two traits that can vary in size. For example, the correlation between intelligence and school grades may be .50. The higher one's intelligence, the higher his school grades are likely to be. The correlation between hours of practice and skill in playing an instrument may be .65. The more your practice, the better you play. Correlations can range from -1 to +1. The correlation between religious fundamentalism and conservative political orientation was .65 in one of my studies. The more strongly a person endorses conservatism the more likely he is to endorse religious fundamentalism. The correlation between fundamentalism and liberalism was -.43; stronger endorsement of liberalism was associated with *weaker* endorsement of fundamentalism. The correlation between age and speed in running may be -.25…the older you are the *lower* your speed. If two traits are unrelated to each other, the correlation will be closer to zero. For example, we'd expect the correlation between eye color and intelligence to be zero. Statistical software programs yield the correlation coefficient and an indication of how likely it could have occurred simply by chance. The software analyzes scores provided for a sample of persons whose scores on traits are obtained by using reliable means, such as questionnaires of several items each. Scientists look for correlations that are high enough to be likely not by chance but because there is a significant, real, relationship between two traits.)

avow warmongering, but conservatives less strongly than liberals. And they both endorse a positive foreign policy, but liberals more strongly than conservatives. Similarly, on Dimension 6, Economics, they both disavow profit (restricted) economics and both endorse balanced (share) economics. On Dimension 10, Environment, they both disavow overusing the environment and both endorse protecting it.

This explained the strange frequency data. Conservatives and liberals are significantly *different* on traits when measured in terms of *correlation coefficients.* *

However, conservatives and liberals are very *close together* in terms of *average group scores.* And furthermore, they tend to fall at the low to neutral end of the range on dimensions that correlate positively with conservatism (all the "A" traits in Table 2) and at the neutral to high end of the range on dimensions that correlate positively with liberalism (all the "B" traits).

I repeated this study with briefer scales and found the same results(1). This replication study involved only 210 questionnaire items. I wanted to see if I could create brief measures of all the dimensions. I used the six best conservative questionnaire items and six best liberal items for each dimension. By "best" I mean the items with the strongest correlations with the liberal or conservative worldview. Two were taken from each scale (a, b and c in the table in chapter 12) on the conservative side and two from each scale (d, e and f) on the liberal side. This study also was of community college students. It included 43 strong conservatives and 49 strong liberals.

In this study, the correlations between these scales and liberal and conservative political orientations were consistent with those of the first study, as were the mean item scores for strong liberals and strong conservatives across the dimensions. The data reminded me of the apparent strong citizen endorsement of public democracy (in the neighborhood of 90 percent endorsement) in my many prior studies. This high proportion had to include both liberals and conservatives.

These findings are similar to those of a study of political attitudes by Jonathan Haidt and Jesse Graham(2). In their study they had 1613 people rate the relevance of various concerns when making moral decisions. Within this study they compared *extreme* liberals with *extreme* conservatives.

The liberals rated harm and fairness higher than conservatives did, while conservatives rated in-group welfare, respect for authority and purity higher than liberals did. However the average scores for both groups were rather close together. For example, liberals had a score of 5.3 on harm, compared to 4.3 for conservatives. Conservatives had a score of 4.4 on Purity, compared to 3.2 for liberals. Both extreme liberals and extreme conservatives considered all five of these concerns to have roughly average or higher importance when making moral decisions.

I considered these findings very encouraging. They suggested that the majority of liberals and conservatives, if not radical ones of either the left or right, are basically on the same page across all the major policy dimensions of political discourse. What we read and hear in the media appears more often than not to be the extreme views of these two political worldviews, perhaps favored by the media on the principle that "everybody loves a good fight". For example, one principle of journalism is "if it bleeds it leads". Violence makes a good lead story for a news publication.

In contrast, if instead of listening to extreme views from the left and right we choose to listen to the voice of strong liberals and strong conservatives as groups, we would probably hear a harmonious blend that would make nice and perhaps even lovely political music. This closeness of attitudes of strong liberals and strong conservatives reminded me of how persons in Rotary committee meetings get along well and come to agreement on policies and programs. There are Rotarians of both liberal and conservative political orientation, including a few at the extremes. But they don't let their differences keep them from cooperating. They discuss and vote on issues, accept majority opinion and take action, all on the same page, all paddling their canoe in the same direction. I wondered if our political leaders could someday do likewise with the ship of state.

If you're curious about your own scores on the several dimensions measured in these studies, you can go to the

Politicalpsychologyresearch.com web site, log in, and complete Study #15, under the "Help Do Research" section. It takes about 20 minutes. You'll get your scores for the conservative scale and the liberal scale for each of the ten dimensions…20 scores, plus a few more.

In this chapter we see evidence that strong liberals and strong conservatives are actually rather close together on all dimensions of political discourse. This implies that we needn't try to change liberals to be more like conservatives or vice versa. We can probably get them to work constructively without fighting over differences in worldviews. In the next chapter we'll review evidence that supports the importance of respecting these differences rather than wasting time and energy debating, arguing, criticizing or making fun of each other.

CHAPTER 14

ARE WORLDVIEWS FIXED OR FLEXIBLE?

MY VIOLIN TEACHER IS QUITE THE CHARACTER. HE LIVES alone in an old duplex. He teaches in his living room, which is filled with keyboard, music stands, bookcases and instruments. He makes electric and acoustic violins in one tiny bedroom. He feeds his cat under the table in his kitchen, which has more violin diagrams on it than room for plates and cups. He stores logs of walnut and maple in his stuffed garage. He rants about politics.

One day after our lesson he played on his computer a tune that he wanted me to learn, Devil Went Down to Georgia, then, knowing my interest in political issues, he clicked to a radio talk show recording. It came from North Carolina, as I recall. A woman host was discussing gun legislation issues with an unmarried man who mentioned that he had a gun hanging on his wall. He said he was still waiting for it to get down off the wall, go out and shoot somebody and come back and get back up on the wall. Guns don't kill people, he reasoned, people do.

The host countered that the issue was that some people, such as criminals, should have to pass a screening process before they could have access to guns. The fellow said criminals could always get guns. She asked if he wouldn't want to make it harder for them by having to pass a screening. As a non sequitur he said that he didn't have children and made some other point. "Aha!", she said. Now she understood. "Your penis doesn't work, so that's why you like guns so much." She added that he wasn't a good debater, that this was clearly not his strong suit, and that he needed to talk to Jesus about this.

This is typical of so many arguments about politics. Liberals make fun of conservatives. Conservatives dig in their heels and counter-argue. The liberal talk show host thinks the bachelor gun-owner should abandon his political worldview and adopt hers. The conservative has a reply for every liberal argument.

Is it worthwhile for liberals to try to convince conservatives to change their worldviews, or for conservatives to try to convert liberals to theirs? Are political worldviews flexible enough to change or are they fixed and inflexible?

Until a few years ago, the field of political science was characterized by the underlying assumption that political attitudes are primarily, if not exclusively, shaped by experience, such as in one's family, in schools, by participating in political party activities, listening to campaign speeches, etc. Psychological studies for many years documented that reminders of mortality tend to shift political worldviews to the right. These reminders are termed "mortality salience". I heard mention of a recent study reported that having a hand sanitizer on the wall of a room in which persons completed a questionnaire measure of political worldviews caused the worldviews to shift to the right, compared to a setting without a hand sanitizer. This made sense to me, because I knew from my studies that disease phobia is correlated with conservatism, as will be discussed in a later chapter. I wondered how easily political worldviews are moved to the left or right by such subtle cues.

I conducted a study to see if questionnaire statements would shift to the right or left respectively if preceded by phrases implying threatening or safe conditions. I selected statements from a prior study that had no introductory phrase. I knew the average score measuring endorsement for each of these phrases. I created a new research questionnaire using dozens of these statements, preceding them with priming phrases. In some cases they were preceded by a threatening priming phrase and in other cases preceded by a non-threatening, reassuring phrase.

For example, the phrase "there is only one true God", can be preceded by the phrase "when nations are warring against each other". In the questionnaire this became the statement "When nations are warring against each other, I am reminded that there is only one true God." This same phrase can be preceded by a low stress phrase, such as "when nations are getting along peacefully with each other". The questionnaire had clusters of 10 liberal items and 10 conservative items preceded by high threat phrases, and then another 10 for each worldview preceded by peaceful, low threat phrases.

When I ran the statistics, I found no differences between how strongly phrases were agreed with or disagreed with when preceded by either high stress or low stress phrases compared to no prime statements. Nor was there difference between the same phrases preceded by high threat and then low threat primes.

This was not what I expected. I thought if a hand sanitizer on a wall could shift a worldview then a phrase such as those that I had written would also cause worldview shifts to a detectable degree. However, there were no significant changes, even when I looked at clusters of 10 items together, which provided a more reliable measure of the liberal and conservative worldviews. Priming phrases showed no impressive effects.

While working on this chapter, my friend Lew at the Oregon Research Institute referred me to a couple of journal articles that he said I had to read. One of them is relevant to the issue of political worldview shift under threatening situations (1). The study demonstrates predicted influence of system (social) threat on how strongly Big Five personality traits relate to self-identification as liberal or conservative. Overall, the relationship between Big Five traits and political worldview is quite small, they found, with lower openness and higher conscientiousness associated with conservatism.

However, the relationship between Openness and conservatism is reduced to an even smaller level in nations where there is higher unemployment and homicide rates, consistent with the researchers' theory that lower perception of safety in persons higher on Openness will shift their worldview to the conservative side.

While this result is consistent with the study authors' theory, it doesn't seem to me to establish a clear causal relationship between threat and worldview. Many other variables could have been involved that weren't measured or included in the data analysis. For example, there were no measures of how aware citizens in the studies were of their nation's homicide rate or unemployment rate, or if they would see such facts as "threatening", or if they perceived their nation to be currently under threat or not due to other conditions. But, nevertheless, the study does hint at the possibility of political attitude shifts under higher or lower threat and an interest in at least some other researchers in this possibility.

Initially, I was disappointed with my findings of no evident change in worldview as a function of priming statements. However, when I gave it more thought, these findings seemed reasonable. I thought about World War II, and how the United States shifted from a basically peaceful foreign-policy to a very aggressive, militaristic foreign policy to fight the axis powers in Europe and in the Pacific. This implied a temporary shift from a basically peaceful, liberal worldview to a more militaristic conservative worldview and then promptly back into a generally peaceful, liberal worldview.

After World War II, the United States immediately instituted peaceful relationships with both Japan and Germany. Instead of blaming all citizens of those nations, we prosecuted only the top leaders for waging war and helped the citizens rebuild their countries. Perhaps if liberals see a threat, they will shift to address that threat, but without changing their underlying views about human nature. Perhaps peace-loving citizens can participate in war temporarily if they see it as necessary for defense. They remain "liberal" but realize, temporarily at least, that there is a real threat and that they need to support the cause of defending their nation.

My thinking on this was consistent with data from the study I had done with Dr. Holly Arrow of the psychology department at the University of Oregon. This is the study I described in Chapter 3. We measured warmongering endorsement with very brief scales in a couple of different ways and found that the results were the same for both techniques. The subjects of study were 244 University undergraduate students, both men and women.

As you may recall, 70 percent of them were willing to participate in war to protect their country as a defensive act. 5 percent were willing to participate in war as an aggressive act, invading other nations to get for our nation whatever we want. 25 percent did not want to participate actively in war in either of these ways, preferring to have international conflicts resolved by peaceful means, such as through the United Nations. The 5 percent figure for these university students was similar to the 6 percent figure in many prior studies as the portion of citizens who endorse warmongering of the aggressive sort.

These issues reminded me also of Hermann Goering's comment after World War II. Goering was Hitler's right-hand man. He expressed the opinion that it was easy to get citizens to participate in war, simply by telling them that they were being attacked. In effect, he was explaining the use of lying and propaganda to convince citizens that war was necessary for defense, even when it was engineered as an offensive, invasive activity, as was World War II by the German Nazi regime. This then reminded me of the United States invasion of Iraq, explained to citizens as necessary to protect them against Iraq's weapons of mass destruction, even when there were no such weapons and the administration apparently knew this.

Most political opinions can be categorized as reflecting either the liberal or conservative worldviews. As argued in Chapter 13, these two worldviews apparently have been necessary for the survival of our species. The conservative worldview is represented by a cluster of traits that protect the in-group from threats, including fear of foreigners, fear of diseases, a willingness to wage aggressive war against perceived invaders and preference for religious beliefs that foster in-group favoritism.

The liberal worldview is represented by another cluster of traits that promote cooperative interchanges with neighboring groups when threat is not too great. This brings benefits from trade of raw materials, finished goods, foods, technologies, information and even genetic material through interbreeding that provides immunity to neighboring diseases.

This theory implies that groups of human primates that had members within their families and clans who represented both of these two worldviews were better able to survive than groups that did not. They had some members who were inclined to fear out-groups and wage war against them. In times of scarcity and threat, these members would be helpful leaders, persuading the others to follow their ideals and actions. In times of low threat and plenty, "liberal" members of the clan, would tend to rise to leadership positions and persuade others to follow their ideals and suggestions for cooperating with neighboring groups.

If this theory is true, we would expect these two worldviews to be grounded in genetics and for individuals who hold these two worldviews to manifest corresponding neurological and physiological differences.

I further reasoned that to reproduce humans we need both males and females. Therefore, it was logical to assume that Homo sapiens clans would also bear offspring that had some "conservatives" and some "liberals", to use current terminology for these two worldviews. To explore this hunch, I designed a simple questionnaire study, asking persons to report how many liberals and conservatives there were in their immediate families and close blood relatives. I had 25 college students fill out the questionnaire.

Of these 25 college students *all* reported that among their immediate blood relatives there were both liberals and conservatives and a few independents. None said their immediate families were all conservatives or all liberals. If political worldviews are shaped primarily by learning, it would be reasonable to expect at least some families to be all liberal or all conservative, but none of the 25 families were. They were all a mixture of these two worldviews.

I've repeated this type of assessment at club meetings; you can do this too. Six to eight people sit around a table over breakfast or lunch. I ask them as a group, how many of you grew up in families, immediate and close blood relatives, where all were conservative, how many where all were liberal and how many where there were some of each. Virtually every time I've done this, the results are the same; the majority grew up in families of some liberals and some conservatives. You can do this little experiment with your friends.

This mixture is consistent with the theory that every small clan needed some liberals and some conservatives to lead the two roles of protection and promotion, alternately, as needed for survival of the group. This appears to be genetic. If it were learned, wouldn't most adults marry persons of political views like their own and raise their children to have their same politic views?

I ran across a couple of articles that hinted at brain and genetic differences between liberals and conservatives and did an Internet search via Google Scholar. I found a treasure trove of recent studies (2-6). Studies such as these raised an uproar of sorts in the field of political science, as they rather convincingly document that political attitudes are heavily dependent upon inheritance, even more than on environment.

Several studies have been conducted on very large samples of twin data, both in the United States and in Australia. These studies measure endorsement of politically relevant phrases associated with the liberal and conservative worldviews. Identical twins are more alike in their endorsement of these phrases than are fraternal twins. The initial studies were challenged by critics, perhaps by political scientists who were reluctant to give up their prior assumptions that political worldviews are shaped by the environment rather than by genetics.

However, subsequent studies addressing all of the objections raised by the critics have confirmed the initial findings and yielded some fascinating results. In general, the summary results across many different political attitudes are that these attitudes appear to be about 53 percent genetically determined, on average, 11 percent determined by family environment and the rest (about 36 percent) determined by unique environmental experiences, such as those one has after leaving home as a child.

Furthermore, longitudinal studies documented that family influence is significant up to about age 21. Then, especially for children who leave home, genetic programming kicks in and heavily influences their adoption of political attitudes consistent with their genetic predisposition, liberal or conservative. These attitudes then remain rather constant for the rest of their lives.

These researchers have even been able to document differences by gender. For males, genetic influences are especially strong for attitudes about X-rated movies, gay rights, capitalism, censorship, school prayer and for political attitudes overall. Keep in mind that these studies simply get reactions of "agree", "disagree" or "undecided" in response to simple one-word or two-word stimuli, e.g. "capitalism", "school prayer" and "living together". For males, the cumulative genetic influence or underpinning of political attitudes so measured is about 58 percent.

For women, genetic underpinning is also strong for attitudes about X-rated movies, but also for attitudes about foreign aid, immigration and school prayer. For political issues overall the genetic component is about 34 percent for women. Of particular interest to me was the very high genetic influence for women of 84 percent for their attitudes about the simple phrase "living together". This implies that females are heavily programmed by genetics to be very concerned about stable families, as we'd expect, as they assume the primary role in raising children.

These studies provide a comprehensive sample of liberal and conservative issues, 14 liberal and 14 conservative, as tapped with words and phrases such as those mentioned above and also "foreign aid", "segregation", "capitalism", "busing", "democrats", "liberals", "republicans", "gay rights" and "military drill". The studies are able to parse out the relative contributions of genetics, home environment and the wider environment beyond upbringing at home to the shaping of citizen liberal and conservative worldviews.

Another very interesting discovery is that specific areas of the brain differentiate liberals from conservatives, or, more accurately, the more active and larger certain brain areas are, the stronger persons tend to endorse liberal and conservative political orientations. In these studies, political orientation is measured quite simply by self-report on a scale from 1 to 5, with one end representing strong conservatism and the other strong liberalism.

The entire brain was surveyed but only four brain structures have been identified in the recent studies that I reviewed. The anterior cingulate cortex is associated with conflict resolution and with stronger liberalism. The right amygdala is associated with greater sensitivity to threatening stimuli, fear processing and with stronger conservatism. This jibed with my psychological studies that had documented a positive correlation between conservatism and fears of many sorts, including disease phobia and xenophobia, which we'll explore in the next chapter. The researchers also pointed out that conservatives are more sensitive to threatening faces.

They found two other brain areas associated with conservatism, the left insula and the right entorhinal cortex. The left insula is associated with feelings of disgust. The entorhinal cortext receives highly-processed input from every sensory system; thus, it may be of critical importance in detecting threats of all sorts. A separate study mentions conservative sensitivity to noxious odors.

The odor issue is interesting for two reasons. Citizens who could "sniff out" rotten meat and other foods unfit to eat would have value for a clan. The Hebrew/Jewish prohibition against eating pork might have its origins in avoiding trichinosis, which is transmitted via pig meat. Having meat blessed by Rabbis might have been a form of sanitary inspection, in part. Kosher meat passed the test.

Also, conservatives are disease phobic, so they could be expected to be wary of and disgusted with diseased foods. My wife is very sensitive to unpleasant odors, very quick to discard old food from our refrigerator, which she cleans almost every weekend. She admits to embracing a mixture of liberal and conservative political attitudes.

This political worldview sensitivity to stimuli has been documented in other studies also. For example, some traits associated with conservatism are more prominent in persons who have greater physiological sensitivity to loud noises and threatening visual stimuli. The traits include endorsement of defense spending, capital punishment and the Iraq war. *Lower* response to threatening stimuli is associated with issues typical of the liberal worldview: endorsement of foreign aid, liberal immigration policies, pacifism and gun control.

A team of fourteen researchers has even begun to tease out specific areas of the human genome that are likely to contain coding for human political attitudes.(7) One such genome area is related to cognitive-behavioral performance, working memory, talking behavior, social learning, fear conditioning, spatial learning, motor performance, and social attitudes, to include pro-social, antisocial and aggressive behaviors. Another area is associated with scores on a psychological test, the Wisconsin Card Sorting test, which measures the ability to display flexibility in the face of changing schedules of reinforcement. Liberals tend to handle such changes more comfortably than conservatives do. Another area that was identified has to do with production of serotonin, which is involved in regulating fear, stress and anxiety. Handling fear has been associated differently with conservative and liberal worldviews. The authors of this research report refer to other areas of research that link olfaction (smell) and political preferences. Another study links disgust, political preferences and sense of smell. Individuals with more conservative political positions tend to have a higher tendency to feel disgust.

The evidence that liberal and conservative political worldviews are largely inherited suggests that trying to change them is impractical. Even though at age 21 or thereabouts citizens who have left their childhood homes are now open to embracing political influences of their culture, the chances are that they will be drawn strongest to features consonant with their inherited predispositions. In effect, it seems that rather than facts or information determining our political worldviews, genetics direct us to choose facts and information consonant with our neurologically-programmed dispositions.

And if liberals engaged in a massive program to convert conservatives to their political camp, we could expect conservatives to counter with an equally vigorous program to draw liberals to their side. The net result would be the same numbers in each camp.

Therefore, our challenge seems to be to understand these two political worldviews well enough to assure that they are expressed constructively and not allowed to overstep their missions of service to their communities. A zookeeper who houses lions and zebras will be more successful if she understands the nature of these two species well enough to not put them in the same pen. Defensive militarism makes sense but hyper militarism, spending excessive amounts of a nation's budget and resources engaging in meddlesome and destructive wars, is counterproductive. Similarly, a liberal preoccupation with health care, welfare, "fair" wages and other expressions of kindness and concern, can be taken to extremes that can similarly overtax a nation's resources.

Our challenge is also figuring out how to unite liberals and conservatives in constructive effort. Communities, states and nations have many serious challenges and problems. They must focus their energies and resources on solutions to these problems rather than wasting them in blocking each other's efforts.

Chapter 15

Fear and Groupthink

I**N THE PREVIOUS CHAPTER WE SAW EVIDENCE FOR GENETIC, IN-** herited underpinnings of liberal and conservative worldviews, including evidence that conservatives are more sensitive to fear and threat. Psychological questionnaires also reflect this sensitivity to fear. For example, consider the Political Fear scale in Figure 1.

FIGURE 1. POLITICAL FEAR SCALE.

1. I worry about terrorist attacks.

2. I worry about diseases coming into our area from foreign places.

3. I worry about military attacks against our nation.

4. I worry about high taxes that could take away my wealth.

5. In international matters I am motivated more by fear than by hope.

6. There may be times when we may need to take military action to keep groups of diseased people from invading our country.

7. In successful business, outwitting competition is a primary objective.

While the last item in this scale does not directly reflect fear per se, it tends to correlate positively with the other items. This scale of seven items correlates positively with conservatism (.52**) and negatively with liberalism (-.19*). [A double asterisk after a correlation means the result could have occurred by chance only 1 out of 100 studies. A single asterisk means 1 out of 20 studies. Scientists disregard correlations that could have occurred more often than 5 percent of the time by chance alone.] Conservatives are more likely to endorse the 7 political fear items. Liberals are less likely to. Conservatism also correlates positively with disease phobia (.45**). Liberalism correlates negatively with disease phobia (-.17*). You will recall the items in the Disease Phobia scale, Figure 2.

FIGURE 2. DISEASE PHOBIA SCALE.

1. I worry about diseases coming into our area from foreign places.
2. People of different language, skin color or nationality are more likely to carry disease than people like me.
3. People living in foreign lands are more likely to carry infectious diseases than people in our nation.
4. People in other states are more likely to carry infectious diseases than people in my state.
5. People in other towns or cities are more likely to carry infectious diseases than people in my town.
6. There may be times when we may need to take military action to keep groups of diseased people from invading our country.
7. We must be very concerned about keeping diseased people from other nearby communities from coming into our territory.

Because warmongering endorsement also correlates positively and substantially with many forms of anxiety, it is fairly safe to assume that psychological measures of anxiety will also correlate positively with conservatism. Consider the correlations in Table 1 between warmongering endorsement and several different types of fear. I did this study several years ago before I was measuring liberalism and conservatism. I used a lengthy measure of anxiety and worry that I had developed and used in my clinical practice.

Some of the statistics below are for other topics that I added to the study, such as Muslims, small creatures and evil spirits.

Table 1. Correlations between warmongering endorsement and conservatism and types of fear.

Political conservatism	.61**
Claustrophobia	.40*
Fear of Heights	.60**
Anxious unless busy	.39*
Unspecified anxiety	.41*
Overall clinical anxiety	.54**
Anti-Muslim	.80**
Fear of terrorism	.54**
Fear of small creatures	.37*
Fear of evil spirits	.40*
Xenophobia	.39*

Thus, warmongering endorsement is robustly tied to fears of all sorts. This seems to support the evidence for genetic, inherited underpinnings of political traits, in this case of traits related to the conservative worldview.

The last trait in Table 1 is xenophobia, fear of foreigners. The items in my Xenophobia scale are presented in Figure 3.

> 1. I would rather live in the interior of my country than near the border.
>
> 2. I would rather live in Kansas, the geographical center of the United States, than in California.
>
> 3. I would rather live in Kansas than in Minnesota.
>
> 4. I would rather live in Kansas than in Texas.
>
> 5. I would rather live in Kansas than in New York.
>
> 6. I prefer not to travel outside the United States.

These items form a reliable scale. I created them based on the assumption that persons who fear foreigners would prefer to live in the center of their country, further from people in neighboring countries. This tendency seems to be borne out with the positive relationship with warmongering endorsement.

Subsequently I received reports of data from the Pew polling organization and other sources that seem to dovetail with this.(1) For example, I ran a correlation between an estimate of guns purchased per capita in a given recent year and whether a state was a border state or in the interior of the country. The correlation was positive and significant (.32*). More guns were purchased by people who lived in the interior of the country than in border states. Correlations don't indicate cause and there could be another explanation for this relationship between gun ownership and locus of residence. But this significant correlation is consistent with the notion that xenophobic people prefer to live in the center of our nation.

And other data is also consistent with the notion that xenophobic people prefer to live further from national borders. For example, the correlation between border state and voting for the Democratic candidate, President Obama in 2012 was also significant (.36*). Obama won more border states than interior states, consistent with the notion that liberals prefer to live in border states and conservatives in interior states. The correlation between blue state (voting Democratic in 2008) and estimated number of guns purchased was also significant (-.30*). Blue state / democratic citizens are *less* likely to purchase guns.

GROUPTHINK

The liberal worldview can be taken to destructive extremes. Providing overly generous union benefits to public employees can outrun state and national budgets. But more often it seems that policies associated with conservatism take the spotlight as subjects of public concern. The most obvious examples are the promotion of war, civilian gun ownership and economic policies favoring wealthy elites, tendencies that are associated with the conservative worldview, as reviewed in Chapter 12, above.

There is a topic of psychological research that may help us explain counter-productive expressions of conservatism and perhaps even some forms of liberalism, such as union activities that generate budget-busting benefits to workers. This topic is what has been referred to in psychological research as *groupthink*.

This concept was studied initially by psychologist Irwin Janis beginning in 1975. He defined groupthink as the tendency of a relatively small group of leaders to lose sight of important circumstances and plan in ways that in the long run were disastrous for the very organizations the leaders were responsible for protecting or promoting.

He was particularly interested in case studies of this phenomenon, such as the failure of Navy leadership to be alert to a possible Japanese surprise attack on Pearl Harbor in Hawaii. Other examples of groupthink have been assumed to underlie the Nixon Administration handling of their burglary of the Democratic Party offices in the Watergate Hotel and subsequent attempted cover-up, President Kennedy's failed invasion of Cuba (Bay of Pigs), and Hitler's invasion of Russia against the better judgment of his generals.

Additional definitions and features of groupthink have been offered by researchers. These reflect thinking characterized by excessive dependence on and deference to top leader opinions, questionable moral underpinnings, self-righteousness, feelings of invulnerability, top leader indifference to criticism, hesitation in underlings to express dissent, ignoring important details and outside corrective information, reassuring each other of the correctness of plans and decisions, and underestimating and despising opponents.

These features of groupthink are suggestive of the facets of authoritarianism. Psychologist Bob Altemeyer developed his questionnaire measure of "Right Wing Authoritarianism", which he believed included three main facets: submission to authority, aggression against groups despised by authority and adherence to tradition and norms.

I developed another definition of authoritarianism as a morality-based preference for a relatively simple, clear authority, versus personal judgment, to explain the world and one's place in it. The 30-item questionnaire measure of the trait so defined has eight facets: Dependence on authority versus personal opinion for doctrine and moral rules, Dependence on authority for safety and comfort, a Worldview of simple good and bad people and being a member of the good, Loyalty to authority, Blind obedience to authority, Dependence on rewards and punishments, Trust in divine authority versus one's own judgments, and Trust in elected officials more than in fellow citizens. All of these facets correlate positively with the total score, indicating that they are all part of the same trait.

In the study of traits reported in chapter 13 there were two clusters of questionnaire items that seemed to reflect some of the facets of groupthink. One included these four: I am totally devoted to my preferred government and religious leaders; In general, the leaders of a group are more important than are the group members; In conversations with others, I prefer the clear guidelines of rules and doctrine to the uncertainties of personal opinions; We should not question persons in positions of authority but rather take them at their word.

These items form a moderately reliable scale that correlated positively and significantly with several other traits measured in this study: conservatism, leader devotion, in-group protectiveness, in-group favoritism, power oligarchy government, authoritarianism, nationalism, Social Dominance Orientation, violence-enabling, violence-proneness, nationalism and disease phobia. This four-item scale correlated negatively with liberalism, violence-prevention, civility promotion, human rights endorsement, egalitarianism, and endorsement of progressive government, common good government and citizen-oriented government.

The other cluster of items that resonate with the concept of groupthink were these six: A primary goal for me is to look out first for my own best interests rather than for other people; I prefer to be part of a group of people who all believe in the same things and worship the same way; What my leaders tell me is the truth *is* the truth; Spiritual truth is more important than scientific truth; When there is a conflict between scientific facts and my religious beliefs, I prefer to ignore the scientific facts; and The more people there are who believe something, the truer that belief is.

This reliable scale correlated positively and significantly with conservatism, personal consumption of resources (rather than conservation), government consumption of resources, conservative tribal beliefs, and endorsement of lying and conniving in politics. It correlated negatively with liberalism, sustainable community endorsement and liberal tribal beliefs.

These two scales were in different sections of the study, so correlations with all of the other traits were inconvenient to run. But, in essence, they reflect the same tendency to correlate positively with conservative traits and negatively with liberal ones.

Thus, it seems reasonable to see groupthink as traditionally defined as a reflection of the conservative worldview. As such, it is reasonable to consider it as an evolved tendency that served an in-group protection function in primitive tribal clans and communities. Groupthink reflects the sort of group thinking that would characterize militant, authoritarian activity in defense of the local tribe or clan. Efficient militarism requires a hierarchical chain of command: unquestioning obedience to those higher up and dominance of those below.

Primitive human groups may not have appreciated the weaknesses of groupthink, as reflected in the failure of the U.S. Navy detecting the Japanese surprise attack on Hawaii or the failure of Hitler's invasion of Russia, but groupthink would have been better in primitive tribes than no planning or organization at all when under threat.

We can think of present-day examples of groupthink, or at least of situations that may very well have been contaminated by groupthink, that led to disastrous results. The financial meltdown of 2008 comes to mind. Top executives at large commercial banks apparently knew about but ignored dangerous signs of risky investment policies. They were making so much money for themselves in the form of salaries, stock options and other benefits that they seemed indifferent to the overall dangers of the reckless policies they were expressing.

They could even anticipate the collapse of their companies without concern because the government tends not to prosecute individual corporate leaders but just fines companies. The leaders could make tens of millions of dollars and walk away from even the collapse of their firms. As an elite, insulated group, they got what they wanted.

Groupthink might also account for the misbehavior of military personnel under stress in combat. Recent publications (2, 3) suggest that the Mi Lai massacre of 500 civilians by U.S. Army troops in South Vietnam was not an aberration. A widespread policy of mistreatment and overkill of enemy combatants and civilians was sanctioned by officers and foot soldiers alike. When this behavior was exposed to the public, the Army tried to cover it up but then understood and corrected for these mistakes. This sort of policy seems to have resurfaced in Iraq in incidents such as the mistreatment of prisoners in the prison at Abu Ghraib.

Perhaps humans developed the ability to manage limited numbers of citizens under their control, such as clans or tribes of scores or a few hundred persons. But it is conceivable that the human species has become so populous and its institutions so large that organizational management demands have outgrown the species' aptitude and skill for managing groups. Perhaps we all have a tendency to identify with a relatively small number of other citizens that we think of as our in-group. Perhaps we have a tendency to look out primarily for this relatively small group and find it difficult to refrain from rejecting and discounting the value of larger groups.

For example, gun owners may identify tightly with other members of the National Rifle Association but discount the importance of the nation as a whole. We have seen how public employees can develop union contracts that are in their own best interests but can jeopardize the common good even of the school students they serve. We have seen how nations overspend, jeopardizing their solvency.

Perhaps an Army sergeant can supervise a dozen soldiers in his patrol but has difficulty extending this concern to civilians in combat areas, putting his own patrol members above the civilians when making combat decisions, and writing off the citizens who are killed or injured as simply "collateral damage", to use the euphemism.

Perhaps liberal citizens have a tendency to coalesce with others of their own political orientation and discount conservatives, in part because they simply can't wrap their minds around a comprehensive political arena of extremely multifaceted complexity. If we are ever going to somehow unite liberals and conservatives in constructive, cooperative political activity, we may have to carefully consider the signs of groupthink and avoid the pitfalls they constitute.

I'm reminded of concerns my wife expresses about the leadership of a nonprofit organization that she has been involved with. She has assumed leadership roles and is quite familiar with the inner workings of the organization. While she works in the local community branch, the organization is of national scope. She describes problems that may reflect the mistakes of groupthink. For example, some leadership elements seem obsessed with status quo, tradition, micromanagement of committees, and even micromanagement of new presidents after serving as president oneself.

I'm reminded also of my own experience as a member of the executive committee of my Rotary club. The club was about 280 members strong at the time. I went to a district conference training meeting to get fresh ideas and came back excited with about 10 ideas that I thought would help us solve many problems that our club had struggled with. I shared my ideas with the committee. None of them were adopted. I complained to a retired district governor of Rotary. He said that changing a big organization is like changing the direction of a big ship. It takes persistent energy and much patience.

Now these may be rather inconsequential examples of groupthink, compared to commercial bank and Army management fiascos. But, any organization can suffer from becoming too insular, too rigid, too concerned with conducting business as usual to look at changing trends. Norman R. Augustine, retired chairman and

CEO of Lockheed Martin Corporation bemoaned the unexpected dramatic contraction of his defense industry just after he assumed corporation leadership (4). This was shortly after the fall of the Berlin Wall and subsequent end to the cold war. He said "Had I been told that within 6 years 40 percent of all the people in the industry and three-fourths of its companies would be gone, I would have said 'not possible'. It happened." He couldn't anticipate the quick fall of the Berlin Wall and imagine the dramatically reduced demand for military materiel that followed.

Another example of poor decision-making is government borrowing. This may be a function of groupthink. Borrowing beyond reasonable levels, at levels that require faith in constant economic growth to sustain, is folly if indefinite growth is not sustainable. The planet is finite. Unions that press for wages and benefits that over-stress private employers or government employers can lead to destruction of the jobs and institutions that union workers depend upon. Constantly escalating tenured school teacher wages and benefits has forced school districts to lay off junior teachers. What's good for the old-timers is bad for the new-comers in the same profession.

Economies that focus too narrowly on short-term profits can destroy the resources and customers upon which they depend, as by clear-cutting forests without replanting, destroying fisheries by overfishing, and writing house mortgages with balloon payment clauses that home owners will not be able to honor due to income limitations. Much criminal behavior can also be classified as reflecting poor decision-making that may be examples of groupthink, especially white collar crime, including embezzlement and investment Ponzi schemes, such as that of Bernie Madoff.

The development and marketing of insecticides and weed-killers can become destructive in the name of immediate profits for the manufacturers, distributors and users. If they inadvertently but knowingly contribute to the demise of a nation's honey bees, which are necessary to pollinate food crops, important segments of the agriculture industry can be jeopardized.

The use of fossil fuels is becoming an inadvertent threat to the environment of the planet, polluting air with global warming carbon dioxide and with mercury and other exhaust particulates. Immediate financial profit for manufacturers and distributors and the benefits of easy transportation and affordable electricity for virtually all citizens implicate virtually everyone.

To the extent that we participate and persist in these behaviors as members of groups, communities, states and nations we can consider this as a form of groupthink. It is behavior that has pleasant short-term benefits for those making the decisions but serious negative long-term side-effects for their communities and eventually themselves.

Thus, causes of poor organizational decisions can include short-sightedness, financial greed, indifference to the overall welfare of one's community, impulsiveness, egocentrism and perhaps even addiction, as in addiction to short-term easy profits, transportation, electricity and other conveniences. An exponentially increasing world population can also be seen as an example of short-sightedness, as the planet has limited space and resources and hundreds of millions of us already lack adequate safety, food and shelter.

Another dimension of groupthink as defined herein, can include psychological techniques that indirectly foster it, such as rationalization, compensation, projection, false advertising and simple lying and conniving. We can justify self-indulgence by rationalizing it: I deserve high wages and benefits because I am special, or because I need them to pursue life, liberty and happiness, or because workers like me in other companies have higher wages than me. I am entitled to health care or food stamps because the United Nations Declaration of Human Rights says all citizens should have food and health care. I deserve a multimillion dollar bonus as a financial corporation executive because executives in competing institutions get them. We must have an increase in our military budget because my success as a commander requires more sophisticated weapons.

Propaganda is another psychological technique that can promote groupthink. Advertising that employs falsehoods or promotes activities, such as the use of fossil fuels and weed-killers that are known to have negative consequences for citizens, has elements of propaganda. Publishing editorials that distort the science of ecology to avoid holding firms accountable for environmental damage does too.

We can compensate for the guilt and worry our poor decisions cause by overindulging in other pleasures or blotting out our capacity to perceive them, as by overeating, overindulging in entertainment or numbing our minds with drugs and alcohol. We can project blame for our poor decisions onto other persons or circumstances. "I drive a car that burns fossil fuels because I live too far from my job to walk or take a bike." "I heat my house with electricity generated by coal-fired generators because everybody in my community does and there is only one electric utility company in our town." "I put weed-killer on my lawn because my wife wants our yard to look as nice as our neighbor's". "I irrigate my crops, even though I know that over many decades the soil will become useless due to salinization from evaporation, because that's the only way I can grow things on my farm."

We can also promote groupthink by simply lying and conniving. "All's fair in love, war and business", is the slogan. In war, lying and deceit are acceptable aspects of military conflict, designed to trick the enemy to gain advantage. For example, Hitler negotiated a treaty with Stalin to protect Nazi Germany's eastern front while attacking Europe to the west. Once he had subdued France and other nations to the west, he violated the treaty and invaded Russia. The Allies built fake buildings and other facilities in one part of England to imply that they would invade France in a location other than the true one. Lying and conniving are not infrequently also used by candidates for political office to gain advantage, both to denounce opponents and to inflate one's own qualifications.

A reliable questionnaire measure of lying and conniving was crafted from seven items in the study of traits that differentiate the liberal and conservative worldviews (Chapter 13).

FIGURE 4. LYING AND CONNIVING SCALE

1. It is smart for my preferred political leaders to lie and cheat if necessary to win elections and hang onto political power.
2. It is wise strategy for leaders of my preferred political party to keep those citizens away from the polls who might vote against us.
3. It is okay for my political candidates to run down and discredit their opponents during campaigns for office.
4. In political campaigns, winning justifies lying and conniving.
5. In political campaigns, belittling your opponent, even with lying, is justified if it will help you win.
6. In times of war, it is worthwhile to use propaganda to demonize enemies.
7. Even in times of peace, it is more important to dominate other nations than to make friends with them.

This scale is very reliable (alpha .91) and differentiates liberals from conservatives. It correlates .36** with Conservatism, -.18 with Liberalism.

ADDICTION?

We could also explore the possibility that many of our poor decisions might be conceptualized equally well as addictions. Addictions can be defined as behaviors that provide short-term pleasures but long-term self-destructive consequences. There's a tendency for one to be aware of the eventual dangers, but to be out of control regarding stopping the behavior without help.

If we conceptualize the behaviors discussed above as manifestations of addictions, then perhaps we could benefit from 12-step treatment programs to change these behaviors. I drive a gas-hog Suburban, even though I know it spews noxious fumes into the environment. "Air sewage", if you will. I keep driving it. What would an adapted 12-step program look like? Here are the 12 steps as abbreviated by the APA Dictionary of Psychology (5):

1. Admit that you can't control the addiction or compulsive behavior.

2. Recognize a higher power that can give help.

3. Examine past errors with the help of an experienced person who has been through the same struggle.

4. Make amends for these errors.

5. Learn to live a new life with a new code of behavior.

6. Help others in turn with the same struggle.

I'll admit that I haven't been able to give up my Suburban, old and beat up as it is (an '86). For me, the 'higher power' I'm comfortable turning to is the universal spirit of human goodness and kindness. However, if I'm honest with myself, my Suburban is only one of my addictions. I'm addicted to flying and electricity, both of which require fossil fuels at present. I'm addicted to paper…for printing documents, professional reports, this manuscript, blowing my nose, reading the news. I'm addicted to my cabin in the mountains, which is 80 miles away and impossible to get to except by car or truck. I'm addicted to concrete, which builds roads, public buildings and house and cabin foundations. Cement for making concrete requires tremendous amounts of energy to create. I'm addicted to chain saws and hedge trimmers, which depend on gasoline, the exhaust from which adds to more than my fair share of "air sewage".

I need a whole community to help me participate in a total overhaul. I need a new type of government to coordinate and finance this overhaul. I need a new type of political party to empower me and others to create this new type of government.

The next chapter will introduce a model for constructively uniting citizens of both liberal and conservative worldviews.

CREATING A NEW TYPE OF POLITICAL PARTY TO UNITE CONSERVATIVES AND LIBERALS

CHAPTER 16

PARTY TIME: CREATING A NEW TYPE OF POLITICAL PARTY; INTRODUCTION AND OVERVIEW

ON FRIDAY NOVEMBER 23, 2012 A LETTER TO THE EDITOR was published in our local newspaper. The citizen referred to recent letters that had referred to red states that should be encouraged to secede from the union and blue states that would be better off without them. He referred to narrow-minded citizens of irrational perspective and criticized the newspaper for "constantly feeding us editorials from liberal idealists". He concluded that we need balance in our nation, and rational thinking, which he thinks is lacking in the local newspaper and in our current government. Instead, he opines, we're fed "constant ultra-liberal versus ultra-conservative banter".

I found this letter interesting, because it dove-tailed with my research findings that show that strong liberals and strong conservatives are actually rather close together on all major issues of political discourse. If we need balance in our nation, it would appear that somehow uniting both strong liberals and strong conservatives, but not extremes of either political stripe, might provide a solution.

What we often see in the newspaper, especially on the editorial page, are heated opinions of extreme left and right positions, each provoking the other and occasionally stimulating pleas for reasonable compromise to constructively address important problems. As mentioned in an earlier chapter, some journalists function from mottos such as "if it bleeds it leads" and "everybody loves a good fight". They sell copy by appealing to our baser natures.

Media coverage of politics thus often gives the impression that liberals and conservatives are miles apart. Research via correlation statistics also gives this impression, with literally dozens of psychological traits correlating positively with liberalism and negatively with conservatism and another batch of traits correlating positively with conservatism and negatively with liberalism. Militarism tends to be endorsed more strongly by conservatives than by liberals. Concern for poor citizens is more strongly endorsed by liberals than by conservatives.

However, we have seen in earlier chapters that research findings further suggest that the majority of citizens are not of extreme political opinions and have reasonable agendas for getting community work done. This suggests that the majority of citizens would respond well to reasonable government leadership that unites rather than sets citizens at each other's throats. We have seen that careful measures of citizen attitudes across 10 major dimensions of political discourse yield average scores for strong liberals and strong conservatives that are actually rather close together.

We have also seen suggestions that the majority of citizens would prefer a government that serves them not as members of special interest groups but as members of the community overall. We have seen that the majority want a peaceful foreign policy, economics that involves sharing wealth to provide a reasonable modicum of services to all citizens, and attitudes of respect toward women.

We have seen that a strong majority of citizens prefer democratic forms of government more strongly than less democratic forms of government, such as monarchy and dictatorship. A review of history also reflects this preference with a gradual progression of governments from monarchies and dictatorships to more democratic forms of government. While some citizens, even some in the United States at present, endorse anarchy, dictatorships and monarchies, greater numbers tend to endorse democracy. Regarding democracy, however, only about 20 percent of Americans endorse government that serves citizens as members of special interest groups. This is the form of democracy we have currently in the United States, with the federal government in particular controlled by very wealthy special interest groups through campaign contributions to legislators through lobbyists. In contrast, 90 percent of citizens endorse a hypothetical new form of government, government that would serve citizens as members of the community overall.

When it comes to the environment, the average strong liberal and even the average strong conservative endorses protection rather than indiscriminate use of environmental resources. International studies show that consistently, across many nations, the majority of citizens see global warming as a serious problem. Thus, the problem does not seem to be one of lack of knowledge or education of the general citizenry but rather the fact that the general citizenry does not have sufficient direct political power to make its will realized in effective public policy, such as by discontinuing the use of fossil fuels to reverse global warming.

Governments in civil societies tend to change slowly. Painfully slowly, when it comes to giving up dependence on fossil fuels, it appears. Therefore, I have surmised that for democratic governments to evolve to a more advanced form, the motivation and willpower will have to come from a grass roots movement. Industries that depend directly or indirectly upon fossil fuels for their wealth and power can support elected official campaign accounts so lavishly that they can control government decisions that protect the status quo for these industries. The grass roots movement will have to inspire common citizens to empower themselves politically. They will have to develop enough power to challenge the current political system with a peaceful but very well-funded system that can compete successfully against the current special interest group dominated one.

This book is intended to serve, in part, as a "How To" handbook to provide rationale and guidance for helping citizens to transform special interest group democracies into common good democracies. A similar handbook to guide citizens living under dictatorships has been translated into over 30 languages and has helped citizens around the world to make transitions from dictatorships to democracy. That handbook, *From Dictatorship to Democracy*, is written by Gene Sharp, an elderly political scientist (1).

I have imagined that a new kind of political party will be the venue through which the new form of democracy, common good democracy, will evolve. In my studies I have included questionnaire items asking citizens directly about a new form of political party that would promote this new form of democracy. A reasonable number of citizens were interested in learning more about such a party if it existed. A reasonable number were also open to considering leadership positions in such a party.

Because of this and for other reasons, I have confidence that this new type of political party will eventually come into being and be successful. It may take a hundred years or several hundred years, but the history of human government is that it gradually evolves to more and more closely deliver what citizens want, and the most central thing they seem to want is a direct voice in government policy.

It may be that the new form of democracy will evolve much quicker than a few hundred years. Modern electronic communications greatly facilitate the flow of ideas and movements. And for the first time in human history we have the technology to quickly obtain reliable and valid measures of citizen opinions on political issues, as is routinely and regularly done by organizations such as the Pew Trust and the Gallup poll organizations.

I envision the polling of party members and of the general public as a critically important dimension of this new political party, and that the results of such polls will form the backbone of the party platform in general and working agenda specifically.

Another reason that I am optimistic about the success of this sort of political party is the success that I have observed in a parallel organization, Rotary International. I have been a member of my local Rotary club for over twenty years and observed its members. They are community leaders and accomplish great things very efficiently, even though politically they are a mix of both liberals and conservatives.

The mission of Rotary International is to do good in the world, specifically promoting peace internationally and providing important services to local and foreign communities. Our local club, for example, raises several hundred thousand dollars each year to support local agencies that fight child abuse. We sponsor high school and university students to study in foreign countries for a year and bring foreign students to our community for similar studies.

We contribute money to International Rotary activities, including the Polio Plus program that has eliminated polio in the Western Hemisphere. This program is a particularly interesting example of how conservatives and liberals can work together. Conservatives tend to be disease phobic. Liberals tend to care about people everywhere in the world. The Polio Plus program appeals to conservatives because it is an effort to fight diseases; it appeals to liberals because it is extending this disease prevention program to people everywhere in every nation. The program is expected to completely eradicate polio worldwide very soon. The next focal goal of Rotary will be to reduce war.

Our club is about 240 members strong and has several committees, including a public service committee that provides direct assistance to maintain public parks, provide food to needy community citizens and build new recreational facilities for children and adults, including playground facilities and a new skateboard recreation facility. Our community service committee provided cash and hands-on assistance for the construction of a new peace memorial honoring Nobel laureates from the United States, the first such public park memorial in the United States.

Rotary meetings, especially committee meetings, are conducted under Robert's rules of order. Most of the work, and specifically the planning processes, is done in occasional committee meetings. Our weekly club meetings involve sharing a meal together, singing a patriotic song and having an invocation. We have an interesting speaker for 30 minutes, including time for question-and-answer. Our club members have included university presidents and professors, city officials, the district attorney and leaders from many prominent local corporations, including lawyers, bankers and business executives.

And our club is only one of about a dozen Rotary Clubs in our local community. Internationally, there are over 2 million Rotarians in clubs in more nations than belong to the United Nations. Our club helped found one of the first Rotary clubs in Russia after the collapse of the Soviet Union a couple of decades ago.

Rotarians pay substantial dues, several hundred dollars a year, as well as making additional voluntary contributions to local and international service projects.

To compete successfully in the current environment in the United States, a new political party would have to have millions of members paying dues sufficient to compete against existing parties in support of its party candidates for political office. Candidates for political office must have considerable funds for television and other advertising in the current political system. A large enough new party could fund the campaigns of its candidates without resorting to special interest group monies, which is critically important to protect against the corrupting influence of money.

A special political campaign advantage that this political party could have is that it would not necessarily need as much money or have to fund as much advertising as traditional candidates must do. I imagine that the new party would groom candidates for elective office and fund their campaigns entirely from party member dues.

Candidates for office would agree by written contract to represent the party agenda if elected, not their own personal agendas or liberal or conservative agendas per se. During campaigns their speeches would focus on the party agenda. The general public would know exactly what that party agenda is because it would be published openly. They would also know where the agenda came from, from polling of the general public and of party members. Thus, the average citizen would know that his or her voice could very well have been heard in such polls and that the party agenda would represent citizen majority interests. The party would not have to "sell" the agenda with expensive television ads, as the agenda would be published in detail, as on a party web site. Thus, the party would need less television candidate marketing time and money and less money for mailings.

I believe that this new form of political party will have to be a grassroots effort with several key features. It will have to function in a way that many citizens find interesting, rewarding, encouraging, inspiring and fun.

It will be important to the success of the new party that its meetings, committee work and other activities be conducted in a manner that enables members to work together with respect, fun and pleasure, so they learn to like and even love working together, month after month and year after year.

It will have to function continuously, not just every four years for a couple of months before an election. It will have to give citizens a sense of personal involvement and appreciation. Research in industry shows that what employees value most about their jobs is feeling in on things and feeling appreciated for what they contribute. This new political party should capitalize on this and give citizens opportunities to feel directly involved, in on things, and feel appreciated for what they do.

Party chapter leaders should give committees responsibility but not micro-manage them. Committees should have responsibilities and authority to carry them out, running important decisions by the executive committee. They should be publically praised and thanked for what they contribute. "Praise in public, criticize in private" is another business management principle that applies. Corrective guidance should be done in private.

I believe Rotary International provides an interesting model for how a new political party could function successfully. Rotary meetings are run well, starting on time and ending on time. They meet weekly and have interesting programs, with good speakers and brief business processes. They have fun.

In addition to my involvement with Rotary, I have experience in our local county psychologist's association, which I helped to found some 35 years ago. We began with a little research questionnaire I suggested. We asked psychologists how often they wanted to meet, what time of day, for how long and what content they wanted the meeting to include.

They wanted monthly meetings that were on a weekday evening and lasted two hours, with a program for continuing education credits. We've been meeting that way ever since, having a guest speaker for 90 minutes, a few items for snacks, and a quick business meeting to handle issues that require votes by members, such as election of officers once a year, awarding appreciation plaques to psychologists and community organizations yearly, etc. In 2013, at my urging, we repeated this poll and got essentially the same sort of results, which we used to adjust our schedule.

Similarly, chapters of the new political party should be careful to measure with good questionnaires what local citizens want in terms of meeting characteristics. Citizens should be given the option to meet twice a month, once a month, once every other month, and on which day of the week and for what amount of time, e.g. 90 or 120 minutes. They should also be given opportunities to decide what the meeting content should include.

My guess is that they will vote for an interesting speaker at each meeting, brief committee reports, a non-denominational invocation to start each meeting and perhaps snacks.

It is important that this be a grassroots movement for several reasons. One is that the party must evolve in a way that is pleasing to the majority of citizens and that can evolve over time in ways that remain true to current citizen desires. It is very important that the party not become ossified and eventually thus irrelevant to citizen needs for direct involvement with their government.

Another important reason for the party to be grassroots is that this will enable local chapters to be true to the needs of local citizens, including their needs as members of ethnic minorities, industrial or agricultural communities or communities characterized by concentrations of young people or older citizens, such as in retirement communities. Thus, what appeals to citizens in one community may vary or differ from what appeals for citizens in another community. Various chapters of the party can take on qualities unique to and successful in their specific communities.

Another reason for a grass roots movement is to spread authority widely across the nation. Authority spread widely assures widespread leadership and protects the organization from being sabotaged by a centralized authority and leadership that can become corrupted in any number of ways, either inadvertently or by design.

Another reason that the party should be grassroots and have a widespread presence throughout states and the nation is that the party should empower citizens at every level of government from city level to the county level, the state level and eventually to the national level. Party members should learn politics from the ground up, first at the city level, grooming candidates for elective office as city counselors and mayor. With experience, they can groom candidates at the county and state levels. Each level of experience and expertise can prepare them for success in higher and wider political arenas.

The party can eventually develop a national presence by networking. Cities can network with each other to form a county party organization and county party organizations can network to form the state party organization. State party organizations can network to form regional networks and eventually a national presence.

The city level party would put up candidates for elective office of city positions, such as city council positions and mayor. The district and county organizations would put up candidates for district attorney, county commissioners, sheriffs and state representatives. The state party organization can put up candidates for state elective office, such as secretary of state, state treasurer and governor. The party can take positions on referenda, initiatives and bond measures that appear on ballots.

Chapters would have to develop bylaws and establish themselves as legal nonprofit organizations, or branches of a larger organization, such as a state or national organization. They will have to clarify their leadership positions, such as president, vice president, secretary and treasurer as well as define various committees to be headed by appointed or elected persons. The bylaws would specify conditions for membership, dues required, officer responsibilities and the functions of various committees. The bylaws would also create a mission statement, a core element of which would be promoting government that serves citizens primarily as cooperative members of the community overall rather than as members of independent and competing special-interest groups.

It would seem important that this party also have as a core element of its mission statement that the common good is to be defined by sophisticated polls of local communities and of party members. These polls can capitalize on the measures of citizen attitudes on various dimensions of political discourse as touched on earlier in various chapters of this book and which will be elaborated in later chapters.

Another key dimension of the bylaws will be conditions of membership, to include a commitment to support the party agenda, perhaps defined by the midpoint between what these polls show is the average opinion of strong conservatives and strong liberals in the party.

Another specification to be included in the bylaws would be the frequency with which polls would be conducted, such as every two years, to assure that the party agenda remains up-to-date with current citizen attitudes about currently important political issues.

Another important issue that should be addressed in the bylaws is the specification that committee meetings and meetings of the whole are to be conducted generally by Roberts Rules of Order in the spirit of democracy to guard against authoritarian dictatorship within the party and to protect the reasonable opinions of all party members on all issues involved in party matters.

Readers familiar with Robert's Rules of Order will appreciate that these rules promote leadership in committees and by the organization president characterized by orchestration rather than authoritarianism. Leaders do not dictate policy to committee or organization members but rather guide members to cooperatively discuss and decide policy as a constructive, respectful and respected group of cooperating participants. As most volunteer organizations in the United States are probably run by Robert's Rules of Order, many members of the new party will be familiar with and skilled in following these guidelines in running committees and the overall organization.

Another issue that the bylaws should address is dues. The party will have several financial obligations, including renting meeting space and purchasing telephone, Internet and related secretarial services, such as postage, paper, hardware and software items.

The party will also need to fund the campaign expenses of party candidates for elective office. This is of key importance to keep special-interest group money out of politics. Thus, the chapter will have to establish a schedule of dues for party members, which may be graduated depending on income.

This chapter has introduced a model for a new political party, one that appeals to both strong liberals and strong conservatives. It is my opinion, based on my research findings, that such a party, as briefly described, will appeal to the majority of citizens, especially if local chapters are designed and run skillfully.

Additional suggestions for how to assure this success are presented in the next chapters. What committees will be necessary? How can public opinion questionnaires be efficiently created and used to define the party platform at the local, county, state and national levels?

How can chapters recruit citizens who are busy just making a living and raising a family? How can it attract and maintain members who have limited time to devote to politics? Could this party evolve out of Rotary International, the League of Women Voters, the Assistance League or other such organizations or will it have to start from scratch? Will local chapters find creative and unique answers to these questions and share their successes with each other?

CHAPTER 17

SPECIFIC SUGGESTIONS FOR CREATING A CHAPTER OF THE COMMON-GOOD DEMOCRACY PARTY; BASIC STRUCTURE AND FUNCTION

As explained in the preceding chapter, the main work of the chapter should be done by committees in committee meetings and work sessions. These committees will be several in number, and probably should include an executive committee, membership committee, program committee, polling committee, ethics committee, candidate selection and grooming committee, strategies committee and networking committee. Consider these suggestions:

EXECUTIVE COMMITTEE / EXECUTIVE SECRETARY.

The executive committee would consist of the officers (president, vice president, secretary, treasurer) and chairs of the various committees. It should meet regularly, perhaps once per month. It should solicit progress reports from the officers and committee chairs, make policy decisions and provide guidance as necessary to committees. It should oversee and promote the overall success of the chapter. It should proceed via Robert's Rules of Order, as should all the committees.

If a chapter becomes large and well-funded enough, it may be able to hire an executive secretary to handle many of the responsibilities of the organization, including record-keeping, bookkeeping, printing, mailing, web site management, communications, etc. Large organizations have many details to attend to that a full-time, intelligent and skillful executive secretary or organizational manager can often handle more efficiently than an informal cadre of volunteers.

Membership committee.

The membership committee should be responsible for clarifying conditions for membership, which then would be stated in the organization bylaws and would be subject to modification from time to time. The membership committee should also be responsible for guiding the organization members in soliciting new members and providing support to new members to help them feel welcome and get actively involved. The committee might provide new members with mentors initially, giving them opportunities to meet and ask questions of current members and to explore committees on which they might serve. This committee might also advise the executive committee on disciplining members who violate organization guidelines

It would be important for current chapter members to understand the conditions of membership and be encouraged to invite prospective members to meetings as visitors. The membership committee should clarify procedures by which prospective members can apply for membership and the steps by which a person can gain membership. For example, the committee may specify a series of activities that new members must complete to gain full membership, such as attending a certain number of meetings, visiting two committee meetings, studying organization pamphlets and perhaps passing a brief written test of knowledge of the organization and signing a pledge of agreement with organization goals and willingness to support those goals faithfully as a member. They would agree to complete periodic polls of desired government services to determine the party platform.

The pledge could include these elements: Respecting the articles of incorporation, bylaws and rules, regulations and ethics code of the party, and accepting and endorsing the primary mission of the party to promote government in one's community, state and nation that serves citizens as cooperating members of the common good rather than as members of competing special interest groups.

More specifically members would agree to accept the party definition of the common good. The common good would be defined by party polls of the public and of party members. The common good would be defined as policies reflected in polls, as determined by majority vote of all party members. I'll elaborate on this below.

Party members would agree to pay their dues on time and serve in party projects and activities as the members are able, given their personal time, resources, talents and interests. Members will agree to promote cooperation rather than competition between party members, especially between liberals and conservatives.

Finally, the party chapter will probably require some statement or measure of political orientation. At first I thought this would be necessary, to facilitate calculation of the midpoint between strong liberals and strong conservatives on party polls. However, after puzzling this over, I decided this was not appropriate or practical, for reason's I'll discuss below. First, let me explain a couple of ways that political orientation can be measured.

The simplest way is by a simple questionnaire such as presented in Table 1a.

TABLE 1A. SINGLE-ITEM MEASURES OF POLITICAL WORLDVIEWS. FOR EACH OF THE ITEMS BELOW CIRCLE ONE NUMBER TO INDICATE YOUR LEVEL OF ENDORSEMENT, USING THIS CODE:

1	2	3	4	5
Strongly disagree	Disagree	Neutral	Agree	Strongly agree

1 2 3 4 5 1. Politically I consider myself to be conservative.

1 2 3 4 5 2. Politically I consider myself to be liberal.

1 2 3 4 5 3. Politically I consider myself to be independent.

1 2 3 4 5 4. Politically I consider myself to be "green".

I found in my studies that responses to the "independent" category tended not to correlate significantly with other traits, implying that independents are basically a-political, relatively disinterested in politics per se. The "green" category tended to correlate positively and modestly with "liberal", but otherwise was not consistently correlated significantly with other traits. As a result, only the liberal and conservative categories held my research interest. These two dimensions appear to be the central ones as far as human political attitudes are concerned.

A party member's political orientation can be measured more reliably with a longer scale. Perhaps the simplest way to do this is to use responses to use both items 1 and 2 in Table 1a. This is done by adding item one to six minus the response to item 2, divided by 2. For example, for a person who marks item 1 "4" and item 2 "1", the math would be 4 plus 6-1 = 9 / 2 = 4.5.

In my studies, I term this the lib-con score. This score has modest reliability (.60). Another way to get a more reliable measure of a party member's score on the liberalism-conservatism continuum is with a longer scale of items that reflect content on political dimensions. A 20-item measure is provided as an example in Table 1b. It has much stronger reliability, an alpha coefficient of .86.

[The alpha reliability statistic is a measure of how well the items in a scale or trait measure spread people apart, or how reliable a given person's score is as a measure of this trait. The higher the coefficient, the more reliable the scale. An alpha coefficient of .80 or higher is good. .90 or higher is excellent. Another way of saying this is that a scale with high reliability is one for which all the items in the scale are truly measuring something in common with the other items. Or, a person who endorses one of the items is likely to endorse the others. Another way of explaining this is to say that the items in the scale truly reflect the way some people think. To find out which people, one computes correlations between this trait and other traits. This yields *validity* data or data giving the traits meaning in how they relate to other traits.]

TABLE 1B. SAMPLE LIBERAL CONSERVATIVE DIMENSION QUESTIONNAIRE.

Technical notes: This questionnaire is based on items selected from the author's studies (1). The Cronbach alpha reliability is .86, mean 3.81, standard deviation .54, range 2.60 to 4.85 on a sample of 55 adult community college students. Higher scores reflect liberal attitudes.

[*Standard deviation* is a statistic that indicates how widely scores range around the mean or average score. It is the range between which, above and below the mean are found 66 percent of the scores. For the above data, the mean is 3.81. Thus, two thirds of the scores in this study fall between 3.81 minus .54 and 3.81 plus .54, or between 3.27 and 4.35. The *range* is the spread of all the scores, in this case between 2.60 and 4.85. For purposes of this manuscript, only technically trained readers need know these details.]

"Please indicate how strongly you agree or disagree with each of the statements below by circling one number for each of the statements below, using this code:

Strongly disagree	Disagree	Neutral	Agree	Strongly agree
1	2	3	4	5

1 2 3 4 5 1. There is only one source of absolute truth, the holy scriptures or writings of my religion.

1 2 3 4 5 2. In general, religion and government should be kept separate.

214 William McConochie

1 2 3 4 5 3. Government should stay out of the way of big business or help big business succeed.

1 2 3 4 5 4. Groups to which I belong should be fair and just to everyone in every nation.

1 2 3 4 5 5. Government should primarily serve the highest social class.

1 2 3 4 5 6. Big money should be kept out of campaign contributions, so that elected officials aren't indebted primarily to their biggest contributors.

1 2 3 4 5 7. With few, if any, exceptions there should be no birth control measures or abortions for the women of our group.

1 2 3 4 5 8. I think that women deserve just as much respect as men in all matters.

1 2 3 4 5 9. War is necessary and desirable to keep a nation united, focused and fully employed.

1 2 3 4 5 10. In foreign policy, our nation should agree to international arms control and pollution control treaties to reduce the dangers from wars, global warming and destruction of forests, ocean fisheries, etc.

1 2 3 4 5 11. Government should primarily assure an environment in which businesses can make profits.

1 2 3 4 5 12. Citizens who have above-average incomes should share them (via taxes) with citizens who make less.

1 2 3 4 5 13. I support the National Rifle Association's interest in citizen access to firearms.

1 2 3 4 5 14. I think cooperation with people from other lands is better than competition against them.

1 2 3 4 5 15. My favored political party should dominate state and national politics to the exclusion of other parties, if possible.

1 2 3 4 5 16. A nation's government should strive to provide

public transportation, job opportunities, and access to housing, food, clean water and health care, and protection from violence to all of its citizens of every social class.

1 2 3 4 5 17. I am totally devoted to my preferred government and religious leaders.

1 2 3 4 5 18. We citizens should be less focused on unquestioning acceptance of political leaders' decisions and more concerned with the government services needed by our citizens.

1 2 3 4 5 19. I am not concerned about global warming.

1 2 3 4 5 20. My national government should fund and encourage research on the design of sustainable communities.

You, the reader, can complete this questionnaire to find your score on the conservative-liberal continuum. Don't mark in your book. Just list your scores for the 20 items on a separate piece of paper. Then total your scores for the odd items and divide by 10. Subtract this score from 6. This will be your C score. Then total your scores for the even items and divide by ten. This will be your L score. Finally, add your C and L scores, and divide this total by 2. This will be your L-C score, your score on the liberalism-conservatism measure. Your score should fall between 1.0 and 5.0. If it doesn't, carefully repeat the scoring steps above until it does. To find the range within which your score falls relative to the norm

TABLE 1C. NORM CHART FOR LIBERALISM-CONSERVATISM SCALE. HIGH SCORES REFLECT THE LIBERAL END OF THE SCALE.

sample of community college adults, use the chart in Table 1c.

Lib-Con score:	Percentile	Range

Range	Percentile	Label
1.00-2.00		"Extreme conservative"
2.00-2.59		"Strong conservative"
2.60 to 3.00		"Weak to moderate conservative"
3.01 to 3.29	10th percentile 3.07	Neutral, between conservative and liberal
3.30 to 3.41	20th percentile 3.30	Neutral, between conservative and liberal
3.42 to 3.53	30th percentile 3.52	Neutral, between conservative and liberal
3.54 to 3.64		Weak liberal
3.65 to 3.87	40th percentile 3.65, 50th percentile 3.78	
3.88 to 4.06	60th percentile 3.97	Moderate liberal
4.07 to 4.17	70th percentile 4.12	
4.18 to 4.29	80th percentile 4.27	Strong liberal
4.30 to 4.39		
4.40 to 4.75	90th percentile 4.43	Very strong liberal
4.75 and up		Extreme liberal

The third column provides labels for the ranges. These are based on the possible ranges of scores. The lowest possible score is 1.00, for a person who strongly agrees with all of the odd items in the scale and strongly disagrees with all the even items. A score of 3 would result from a person who marked all of the odd items "3, Undecided" and all of the liberal items 3. Thus, this is the Neutral range. The highest possible score would be a 5, for a person who strongly disagreed with all of the odd items and strongly agreed with all of the even items. Finding reasonable labels for all of the possible ranges on this scale was a bit of a challenge. Other labels might be preferable. But this issue needn't bog us down.

The sample of community college students on which this scale was normed included 13 persons who considered themselves to be strong conservatives, agreeing or strongly agreeing with the questionnaire item in Table 1a asking whether they considered themselves to be a political conservative. Their scores were compared to those for the 20 strong liberals in the group.

The mean score for the strong conservatives on the lib-con scale was 3.43, in the "Neutral" range, not in the clearly conservative range, judging by the content of the questionnaire items. The mean score for the strong liberals was 4.24, in the "Strong liberal" range.

I puzzled over my initial idea that party agenda items would be defined as the mean of the mean scores between strong liberals and strong conservatives on polls of response options, as discussed above. Response options are government policies or programs that the party determines by research to be worth consideration.

I thought it would be necessary to know each party member's political orientation for two reasons: to identify "strong liberals" and "strong conservatives" for determining the mid-point between the mean scores for both of these groups on response option polls; and to eliminate the votes of extreme liberals and extreme conservatives, to guard against members faking extreme positions on the political orientation measure in order to distort decisions on response option polls in their favor.

However, this approach had some serious drawbacks. One was that it was hard to decide who would be a "strong liberal" or a "strong conservative", e.g. by setting scores in Table 1c, above. One could argue as to what the proper cut-off scores should be. More important, it seemed inappropriate to limit decisions to just these two groups from among all party members. If only the scores of strong liberals and strong conservatives were going to count, why would other party members bother to vote? They'd feel disenfranchised.

So, it seemed to me that whether a given response option "wins" an poll election should be determined simply by the highest vote, if among two or three options, and by a vote of at least 51 percent of those casting ballots, if on a single-option or a multiple-option ticket. And all party members should be given a reasonable opportunity to be familiar with the poll items and issues and to vote on them. See additional information on this in the Epilogue chapter at the end of the book.

The 20-item scale results can be interpreted as reflecting the similarity between strong liberals and strong conservatives as found in the studies reported in prior chapters. From a scientific perspective, these measuring issues can be analyzed further.

For example, the ten items in this lib-con scale designed to reflect conservative attitudes correlate more strongly with conservatism as measured by the single "politically, I consider myself to be conservative" item in the questionnaire than do the ten items designed to reflect liberal attitudes correlate with liberalism. Thus, in this sense, we might consider the conservative items to be truer measures of conservatism than are the liberal items measures of liberalism. In spite of this, the strong conservatives in the study tended to disavow the conservative items and endorse the liberal items in a manner that moved their mean score as a group (3.43) into the neutral range, close to the liberal perspective.

Why this is so is a puzzle. But, even without knowing the reason, it is important to appreciate that conservatives, as a group, are not that different from liberals on specific policy issues, as measured by questionnaire items. Keep in mind that this is the phenomenon documented in questionnaires totaling over 800 political policy issues, as reported in earlier chapters. The present questionnaire findings are not an anomaly. They are consistent with similar political agenda questionnaire findings on a sample of over 150 community college and university students and on samples of Occupy members and churchgoers. Conservatives and liberals do differ significantly from each other on questionnaire measures of political policy issues, but not by much.

The implication is that strong liberals and strong conservatives can be expected to work cooperatively and closely together to solve important and necessary community problems in the political arena, much as they do as members of Rotary International, for example. Rotarians are not an anomaly either.

While we have handy the mean scores for strong liberals (4.24) and strong conservatives (3.43), we can compute the midpoint between them, simply by adding them and dividing by 2, 4.24 + 3.43 = 7.67 / 2 = 3.84. 3.84 is in the "Moderate liberal" range in the Norm Chart (Table 1c). In terms of policies, then, one can conclude that the party agenda based on this sample of 55 students would consist of promoting the even-numbered items in Table 1b, but with moderate intensity, not fanatical energy.

However, I don't think this is the best way to go, as I explained immediately above. I think the party chapters should ask members to complete the 20-item political orientation scale, or one like it, for research purposes. The member should be told his/her score, but otherwise the information should be kept confidential.

Party members should be expected to agree as a condition of membership to accept all other party members as their respected political "equals", regardless of their political orientation. As long as party members respect party behavior codes, e.g. refraining from extreme political rants or demonstrations, disruptive activities or other incivilities, they should be respected and accepted in committee and other activities.

Committees should be made up of approximately equal numbers of liberals and conservatives, to assure respect for both worldviews. Party officer positions should also be equally open to members of both worldviews, e.g. by having at least one liberal and one conservative candidate on each slate at election times.

For an actual new political party such computations should be based on much larger samples of party members and samples that are fairly representative of party members. For example, the sample for a large city, or a county or state, should include men, women, blacks, whites, Hispanics, Asian Americans, Native Americans, urban dwellers and country dwellers, assuming there are members in the party from all these groups. Indeed, ideally, the numbers should be calculated on *all* current members of the party organization.

Measuring party member political worldviews using a 20-item measure is probably preferable to the single-item measures in Table 1a. The reason is that the liberal and conservative worldviews are complex, including many facets. A given citizen may not realize exactly what his attitudes are on all of the facets, so his response on a single-item measure of liberalism or conservatism might be a rather rough guess or estimate. A 20-item scale provides a sample across ten of these facets for the liberal worldview and ten for the conservative. This gives the citizen an opportunity to indicate a more robust measure of his or her worldviews.

In the next chapter we'll explore the functions of one of the most important committees of the new party.

Chapter 18

Functions of the Polling and Research Committee

One of the most important committees will be the polling and research committee. It would be responsible for creating polls, analyzing and summarizing the resulting data and making this data available to the executive committee for use. Polling should include polls of the general public and then polls of members.

Specifically, polls of the general public should solicit input on issues of political importance perhaps every two years. These issues might include tax policies, infrastructure maintenance programs, public employee salary and benefit schedules, Justice Department policies, programs and facilities, and other issues typically addressed by governments.

The results of this poll would then be used to create response options, possible specific policies and services that government might enact to address the issues clarified in the poll of the general public. These response options would then be presented to party members to determine which options are most preferred, as by a vote of at least 51 percent (simple majority). These preferred options would then become the party platform.

As I was writing this chapter I attended a conflict resolution studies convention at Oregon State University where I gave a paper on the relationship between violence and fear. As part of the day's activities we were taken on a tour in the library of the entire works of Linus Pauling and his wife Ava Helen. We saw a replica of his office in the chemistry department at California Institute of Technology where he studied and taught for many years after undergraduate studies at OSU. Both of his two heavy gold Nobel medals, one for chemistry and another for peace promotion containing nuclear weapons testing, were there for us to pick up and admire.

We were given free copies of two books, one he wrote and one on his selected writings. He was a strong advocate for high-quality and honorable governments and opined that "The principle upon which a true democratic system operates is that…correct decisions are to be made by the process of averaging the opinions of all the citizens in the democracy."(1) I found this interesting, as it dovetails, in a sense, with the process proposed above for pooling the votes of both liberals and conservatives.

Pauling was a highly respected scientist and thinker who had been successful in a wide variety of endeavors for many decades. Thus, I respect his thinking on this matter of political policy decision-making, with some qualification. If liberals and conservatives were to vote on issues separately, then taking an average between them might make some sense.

However, as the Common Good Party melds both liberals and conservatives in its membership, this averaging seems an unnecessary complication. Averaging furthermore seems unnecessary in light of the research findings presented in earlier chapters as to the relatively close positions that liberals and conservatives, on average, take on virtually all major dimensions of political discourse. So, as I recommend, the party would determine its platform based on polls of party members, using majority vote to carry issues. These would lead to specific recommended government policies and programs.

These specific recommended policies and programs would be the focus for party candidates to promote if and when running for elective office. If elected to office, for example as a city counselor or State or Federal Representative, they would continue to promote this party agenda in that arm of government.

General characteristics of good polls.

Briefly, polls should be comprehensive and cover the full range of probable and possible issues currently evident in citizen minds. Focus group interviews, reviews of recent newspaper editorials and letters to the editor and similar procedures can be employed to assure comprehensive, currently relevant poll content.

Poll questionnaire items should be phrased in a manner that will provide a full range of quantified response options, from strongly disagree to strongly agree, so that the full range of public opinion is reliably measured. Each general topic should be measured with more than one question, which also will help assure reliability. The questionnaire items should be written clearly and simply enough for the majority of citizens to understand.

Questionnaires should be divided into sections, each introduced with a paragraph or two of background material to familiarize the poll taker with the issues addressed in the questions that follow.

Consider the example in Table 2.

Table 2. A section of a hypothetical citizen poll.

This questionnaire section addresses kindergarten through high school public school issues in our community. There have been many discussions in recent years about budgeting, numbers of administrators, ancillary services and programs, buildings and facilities, class sizes, teacher salaries and benefits and underfunded pension obligations. More information about the issues involved is available on the Chapter web site, CGPChapter123oregon.com.

Please circle one number, 1 through 5, to indicate how strongly you agree or disagree with each of the statements below, using this code:

1	2	3	4	5
Strongly disagree	Disagree	Neutral	Agree	Strongly agree

1 2 3 4 5 1. For grades 1 through 6, class sizes should be no larger than 22 students.

1 2 3 4 5 2. For grades 7 and 8, lecture class sizes should be no larger than 28 students.

1 2 3 4 5 3. For grades 9 through 12 class sizes should be no larger than 40 students.

1 2 3 4 5 4. As general policy, gym, music and art classes should not be cut from the curriculum when budgets get tight.

1 2 3 4 5 5. As general policy, counseling, school nursing and shop and homemaking classes should not be cut from the curriculum when budgets get tight.

1 2 3 4 5 6. As general policy, the same adequate portion of the annual budget should be maintained for maintenance of the physical plant of the school system (building repairs, heating, lighting, plumbing, etc.).

1 2 3 4 5 7. A school lunch program with cafeteria services and items for purchase at affordable prices should be developed for our local high school.

This hypothetical citizen poll is focused on public school issues and is rather specific on the first six items. Item seven is more general. How general or specific the items are can be decided as you draft a given poll, depending on the state of current public opinion on issues. Opinion might be diffuse and general on issues when they first arise, but then more specific when an issue has been discussed and debated for some weeks or months. For example, a town that has no public parks will initially consider the general affordability of parks and where they might be located. Later in the discussion, the citizen might be invited to weigh in on specific budget questions, such as a bond amount, how much the bond would increase taxes for the average citizen and for how long, and how strongly the citizen supports each of three specific possible park locations.

Polls specifically for party members are based on the results of the polls of general citizens. These polls are designed to measure support for various possible government policies and programs for delivering on the desires for services expressed by citizens in their poll. These policy and program options should be crafted very carefully, after thorough research and deliberation. Therefore, the members of the polling committee should be well-educated and well-versed on issue topics. They should be willing to do research on issues, reading, studying public documents, conferring with consultants and experts, university professors, etc. and perhaps even attending conventions focusing on issues in question.

The better this work is done, the better the ultimate party elected representatives, mayors, and others can serve the community, for their mission will be to promote the policies and programs chosen by party members via the party member polls. Thus, it is critically important that poll committee members be dedicated, energetic and skillful in researching issues and crafting well-designed government service response options. These response options, ideally, will someday become community law, regulation or policy. So, they need to be crafted carefully.

This crafting may be rather simple at the small town level but will have to be more sophisticated at the city, county, state and Federal levels. Thus, it will behoove the party to develop sophisticated collaborations with other facets of the party and of the broader community so the research done can be an economical, well-coordinated collaborative and effective effort. For example, eventually, a state party organization may be able to promote a state level well-funded polling committee that works full time with full-time paid professional staff to craft a wide range of response options that various city and county organizations can use in their respective polls.

These state-level polling committees might have several subcommittees specializing on various areas, such as school systems, roads and bridges, economics (to include banking, taxation and pension fund investing), public utilities (gas, water, electric, sewer) and public recreational facilities (including fishing, parks, ski areas, etc.). The staffing of these committees would vary in expertise as appropriate, with academic degrees and work experience appropriate to each topic area.

The party member polls would have a format similar to the polls of citizens, with various sections introduced with paragraphs of background information. Consider the example in Table 3.

TABLE 3. A SECTION OF A HYPOTHETICAL PARTY MEMBER POLL.

This questionnaire section addresses issues of class sizes in kindergarten through high school in our community. A recent poll of the general public resulted in endorsement by the majority of citizens for class sizes no larger than 22 for grades 1 through 6. More information about the issues involved is available on the Chapter web site, CGPChapter123oregon.com.

Please circle one number, 1 through 5, to indicate how strongly you agree or disagree with each of the statements below, using this code:

1	2	3	4	5
Strongly disagree	Disagree	Neutral	Agree	Strongly agree

1 2 3 4 5 1. When budgets are strong, and student enrollment is growing, more classes and teachers should be added when class sizes grow to 28, thus bringing the maximum size down to the recommended maximum of 22.

1 2 3 4 5 2. When budgets are weak, administration, and teacher salaries and benefits should be trimmed as necessary to maintain all facets of the school program and class sizes of 22 maximum.

1 2 3 4 5 3. When budgets are weak from the tax base, the school system should actively pursue other sources of funding and program support, such as using volunteer teacher assistants, fund-raising auctions and direct solicitation of financial support from local charitable organizations.

1 2 3 4 5 4. Budget plans for each school year should be prepared by school administrative personnel and presented via the local newspaper in detail three months in advance of final decisions for a ratification vote by the general public.

It is clear in the Table 3 example that controversial issues will inevitably be a part of such polling. Public employee salaries and benefits are a hot topic and probably always will be. The new party must have the courage and expertise to confidently and competently address and grapple with any and all of the many issues that are faced by governments. There are always tough issues to be handled, tough choices to be made.

As mentioned earlier, polls specifically for party members will represent *response options* for government policies and programs to address issues raised by the general public. Response options should be carefully crafted. Crafting these options should rest heavily upon detailed and sophisticated information, as can be provided by party experts in various fields. These experts should be well-versed in topic areas for which they are responsible.

Polling experts in the party should seek current sophisticated information from other professionals, whether in the party or not. For example on issues of economics, revenue, taxation and budgeting, party members could gain information from university professors in economics and accounting, and from the state treasurer's office and federal budget offices, such as the General Accounting Office.

Committee members responsible for crafting options on issues such as infrastructure development and maintenance should have appropriate credentials, such as ones in civil engineering, and be skilled at gaining suggestions from practicing engineers in related fields, such those contracting with the airline, highway and railroad industries.

Committee members responsible for crafting options regarding public employee salaries, benefits and working conditions, should be well-qualified with backgrounds in public service, union activities, human resources, economics, and/or similar fields. They should have expertise in communicating with experts from the community who serve in these various fields or study them, as university professors, consultants, etc.

CHAPTER 19

PROGRAM, MISSION AND ETHICS, STRATEGIES AND NETWORKING COMMITTEES

PROGRAM COMMITTEE.

The program committee would be responsible for finding interesting speakers for chapter meetings, assuming that this will be a feature of monthly meetings. These meetings may occur once a month. Speakers might include current elected and appointed officials, such as city mayors, sheriffs, counsel persons, state representatives, university presidents, district attorneys, and state governors, treasurers, etc. They might also include university professors, especially from departments of political science, ecology sciences, political philosophy, criminal justice, economics, sociology, history and other fields with immediate political implication. The committee should clarify desired features of such speeches, such as speaking slowly and clearly, allowing 20 minutes for lecture and slides, preparing slides with large enough font to be easily read, and allowing15 minutes for question-and-answer. The committee should prepare guidance material and present it to speakers to follow. His committee should also be responsible for arranging for audio and visual materials as needed by speakers. The committee should schedule speakers well in advance, perhaps for as much as four months out.

Speakers should talk on topics that are of direct current relevance to the political issues of interest to party members. Indeed, party members might be asked to fill out a brief rating form for each speaker they listen to, to help the program committee measure the interest value of each speaker to the party chapter. This information can help them choose good speakers.

Mission and Ethics Committee.

A mission and ethics committee would be responsible for drafting, revising and interpreting the underlying mission statement, code of ethics and related documents of the chapter. Eventually the State party organization will probably craft such documents that all chapters in that state might choose to adopt.

There are many potential sources of examples of ethical codes that chapters and State organizations can refer to in creating a code of ethics and related documents. One is the United Nations Declaration of Human Rights, which includes the rights of citizens to have a viable voice in the governments under which they live, as presented in Table 4.

Table 4. Article 21 of the United Nations Declaration of Human Rights

---

Article 21

Everyone has the right to take part in the government of his country, directly or through freely chosen representatives.

Everyone has the right of equal access to public service in his country.

The will of the people shall be the basis of the authority of government; this will of the people shall be expressed in periodic and genuine elections which shall be by universal and equal suffrage and shall be held by secret vote or by equivalent free voting procedures.

The chapter or State organization can adopt and modify principles in other sources for use in the party code of principles. For example, item 21-1 might be transformed into:

Every party member in good standing has the right to take

part in the polls of party members by direct and private completion of said polls.

Or, more broadly:

Every party member in good standing has the right to participate in the activities of the party, including the right to take part in the polls of party members by direct and private completion of said polls.

Item 21-3 of the U.N. Charter could be transformed into:

The will of the people shall be the basis of the authority of government. For our party, this will shall constitute the common good, as measured by party polls, and will be promoted by representatives from our party who are elected to public office.

Within the party the common good shall be defined as the will of party members as measured regularly and at least every two years, by reliable and valid polls of relevant and current community issues.

There are other sources of ethical codes that can also be used for guidance in forming the chapter and larger party organization codes. For example, the American Psychological Association has a detailed code of professional ethics for its members. These include protections of privacy for participants in research studies and clear disclosure of how the research results will be used. These principles could help craft a party ethical principle or code principle such as:

All polls designed and administered by the party shall include introductions explaining the purpose of the poll, any expected discomfort for participants completing the poll, how the poll data will be used and how participant privacy and confidentiality will be assured, as well as how the participant can gain further information on their scores, etc.

Party member poll data will be summarized and published

only as aggregate information, and personal identity of participating members will be kept strictly confidential or accessible only by an identifying code known only to the participating individual and key party research personnel.

In addition to the United Nations Declaration and the APA ethical code, the simple code of ethics of Rotary International might be considered. This consists of four questions that Rotarians are expected to refer to when making decisions in their personal, career and Rotary activities:

- Is it the Truth?
- Is it fair to all concerned?
- Will it build goodwill and better friendships?
- Will it be beneficial to all concerned?

Whether and how a chapter might incorporate these principles will be up to the chapter. Perhaps you, the reader, can think of a way.

The ethics committee of each chapter should create the ethics code and serve as a reference body to the chapter. Or, if the chapter simply adopts a code of ethics from a state or national branch of the party, the local ethics committee can serve simply as a guiding body, hearing cases within the chapter that involve ethical concerns and advising the executive committee on recommended actions.

SAMPLE ETHICS COMMITTEE PRINCIPLE: COOPERATION VERSUS COMPETITION.

It is recommended that the chapter poll its members to gather data upon which to create its mission statement and code of ethics and related fundamental philosophical positions and worldview. Based on my research, I expect that the majority of general public and of party members will want the party to promote a cooperative rather than competitive worldview both within the party and within the community. This is not to say that humans aren't competitive, but merely to suggest that it will be important for party members to emphasize cooperation and to guard against excessive competition. Cooperation can be promoted within the party and within the broader community. Even businesses can compete in a civil, kind manner, as do athletes when coached to display good sportsmanship.

In this vein, the party may choose to promote cooperative negotiations between businesses and unions, and between government agencies and unions. For example, the party may advocate for cooperative negotiations between public school teacher unions and school systems rather than competitive tussles resulting in strikes, lawsuits and battles over taxes.

More broadly, it is expected that the party will promote an atmosphere of such cooperation between all government agencies and unions or other groups with which the government agencies contract. For example, Medicare negotiations with pharmaceutical companies for medications will probably be a focus for cooperative negotiations to keep medical services affordable for citizens.

Such cooperation can be promoted in different ways. For example, more cooperative procedures might be found for managing public school policies and programs. A policy of proportional budgeting rather than contract-driven budgeting might be tried. In such a program, each aspect of the school system is maintained regardless of available funding. If funding increases, all aspects of the system get their fair proportion of it. If funding decreases, all aspects take their fair portion of cuts.

Other options could be explored. A policy might be promoted to enable school districts to put public school teaching services up for bid by competing unions. A given teacher might be willing to work for either of two such unions. One union might underbid the other and get the contract to provide teaching services to the school district for the next contract period, perhaps six years. The teachers working for the successful union might then make contributions to Social Security for retirement benefits rather than to a union or State pension fund, so that if they don't work for the school district beyond six years they would still have accrued retirement benefits.

Another more general way that cooperation rather than competition could be promoted might be via a new state and national law that renders any contract between government and a non-government entity, such as a union or construction contractor, to be invalid if and when the contract is no longer in the best interests of the common good, as determined by a court of law.

For example, in Oregon some decades ago the State made a contract with public teacher unions to guarantee an assumed 8 percent per year gain in invested pension funds and corresponding benefits to union members. But, in subsequent years the invested funds, though thoughtfully invested, did not gain an average of 8 percent. But, the state by contract was still obligated to pay benefits as if they had gained 8 percent. Under current law, the State could not get out of the contract.

In retrospect, this contract was made unwisely, for no one can guarantee future return levels on investments. The State should be able to protect citizens of the state from an obligation made foolishly by a state agency. A constitutional provision that would give the State the power to nullify contracts that turn out to be clearly not in the interests of the common good might solve this problem more gently than by bankruptcy of the state.

Many U.S. States have billions of dollars of unfunded obligations to public employees by reason of such contracts, where the funds set aside have not grown via investments sufficiently to cover the obligations. This is a serious problem that can contribute to the bankruptcy of a State government. It suggests that many contracts may have been made in a manner that clearly jeopardizes the common good.

Finding mechanisms for avoiding such economic problems seems to be of utmost importance. If current political systems and political parties do not address such problems, some other entity will have to. The new party, dedicated to serving citizens of the community overall and thus the common good, could consider addressing such challenges.

STRATEGIES COMMITTEE.

A strategies committee may be valuable to plan general party activities and efforts. These topics may include planning an election campaign for one or more party members who have been chosen as candidates. Planning special events, such as conventions might be another. For example, the chapter may want to host a county convention of party chapters. Another special project for the strategies committee might be engineering a trip by a panel of party members to the state or national Capitol to visit with sitting elected officials or other government agencies. This project may require a special fund-raising event to finance the trip.

Another project for a strategies committee might be a periodic examination and assessment of the overall status of the chapter, assessing its strengths and weaknesses and planning for improvements, growth in membership and exploration of new foci for the chapter. It might recommend to the executive committee an increase in membership, an increase in dues, a revised or graduated dues structure to enable more members to join, a new meeting place for chapter meetings and new local service projects. The strategies committee might see a need for other new committees that it could recommend to the executive committee, such as a committee to select and carry out service projects.

NETWORKING COMMITTEE.

A networking committee is recommended for promoting constructive relationships with other chapters, with county and state party organizations and with non-party organizations, such as the media, local governments and college and university departments of law, civics, political science, education, psychology, sociology, anthropology, business, economics, civil engineering, environmental science and community planning.

The chapter may help citizens in a nearby area form a new chapter. The networking committee could work with the strategies committee to sponsor a joint meeting of several adjacent chapters. This committee might assume responsibility for networking with the outside community in general, as by handling public relations for the chapter. Public relations can include public service announcements, public media communications and appearances, and arranging for school students to serve internships with the chapter. It would be important to publish the party agenda periodically, as on a chapter web site and in newspaper articles.

In this chapter I have presented specific suggestions for several committees. In the next chapter I present suggestions for a candidate grooming committee. How will a common good party screen and groom candidates for elective office in community, state and national governments? Can psychological tests help in selecting candidates for office who are likely to be noble and effective and unlikely to be corrupted by money and power? How can academic skills, experience in party leadership and in community experience be woven into the formation of good candidates?

Chapter 20

Selecting and Grooming
Candidates for Elective Office

The civil war in Syria was still raging, but the article headline on page A7 of our local newspaper on December 21, 2012, the shortest day of the year, read "Caring for wounded emerges as health crisis for postwar Syria"(Register Guard, Eugene, Or). The photo showed a 4-month-old boy lying on a hospital cot, mouth agape, apparently comatose with his head bandaged, mother sitting nearby. He had brain damage, hit by shrapnel from a bomb dropped on his village by the president of his country, Bashar Assad. Assad was fighting for his political life, willing to kill even his own people to cling to power.

The Common Good Party, as I imagine it, will seek political power in the conventional way through party members elected to political office. They will sponsor candidates for elective office at all levels of government, from the local to the national. Thus, selecting good candidates to run for office is of utmost importance, especially when selecting candidates for president of one's nation, for presidents wield great power. They can use this power for good, or, as we see in Assad's case, for evil.

How should party candidates be screened and groomed for elective office in the city, county, state and nation? What is the simplest way to do this? What are more detailed ways? How might psychological tests help in selecting candidates for office who are unlikely to become warmongers at worst and ideally noble and forward-looking leaders at best? Chapters will devise their own ways to do this, but let me offer some suggestions.

The party chapter, or networks of chapters, such as all those in a given city, will select and groom candidates for elective office, first locally, and eventually for county, state and national office.

The simplest way to find and prepare party members for public campaigns will be by giving them opportunities to lead within the party. They will be appointed and elected to serve in leadership positions within the party. Chapter officers will be elected by chapter members from slates of candidates. These slates may be created by small ad hoc committees appointed by the board of directors for this purpose. Committee chairs may be appointed by the board as well, unless there are many persons striving for such positions, in which case elections would be appropriate. Typically, persons will gain leadership skills by serving as committee members, then chairs. Success in these roles can lead to running for a position as an officer, such as vice president, secretary, treasurer or president of the chapter.

Persons who prove themselves able leaders within the party, rising from committee work to chapter leadership, can be sponsored by the chapter or a coalition of chapters to run for a local public office, such as city council person, utility board member or mayor. Party members successful in these elective offices can then run for county and state elective positions. Persons who are successful in state government positions can be sponsored by the party for federal positions.

Party chapter members will bring varying degrees of expertise to the chapter from their academic and work experience. For example, a member may have majored in government as a college undergraduate, earned a subsequent law degree and practiced in law and union negotiations. Such background may strengthen a member's qualifications for elective office.

A person may work on and lead committees within the party and eventually as chapter president for a year or two. He or she may also serve on city committees as a volunteer and be doing all this while maintaining a law practice or running a business in the community.

This person may then ask the party chapter, in coalition with other local chapters, to sponsor him/her as a candidate for city mayor. If there is more than one party member who is interested in running for public office, several can run for sponsorship within the party first. In most cases, a coalition of chapters will sponsor a member for public office.

The party will assume responsibility for a sponsored member's campaign, including financing it. The campaign would be financed only from party member dues. This is critically important. Money can corrupt, or at least buy loyalty. Candidates must be loyal to the interests of those who fund their campaigns. If special interest groups fund them, candidates must cater to those groups once in office. One could argue that the Common Good Party is a special interest group, of sorts, and it is.

But, the loyalty it exacts is adherence to the party agenda, as defined by party member polls. Candidates who accept party funds and endorsement will agree by written contract with the party to represent its agenda if elected, and to accept no campaign funds or other special interest group monies from any sources other than the party while running for office or once in office. This is the party's mechanism for keeping "money out of politics", specifically special interest group money.

Party candidates who are elected to office will be obligated to promote the party agenda. They'll be expected to do this in their votes on legislation and in proposing legislation. While campaigning, they will be expected to speak to the party agenda, not to their own personal agendas. If they have novel political agenda ideas, those ideas should be vetted through the party, and, ideally, through polls of party members. Of course, some novel ideas may arise in crisis situations that demand quick attention, but the basic principle of vetting new ideas through the party is to be honored as far as practical.

In terms of money needed for campaigns, there is reason to believe that the Common Good Party will need less campaign effort and expense than other parties, because its polling processes, which include polling of the general public, assure that its agenda will appeal to the majority of citizens.

In addition, by publishing the party agenda, and by the party's policy of promoting party-sponsored candidates who are obligated to promote this agenda, the party assures the public that "what it sees is what it will get". What candidates say they will do in office is what they *will* do...promote the party agenda as published. Thus, it should take less advertising to "sell" party candidates, and thus less money.

But, campaigns do cost much money, so the party will have to have literally tens of thousands of members at the state level to have sufficient money to fund candidate campaigns. The party will need tens of millions of members at the national level. So, the party will have to be designed and managed in a manner that has consistent and substantial pubic appeal. All chapters will be expected to appreciate this challenge and take it seriously.

The party may want to augment or refine the candidate selection process in various ways. For example, it may wish to set lower and upper age limits for various offices, such as ages 30 and 60 for city mayor and 45 and 55 for President of the United States. It may create residency and citizenship conditions or educational conditions that are more restrictive than those established by pubic charters.

It may even add intelligence, personality and attitude conditions, as can be measured by reliable questionnaires and rating scales. The present author has substantial experience in developing and using such questionnaires. The remainder of this chapter will explain how such questionnaires can be developed specifically for use in the political arena.

I have developed scales for screening job applicants, first specifically for the heavy trucking industry and then for jobs in general. These batteries of tests include measures of verbal and spatial intelligence, memory, the Big Five personality traits (conscientiousness, extroversion, agreeableness, openness and emotional stability), business management aptitude and preferences and job problem behaviors (e.g. substance abuse tendencies, anger management problems, theft tendencies, etc.). They include measures of English grammar, basic arithmetic and high school level science and chemistry. These batteries are available in their entirety on web sites, such as Testmasterinc.com.

Such tests have been used in industry for over 80 years and have proven to be the most valid method for selecting employees, e.g. compared to just interviews or work experience. More specifically, intelligence and conscientiousness are the traits most consistently associated with good work performance, and across all sorts of jobs.

Thus, a Common Good Party chapter or state association of chapters that wants to capitalize on this information might want to add measures of various traits that have been shown by research to predict desired performance. They could require candidates to have certain minimum scores on various trait measures.

Consider these tidbits of information related to politician qualifications. An attorney friend of the author went to law school with a fellow who ended up in national politics. The attorney friend has expressed dismay at this, as this classmate seemed to him to be one of the least intelligent in his class.

Dr. Lew Goldberg, another friend of the author, is a world-renowned expert on the Big Five personality traits. Dr. Goldberg studied these traits at the Oregon Research Institute for decades and developed detailed measures of them, including a questionnaire that provides reliable measures of 9 facets within each of the five main factors (conscientiousness, extroversion, etc.). He termed this measuring instrument "AB5C". Lew studied the personality traits of about 800 local adults to develop this and other measures and to study their relationship to other traits, such as preferred job activities.

I was familiar with this process, in part because I served as one of the 800 subjects over several years, completing questionnaires for Dr. Goldberg. Upon request, Dr. Goldberg made his data files available to me for the AB5C instrument and for the Strong Campbell Interest Inventory. I ran correlations between the two and noted the personality traits of persons who expressed interest in being politicians. Persons who expressed interest in being politicians were notable for their *lower* scores on conscientiousness. They seemed to be persons who would rather tell others how to do things than do the work themselves.

So, from these two anecdotal examples, it would appear that one cannot assume that everyone who wants to be a politician is necessarily well-suited for the job, just as not everyone who wants any particular job is necessarily a good candidate for that job. My most detailed experience with this issue was in the trucking industry, where the use of my battery of ten tests measuring intelligence, personality and factual knowledge traits reduced accidents dramatically. Using my other battery of tests (the "generic" battery) in a semiconductor company caused the engineers there, who had come from many other "fabs" (semiconductor fabrication facilities) around the country, to report that in their informal opinions they had the best workers in the industry.

So, if the Common Good Party wants to maximize the success of its candidates for public office, it may want to consider using questionnaires that measure relevant traits. While this may seem a bit radical, in my opinion, the Common Good Party will improve its image in the public eye if it goes to the trouble to carefully screen its candidates for office using quality psychological measures. As I mentioned at the beginning of this section on how to craft a new type of political party, it may take hundreds of years for nations to transition from special interest group democracies to common good democracies.

The airplanes of the 21st century are technologically much more sophisticated than their initial prototypes were a hundred years prior. This rapid progress in flight sprang up as a result of scientific research on aerodynamics and related fields. Political parties a hundred years from now can be more sophisticated too, if we use science as our guide.

Warmongering-proneness of a candidate for political office can be measured with the Warmongering-proneness scale as described in Chapter 3, above. This scale is presented in Figure 2. As this is an indirect measure of the warmongering trait. It is a measure of warmongering-*proneness*, a tendency to be more likely than others to endorse or manifest warmongering, given the opportunity. You will see in the content of the items reflections of the many traits that correlate significantly with warmongering endorsement. For example, items one through five are intended to measure the five dimensions of social disenfranchisement. Items 6 through 14 are facets of violence-proneness as measured by my 58-item scale of that trait.

FIGURE 2. WARMONGERING-PRONENESS SCALE.

Circle one number (1-5) for each of the items below to rate the person, thinking carefully of the specific objective evidence that supports your rating. Consider statements made by the person or behaviors while seeking leadership or acting as a leader. Consider friendships, favors accepted or given and overt affiliations or group memberships. For historical figures, mentally translate each item into the past tense. For example, read item 1 as "<u>Did</u> the person belong to a group....etc."

Use the following code:

1	2	3	4	5
Definitely not true for this person	Probably not true for this person.	Uncertain or between 2 and 4	Probably true for this person.	Definitely true for this person.

1 2 3 4 5 1. Does the person belong to a group, organization or social class that feels helpless?

1 2 3 4 5 2. Does the person belong to a group that feels a sense of injustice?

1 2 3 4 5 3. Does the person belong to a group that feels distrust in other groups?

1 2 3 4 5 4. Does the person belong to a group that feels vulnerable?

1 2 3 4 5 5. Does the person belong to a group that feels superior to other groups?

1 2 3 4 5 6. Is it likely that the person feels like a failure in careers longed for or engaged in?

1 2 3 4 5 7. Does the person tend to think rigidly, inflexibly, unable to consider alternative points of view, alternative courses of action?

1 2 3 4 5 8. Does the person seem to have a lack of guilt for wrongdoing either by him/herself or by persons with whom he/she closely identifies?

1 2 3 4 5 9. Does the person seem preoccupied with or frequently concerned about being rejected by others?

1 2 3 4 5 10. Does the person engage in activities that suggest pleasure from hostile acts, such as participating in or watching violent sports, or recreational activities?

1 2 3 4 5 11. Does the person seem to have a reservoir of unresolved anger. For example, does he/she bear grudges? Are there persons or groups with which he/she seems

constantly at odds?

1 2 3 4 5   12. Does the person have gun skill and access to guns? (Or to other common combat weapons.)

1 2 3 4 5   13. Does the person seem unwilling to ask for help with personal or business problems, to carefully consider helpful suggestions or other offers of assistance?

1 2 3 4 5   14. Does the person show an unwillingness to help reduce violence in the community?

1 2 3 4 5   15. Does the person seem comfortable lying and/or using propaganda?

1 2 3 4 5   16. Does the person seem interested in dominating other individuals or groups?

1 2 3 4 5   17. Does the person seem to think it is his/her position, right or duty to dominate others?

1 2 3 4 5   18. Does the person hold membership in groups or organizations who advocate dominating other groups?

1 2 3 4 5   19. Does the person maintain an authoritarian stance vis a vis other persons or groups?

1 2 3 4 5   20. Does the person associate with or endorse groups that advocate authoritarian views, opinions or actions?

1 2 3 4 5   21. Does the person hold fundamental religious beliefs, e.g. that there is only one true God and that anyone that disagrees with this belief is wrong?

1 2 3 4 5   22. Does the person disavow kindly religious beliefs, e.g. that all peoples should strive to cooperate and compromise to get along together?

1 2 3 4 5   23. Does the person advocate or condone anarchy forms of government?

1 2 3 4 5   24. Does the person advocate or support military dictatorship forms of government?

1 2 3 4 5 25. Does the person advocate government serving special interest groups rather than citizens in general?

1 2 3 4 5 26. Does the person have a messianic self-image, a sense of personal destiny or duty to achieve great things?

1 2 3 4 5 27. Does the person lack a college education? (Or other advanced education typical of his/her time and culture.)

1 2 3 4 5 28. Does the person lack verbal intelligence? Be careful in rating this one. Don't assume that a person is not intelligent just because they have done a few "stupid" things. High verbal intelligence is often reflected in traits and activities such as sophisticated conversation, good memory, comprehensive awareness of relevant information, high grades in school, high levels of formal education, significant achievement in career activities, etc. Don't assume the person has high verbal intelligence just because they have a college degree.

1 2 3 4 5 29. Does the person disavow endorsement of human rights, e.g. prisoner of war rights and equal status for women?

1 2 3 4 5 30. Does the person disavow international global warming treaties? (Or similar international accords.)

1 2 3 4 5 31. Does the person disavow international arms control treaties? (Or similar international accords.)

1 2 3 4 5 32. Does the person disavow endorsement of fossil fuel conservation and eventual replacement with renewable, non-polluting fuels? (Or similar conservation and sharing internationally of fuel resources of his/her time and culture.)

1 2 3 4 5 33. Does the person disavow conservation of forests and fresh water fisheries?

1 2 3 4 5 34. Does the person disavow public democracy, direct

participation by the public in government policy decision-making?

1 2 3 4 5 35. Does the person disavow a kindly foreign policy, e.g. fighting terrorism with non-military means more than military ones?

1 2 3 4 5 36. Does the person disavow a kindly foreign policy helping other nations achieve their goals?

1 2 3 4 5 37. Does the person disavow support of the United Nations organization? (Or for other similar efforts to promote international cooperation and peace.)

1 2 3 4 5 38. Does the person have a disagreeable personality, being oppositional, irritable, contrary, argumentative or unsupportive of others?

1 2 3 4 5 39. Does the person have tendencies toward anxiety, depression or other signs of emotional instability?

1 2 3 4 5 40. Does the person have strong trust in top government leaders and cabinet members?

1 2 3 4 5 41. Does the person advocate unquestioning loyalty to such leaders?

1 2 3 4 5 42. Does the person think spending for military activities should be increased?

1 2 3 4 5 43. Does the person disavow the idea of his/her national budget being determined by direct vote of the citizens?

1 2 3 4 5 44. Does the person think his/her nation should try to control the world with military power?

1 2 3 4 5 45. Does the person advocate retaliation against wrongdoers?

1 2 3 4 5 46. Does the person advocate access to and use of nuclear weapons or other very destructive weapons, if needed to achieve military ends?

1 2 3 4 5 47. Does the person have interest in military activities,

manufacturers, armed forces, weapons?

1 2 3 4 5 48. Does the person enjoy war movies, war stories, or hostile video games? (Or other such theatrical entertainment of a bellicose theme.)

1 2 3 4 5 49. Does the person think war is a noble and glorious activity?

1 2 3 4 5 50. Does the person think that powerful nations in the past have been justified in killing peoples in underdeveloped countries to get control of their gold, silver, land or other resources?

The scores for several leaders are presented in Table 3. You can judge the warmongering proneness level of a candidate by comparing his/her score with those in this table.

TABLE 3. WARMONGERING-PRONENESS SCORES FOR POLITICAL LEADERS.

Nelson Mandela	1.61
Mahatma Gandhi	1.71
Jimmy Carter	1.73
George Washington	1.82
Harry Truman	1.84
Lincoln	1.92
F.D. Roosevelt	1.98
Bill Clinton	2.09
J.F. Kennedy	2.10
Teddy Roosevelt	2.12
John Kerry	2.14
Winston Churchill	2.20
D. Eisenhower	2.29
Woodrow Wilson	2.47

Lyndon Johnson	2.56
G. H. Bush	2.60
George Patton	3.11
N. Bonaparte	3.64
Alexander the Great	3.73
Genghis Khan	3.98
G. W. Bush	4.00
Attila the Hun	4.04
Stalin	4.21

Members of the Common Good Party who are quite familiar with a candidate can rate the person on the warmongering-proneness scale. Several careful ratings should then be averaged to obtain the final score. Scores in the low range, perhaps below 3.00 would be desirable and would help to assure that the candidate will not be a warmonger or support warmongering legislation.

There are other problematic behaviors that the party should be alert to and avoid in candidates for public office, such as substance abuse tendencies, anger management problems, money mismanagement (personal or business), theft or embezzlement tendencies, unreliability (late for or absent from meetings), sexual indiscretion tendencies or tendencies toward laziness and selfishness.

The leader should be fairly high on all of the Big Five personality traits, as business managers in general tend to be. They should be comfortable in public speaking and attending social functions and meetings with strangers and with the general public (extroversion). They should be conscientious, attending to detail, being well-organized, willing to work hard and responsibly (conscientiousness). They should be agreeable, sociable, willing to compromise rather than argue and intimidate (agreeableness). They should be open to learning new things, hearing others' opinions, comfortable with new and unfamiliar information (openness).

They should be emotionally stable under pressure (not prone to severe depression or anxiety).

Candidates should be skilled at leading and participating in meetings. They should know and follow Roberts Rules of Order when appropriate. They should be tactful, supportive and polite. They should have a sense of humor, be respectful of others, be good listeners, know how to choose reliable and competent assistants, know to praise in public and criticize in private. They should be likeable and pleasant. They should keep their personal life in order. They should be well groomed.

Some of these traits can be measured with reliable questionnaires that candidates could be required to complete. Many of these traits can be assessed simply by ratings of them by fellow party members who know them well after years of working together. Tests may be more objective and thus a better technique. Chapters of the party will have to make such choices.

In this chapter of the book I have emphasized screening candidates for warmongering-proneness, as it is a very important trait to avoid. In the next chapter, I'll explain how chapters can rate candidates on the inverse of warmongering-proneness, constructive leadership attitudes.

Chapter 21

Constructive Leadership Traits

I MET A FELLOW, I'LL CALL HIM "RON", AT A PARTY ON CHRIST-mas Eve, 2012. I'd seen him before with this neighborhood crowd but hadn't had a chance to get to know him. This evening we had time to talk. I asked what he did for a living. Ron explained that he has a company that provides video gaming services to the State of Illinois. I kept asking leading questions and he kept talking. The State of Illinois is very corrupt and it is no accident that four previous governors have been or still are in prison. The problem stems largely from authority vested in local communities to tax without public approval. He said that even park districts can levy such taxes, which in Oregon would require a bond measure approved by citizen vote. In Illinois building codes are unique to each community. Mayors rule communities like fiefdoms. Businesses pay bribes as standard practice, supporting mayors in return for permission to do business in the community. Ron admitted that his business too must pay bribes to succeed in that environment, though it runs against his underlying moral principles.

He said that many states now emulate our gaming industry in Oregon. He helped start this industry in Oregon 20 years ago, which has qualified him now to provide similar services to other states. Gaming is now essential to balancing the Oregon State budget, contributing a billion dollars per year. He said that Illinois is in deep financial trouble; the recession has lowered tax revenues. The State lacks sufficient revenue to pay public employee salaries and other current operating expenses, let alone contributions to pension funds.

I thought about this. I saw an interesting leadership problem.

Government leaders must work within a specific political culture. In Illinois, according to my acquaintance, Ron, this culture apparently requires functioning within a bribery system. Politicians must be willing to ask for and accept bribes. Business leaders must pay bribes to politicians. But this must be done adeptly enough to avoid prosecution. Otherwise one can end up in prison, as several governors have.

The next day, Christmas, I received a gift from my wife, *The Generals,* a non-fiction book by Thomas E. Ricks. It explores in detail the history of demotions and promotions of U.S. Army generals over the past seven decades, beginning in World War II. It also explores a changing trend from many demotions and promotions in leadership in the early decades to very few in more recent decades. General George C. Marshall, Chief of Staff during World War II took advantage of the policy during his command that permitted quick demoting and promoting.

In the prologue, World War II general George Patton is quoted as saying "Personality plays a tremendous part in war." Marshall had specific personality and other traits that he looked for in promoting officers to high rank: good common sense, knowledgeable through study of the military profession, physically strong, cheerful and optimistic, energetic, extremely loyal and determined in action. The book doesn't explain how he arrived at this list, but presumably he fashioned it from personal experience and perhaps via logic, imagining the qualities he would need in officers under him to maximize success in combat.

Apparently in combat there is much more to effective leadership as a top general than simply giving commands to junior officers. How well an officer carries out commands he is given depends on his personality and other traits. If he doesn't have the right traits for the job, he won't be able to perform to the levels desired. For example, one general in Normandy found a subordinate general hiding in a ditch to avoid enemy fire. The superior officer berated the other, telling him to get back to his headquarters; he couldn't command from a ditch. The junior officer appeared to lack common sense.

What traits characterize successful elected politicians? What traits should the Common Good Party look for in selecting candidates for public office? Effective leadership requires a variety of personal characteristics suitable to the job and to the specific culture in which one will have to function. A given West Point graduate might be able to graduate high in his class, function well in desk jobs and advance in rank in peacetime but not function at all well in combat jobs in times of war. Of 44 generals involved in a large pre-combat simulated war exercise in World War II, only 11 were found suitable enough to lead units in combat. They had succeeded in non-combat leadership but were judged to lack traits needed for the many demands unique to combat duty.

It seems from this example that the personality traits that a successful politician must have in one setting might be different from those in another. What works in one political culture may not work in another. What works in Illinois may not work in Oregon. What works in a rural county may not work in an urban one. And, unlike George Marshall's situation, the Common Good Party will be looking not for compliant subordinates to follow commands. Rather, it will want persons who are familiar with the party agenda and can and will promote it skillfully. And candidates must be able to function independently, in an environment removed from the party chapter meetings in which they gained their initial leadership experience.

The mayor's office will be an environment that differs from that of a county commissioner. The environments of these offices will differ from that of a state representative, which in turn will differ from that of an office in Washington, D.C.

But let's not get too complicated. Let me simplify. I'll make some general suggestions for choosing candidates based on my experience as a psychologist having assessed a wide variety of traits for clinical and job placement situations.

The Party will develop its specific procedures for selecting party candidates to run for elective office. These procedures may vary from chapter to chapter and state to state, and, for that matter, from nation to nation, assuming that the party finds wide appeal. Generally, as explained earlier, the candidate selection and grooming committee will be responsible for this. The tasks will include selecting or creating procedures it will be recommending to the party executive committee and then to the membership for approval. The committee also will be responsible for overseeing the assessment of individual candidates.

Candidates might have to fit into age ranges established by the party, such as between 28 and 65 years old for city mayor. Candidates could be required to provide copies of school transcripts, letters from prior employers, and a detailed job history. Candidates could be interviewed on their knowledge of the elective office concerned, how they'd handle various challenging job scenarios, and how they plan to balance work and personal life. They should be asked how they would handle offers of money from special interest groups in return for legislative favors. A medical report of general health might be required, as might a credit report and an essay addressing several job-related issues. The candidate might be asked to explain future aspirations in government service and to describe his/her personal financial management activities and future plans.

The committee could use psychological questionnaires or other tests, as by contracting with a local psychologist or some other responsible professional to do face-to-face assessments. Committee members should be familiar with the various ethical concerns relevant to such assessments. These are elucidated in the American Psychological Association code of ethics, which can be obtained from that organization. These principles include informing persons of the purpose of the testing and assessment, maintaining an appropriate degree of confidentiality of results, possible discomfort that the person might experience via the assessment, how the test results will be used and how the person can obtain more information about the procedure or results.

Basically, the party should have candidates that have characteristics that qualify a person for political leadership and also political attitudes consistent with the political philosophy reflected in the party agenda. These characteristics have been touched on in the previous chapter.

The specific traits that political candidates should have can be assumed by experienced party members, decided by detailed discussion, deliberation and debate within the party, determined by research, guided by recommendations from outside experts or by a combination of such means.

Candidates' years of service within the party will reveal how well they resonate with and support the many facets of the party agenda as defined by party polls. How well do they promote the common good? How well do they run a committee? How well do they perform on the executive committee? How poised and persuasive are they in public speaking? How well do they interact with the broader community on party business? Skill in all these areas will characterize the strong candidate for elective office.

Regarding use of tests and questionnaires, I can offer specific suggestions. The traits I recommend include high verbal intelligence, relatively high scores on the Big Five personality traits (conscientiousness, extraversion, agreeableness, openness and emotional stability), and moderate to high business management aptitude. Good business managers tend to be high on all of the Big Five traits. The candidate should be free of what might be generally referred to as problematic traits, such as criminal tendencies, anger management problems, substance abuse problems (alcohol, prescription or street drug abuse), sexual misbehavior, embezzlement tendencies, etc.

Political attitudes should include assessment of warmonger-ing-proneness, especially for candidates for national offices. They should include constructive leadership attitudes. This will be described in detail below.

The political attitude traits should include measures of the ten or twelve basic areas of political discourse previously discussed, including foreign policy, preferred type of government, group relations, gender attitudes, religious beliefs, environmental concerns, and perhaps measures of policies and programs for health care, Social Security, tax and national debt, and perhaps even xenophobia, same-sex marriage and civilian violence management (e.g. gun ownership and violent video and movie policies).

Candidates should have a profile on the party agenda polls similar to that of the majority of citizens and party members. These are the polls that most recently define what citizens and party members want from government. Such polls will be discussed in detail in the next chapter.

These many traits are probably most reliably measured with well-designed tests and probably ones administered, scored and interpreted by professionals, such as psychologists trained in assessment. In many small communities and in many nations without psychologists, this sort of assessment may not be convenient, but with the Internet, such assessment can be made available to an increasing range of communities. If neither of these two options is available to the party or a chapter, then party officers will have to develop informal procedures for estimating candidate scores on these many traits.

A psychologist or other trained psychometrician can use a variety of tests to assess candidates for the party. I will briefly describe tests that might be used in the United States. Other tests of similar design can be selected for other nations. For intelligence, the Wechsler Adult Intelligence Scale would be a reasonable option. Probably just the Verbal sections would suffice. Scores of 120 or higher would be desirable.

For the Big Five personality traits there are several available tests commercially available including the BFI. It is a 44-item measure that provides scores on each of the five facets separately and is normed on tens of thousands of adults over the Internet. It is in the public domain and is available free on my web site (Testmasterinc.com). It can also be administered and scored by a psychologist, using the instructions in the manual, which is also available on this web site. Above-average scores are recommended on all of the Big Five (conscientiousness, agreeableness, openness, extroversion and emotional stability). The very detailed Big Five 45 test on my Testmasterinc.com web site is another option, though rather long. It has 455 items and provides scores on 45 scales, nine for each of the five factors (extroversion, etc.). This is Dr. Goldberg's AB5C instrument, which is in the public domain.

Business management aptitude can be measured by various tests but without additional research, it is uncertain whether this aptitude would be relevant for politicians. Perhaps a test measuring the facets of political activity could be developed, modeled after my Business Management Aptitude and Business Activity Preferences tests. I'd be willing to advise the party if it comes to this.

Job problem behaviors can be assessed by various questionnaire measures, including my Job Problem Behaviors scale, also known as the Job Opinions Scale. It is a 58-item measure of seven areas of problem behaviors: anger management problems, substance abuse tendencies, laziness, turnover, theft tendencies, etc. It is available on the Testmasterinc.com web site and can be administered offline. Low scores on the seven facets of this scale are desirable. Sexual misbehavior tendencies can be assessed via interview exploring past and current sexual behavior and attitudes. These problem areas can probably be assessed accurately for party candidates for elective office simply by observing candidates in party activities for many months or years before selecting them. Thus, tests for these traits or tendencies might be unnecessary.

Most of these traits can also be assessed via tests directly available over the Internet. I am not familiar with all possible such tests, but I have many of my own that can be used or considered as examples. Several of these are available on my Testmasterinc. com web site, as mentioned above. In addition to this site, I have a detailed measure of verbal intelligence available on the FunEducation.com web site. It is a measure of verbal intelligence modeled after the Wechsler test areas. It has five sections of 40 questions each: vocabulary, information, similarities, arithmetic and comprehension. It has been normed on over 100,000 persons from around the world and has high reliability for all age levels, even for children.

As mentioned above, measures of the politically relevant traits discussed above also should be assessed, including warmongering-proneness, constructive leadership attitudes and measures of the ten basic dimensions of political discourse. These are also available on my Politicalpsychologyresearch.com web site. These appear in the form of research studies, which can be accessed by logging in and going to the Help Do Research page.

Warmongering-proneness can be measured by having several raters familiar with the candidate rate him or her on the scale for this dimension, which appears as study #6. Similarly, constructive leadership attitudes can be assessed via the rating scale in study # 7, described below. Brief but reliable measures of the ten dimensions of political discourse are available as a questionnaire of about 200 items that the candidate himself can complete as study #15.

Finally, candidates should be assessed in terms of their attitudes or opinions on the specific desired government services that define the party or chapter's current political agenda. This can be easily determined simply by examining a candidate's completed party questionnaires used for this purpose. Such questionnaires will be addressed in the next chapter.

The results of these different instruments are gathered by the psychologist or other psychometrician who then summarizes the information in a written report provided to the candidate assessment committee. This committee then makes final recommendations to the executive committee. The information for one or more candidates is then summarized for consideration by party members when casting votes for the candidate. These votes are within the party, to choose whom to sponsor in public elective office campaigns.

As an alternative to a psychologist or other psychometrician, the candidate selection committee may simply rely on committee members to gather the needed information on candidates. They may choose to use tests, as described above, or other means to estimate the traits they deem important. They may use some or all of the traits recommended above or develop another group of traits. They may design their own rating scales for summarizing data and opinions of committee members across the dimensions or traits deemed important. I would be willing to help do research and design a questionnaire to measure traits specific to political leadership aptitude.

In addition to or instead of traits as discussed, the committee will probably consider the applicant's academic and work background, history of service within the party and general reputation in the community, as reflected in community service organization, professional or business activities.

Eventually, the Party may choose to create its own web site on which its own selection of assessment tests will appear. This may be a state party service or a national service provided by the party. It could use my tests or other tests of the Party's choosing, with arrangements for permissions and fees made with test authors as appropriate.

A special advantage of the Party having its own site would be that it could save the data to file automatically and conduct research studies to perfect the battery of tests, as by later adding performance ratings for candidates to measure validity of the assessment instruments as predictors of desired behavior. Having its own site would decrease the Party's dependence on outside resources.

The Constructive Leadership Attitudes scale.

Another instrument available on my web site can also be considered for screening and selecting candidates for political leadership. It is on the same web site as study # 7. It is, in effect, the inverse of the warmongering-proneness scale. This Constructive Leadership Attitudes scale has not yet been normed, so I don't have reliability or validity data for it, but I am quite willing to work with groups who can help do this research.

This research will be as described in the preceding chapter. Persons who are familiar with political leaders, current and past, from reading biographies and other detailed accounts of leaders will rate them on the instrument. When many scores are available for a wide range of leaders, perhaps 20 or 30, some admirable ones and some judged to be failures, then independent scores on leadership competence will be obtained via another group of raters and correlations will be run between the scores obtained by the two processes.

I expect the reliability and validity statistics will be very similar to those for the Warmongering-Proneness scale. If they are, then this new instrument will provide a good measure of desirable candidate traits. The Common Good Party could use it to screen its candidates for elective office. Indeed, if the Party wants to use just one questionnaire to assess candidates for elective office, this one, once validated, would probably be the most useful.

The items and scoring instructions for the Constructive Leadership Attitudes scale are presented in Figure 1. This scale differs in format from the Warmongering-proneness scale in one important respect: it includes some reverse-scored items. These are items that measure the opposite of constructive leadership. As such, they must be reverse-scored, as described in the notes at the bottom of the Figure.

FIGURE 1. CONSTRUCTIVE LEADERSHIP ATTITUDES SCALE

INSTRUCTIONS:

For a leader you know very well, as from media articles, voting record, public speeches, writings and other behavior, make ratings on the items below using this code:

1	2	3	4	5
Definitely not true for this person	Probably not true for this person.	Uncertain or between 2 and 4	Probably true for this person.	Definitely true for this person.

1 2 3 4 5   1. Endorses the idea of government that serves the best interests of the community overall more than special interest groups per se.

1 2 3 4 5   2. Is dedicated mainly to serving the "common good", what is good for all groups of people in the community.

1 2 3 4 5   3. Supports policies and programs that help disadvantaged or weak citizens in the community.

1 2 3 4 5   4. Promotes the idea that everyone should have an effective voice in group decisions.

1 2 3 4 5   5. Encourages all persons affected by government decisions to have a say in those decisions, as via referenda presented by government and initiatives sponsored by citizen groups.

1 2 3 4 5   6. Promotes and encourages all groups of citizens to vote

262 William McConochie

in elections.

1 2 3 4 5 7. Promotes local citizen direct control over local government policies, programs, taxes and budget decisions.

1 2 3 4 5 8. Believes that government is a necessary and constructive aspect of society.

1 2 3 4 5 9. Does not promote either highly limited government or overly-domineering government.

1 2 3 4 5 10. Promotes good, balanced government services and programs, not favoring some services or programs at the expense of other services.

1 2 3 4 5 11. Promotes a positive, helpful foreign policy.

1 2 3 4 5 12. Believes nations should cooperate with each other more than compete against each other.

1 2 3 4 5 13. Believes one's nation should be generous in sharing resources and wealth with weaker nations.

1 2 3 4 5 14. Promotes aggressive war, starting wars against other nations.

1 2 3 4 5 15. Believes in striving to be the most powerful nation in the world, and that "might makes right".

1 2 3 4 5 16. Promotes regular increases in military budgets even in peacetime.

1 2 3 4 5 17. Believes that some nations deserve severe punishment, such as bombing of civilians.

1 2 3 4 5 18. Believes in torturing prisoners if necessary to get information out of them or to extract confessions.

1 2 3 4 5 19. Is indifferent to genocide, deliberately engineered deaths of large populations of civilians via starvation, war or other means.

1 2 3 4 5 20. Has a criminal record or associates with known or suspected criminals.

1 2 3 4 5   21. Seems to enjoy observing or participating in violent entertainment or recreation.

1 2 3 4 5   22. Seems to feel rejected socially by persons or groups by which he/she had hoped to be accepted.

1 2 3 4 5   23. Tends to strongly support and admire top government leaders, regardless of their policies.

1 2 3 4 5   24. Believes that wrong doers should be punished and rewards provided only to those who comply with leader ideals.

1 2 3 4 5   25. Believes that there are "good-guys" and "bad-guys" and that he/she is one of the "good-guys".

1 2 3 4 5   26. Thinks that only his/her religious beliefs are the right or good ones and that persons who think otherwise are wrong.

1 2 3 4 5   27. Believes that God is more likely to punish than to forgive wrongdoers.

1 2 3 4 5   28. Believes that government and religion should be closely intertwined rather than separate aspects of society.

1 2 3 4 5   29. Believes that God appears in different forms for different peoples around the world.

1 2 3 4 5   30. Is tolerant and respectful of religious beliefs different from his/her own.

1 2 3 4 5   31. Believes in the Golden Rule, in treating other persons as you would have them treat you.

1 2 3 4 5   32. Is more likely to endorse than to reject human rights treaties.

1 2 3 4 5   33. Endorses individual women's rights to make their own personal childbearing decisions.

1 2 3 4 5   34. Endorses citizen rights to privacy, a fair trial and freedom of speech, even speech critical of government

leaders.

1 2 3 4 5 35. Endorses sustainable policies and programs to protect the environment and plant and animal species at risk of extinction.

1 2 3 4 5 36. Endorses limiting and reversing global warming, air pollution and other such threats to plant, animal and human survival.

1 2 3 4 5 37. Promotes programs to replace fossil fuels with hydrogen, solar or other non-polluting energy.

1 2 3 4 5 38. Promotes birth control to limit human population growth to sustainable levels only.

1 2 3 4 5 39. Endorses the concept of public school budgets protecting all aspects of a balanced program, sharing each school dollar proportionally.

1 2 3 4 5 40. Endorses the concept of public school budgets preserving all programs and reasonable class sizes over teacher union contract demands.

1 2 3 4 5 41. Under tight public school budgets, values the needs and desires of parents and children over the desires of tenured teachers.

1 2 3 4 5 42. Talks often of feeling vulnerable to threats.

1 2 3 4 5 43. Seems especially concerned about persons or groups that he/she believes cannot be trusted.

1 2 3 4 5 44. Often seems to think he/she or his/her constituents have been treated unjustly.

1 2 3 4 5 45. Seems concerned that a group he/she is in may become helpless unless special steps are taken.

1 2 3 4 5 46. Promotes the idea that his/her group, political party or nation is superior to other ones.

1 2 3 4 5 47. Promotes the idea that his group is vulnerable to domination or mistreatment by other groups.

1 2 3 4 5 48. Tends more often to agree and compromise rather than disagree and argue when in conflict with others.

1 2 3 4 5 49. Promotes discussion and negotiation more than demands and intimidation when dealing with opposing groups.

1 2 3 4 5 50. Has a reputation for being nice, generous and kind toward strangers, minority groups, the unfortunate and the needy.

1 2 3 4 5 51. Tends to remain calm and poised when under threat.

1 2 3 4 5 52. Rarely or never seems unusually anxious or depressed.

1 2 3 4 5 53. Seems emotionally and psychologically stable and healthy.

SCORING INSTRUCTIONS:

1. Reverse score items 14-28 and 42-47 by subtracting obtained score from 6.

2. Add scores across all 53 items to get total raw score. The lowest possible score is 53, highest 265.

3. Divide by 5 to get mean item score. The lowest possible is 1, the highest 5.

4. Compare to tentative scale below:

1.0-1.8	1.9-2.6	2.7-3.4	3.5-4.2	4.3-5.0
Very low	Low	Average	High	Very high

This scale can be modified before research on it is done. Some items might better be removed. Some new ones, such as about pubic health care and taxes, might be added. I would be happy to work with persons and groups who are interested in creating the Common Good Party and doing studies to perfect this scale for their use.

The alert reader will realize that there is a complication with using this and perhaps most such instruments for screening candidates. Any candidate who has read this book and is familiar with the Constructive Leadership Scale can figure out how to take it in a manner that will assure a high, desirable score for him or herself.

Thus, the Common Good Party may have to create its own "private" versions of such scales to minimize cheating by candidates. Or, the Party may have to rely on rating scales to measure traits and develop careful methods for selecting objective, fair raters. These raters would be party members who know the candidates well from working with them over the years within the party.

Assessing executive ethics

Other traits can be considered when assessing candidates for political office. Perhaps one of the most important is executive ethics. Consider, for example three scales of ethics I created, scales measuring In-group Elitism, Messianic Nationalism and Common Good Concern, to use the labels I have given them.(1) In their full versions they have 14 items. Brief 6-item measures of them, presented in Figure 2, provide reasonably reliable scales. These brief scales give a flavor of what is measured.

Figure 2. Three brief scales of executive ethics. Note: r means the item is reverse-scored.

In-group Elitism scale.	
1.	Corporate executives are more deserving of government favors, such as bailouts and tax deductions, than are citizens who claim physical or mental disabilities.
2.	I like the athletic coach slogan: "Winning isn't everything, its the only thing."
3r.	I like the motto: "Service above self." (reverse scored)
4.	It is reasonable for national authorities to sanction torture of suspected terrorists to get information from them.
5.	I seldom say 'thank you' to other people.

6.	I believe in the superiority of my own ethnic group.
Messianic Nationalism scale.	
1.	Most years I give money to charitable causes
2.r	Our government best serves our nation by serving special interest groups.
3.	I sometimes feel a divine inspiration to lead.
4.	Religion should play the most important role in civic affairs.
5.	I believe in government by law with the consent of those people governed.
6.	Our nation's religion is better than all other religions.
Common Good Concern scale.	
1.r	In general, corporations should be freer of government regulation in order to compete most effectively in the world economy.
2	I support the missions of the United Nations.
3	I believe the United Nations Universal Declaration of Human Rights is a proper guide for our nation.
4	I support government programs promoting health care and public education for all citizens.
5.	The government ought to take responsibility for the individual and social welfare of its citizens.
6.r	Our nation is better than all other nations.

The value of such scales for screening candidates is evident in the significant correlations between them and many other traits, presented in Table 2.

TABLE 2. RELATIONSHIPS BETWEEN THREE EXECUTIVE ETHICS SCALES AND OTHER TRAITS. ** = SIGNIFICANT AT .01 LEVEL, * AT .05 LEVEL.

Trait	In-group elitism	Messianic Nationalism	Common Good Concern
Warmongering endorsement	.56**	.31**	-.54**
Violence-prone-ness	.36**	-.09	-.08
Positive Foreign Policy	-.46**	-.27**	.63**
Valuing Religion	.09	.55**	-.29**
Religious Funda-mentalism	.39**	.53**	-.52**
Kindly Religious Beliefs	-.27**	.00	.41**
Special Interest Group Favorit-ism	.71**	.08	-.57**
Meta-religion endorsement	-.18*	.07	.35**
Public/Common Good Democ-racy endorse-ment	-.45**	.13	.19**
Authoritarianism	.51**	.36**	-.47**
Human Rights Endorsement	-.35**	-.14*	.58**
Environmental Concern	-.39**	-.19**	.59**
Extroversion	-.02	.14	-.08
Agreeableness	-.37**	.02	.28**
Conscientiousness	.00	.14	-.14
Openness	-.20**	-.19**	.31**

| Political conserva-tism | .31** | .45** | -.69** |
| Political liberalism | -.27** | -.35** | .55** |

Persons higher on In-group Elitism tend to be higher also on warmongering endorsement, violence-proneness, religious fundamentalism, special interest group favoritism, authoritarianism and political conservatism. They tend to be lower on common good concern, positive (peaceful) foreign policy endorsement, kindly religious beliefs, meta-religion endorsement (endorsement of friendly relationships between believers of different world faiths), endorsement of common good democracy, human rights endorsement, environmental concern, and the Big Five agreeableness and openness traits. They also tend to be lower on political liberalism. Thus, it would be wise to avoid candidates for elective office who have average or high scores on in-group elitism.

Persons who are higher on Messianic Nationalism tend to be higher on warmongering endorsement, valuing religion as a comprehensive guide to one's life, religious fundamentalism, authoritarianism and political conservatism. They tend to be lower on Common Good Concerns, Positive Foreign Policy endorsement, Human Rights endorsement, environmental concern, openness and political liberalism. Thus, it would be wise to avoid candidates with average or higher scores on Messianic Nationalism.

Finally, persons who are higher on the Common Good Concern ethic tend to be higher on Positive Foreign Policy endorsement, kindly religious beliefs, meta-religion endorsement, public or common good democracy endorsement, human rights endorsement, environmental concerns, and the Big Five traits of agreeableness and openness. They also tend to be higher on political liberalism. They tend to be lower on warmongering, valuing religion comprehensively, religious fundamentalism, special interest group favoritism, authoritarianism, conscientiousness and political conservatism. Thus, overall, it would be wise to endorse candidates with high scores on Common Good Concern.

It can be informative to note the frequency of persons who manifest traits. In the sample of 196 college and university students used for the above statistics, only 2 percent had scores above 3.5 on In-group Elitism. 14 percent had scores above 3.5 on Messianic Nationalism. 46 percent had scores above 3.5 on Common Good Concern. This data suggests that most candidates for public office in the Common Good Party may have relatively low scores on In-group Elitism and Messianic Nationalism, while 45 percent or more may have high scores on Common Good Concern.

These three executive ethics scales again reflect differences between liberals and conservatives, or, more accurately, between liberal and conservative worldviews. But keep in mind the fact that strong liberals and strong conservatives, as groups, are actually rather close together on virtually all traits on which they differ, as presented initially in Chapter 13, above. For the 196 college and university students in the study of executive ethics this phenomenon is again clearly evident, as presented in Table 3.

TABLE 3. MEAN ITEM SCORES FOR STRONG CONSERVATIVES (C) AND STRONG LIBERALS (L) ON SEVERAL TRAITS ON WHICH THEY TEND TO DIFFER SIGNIFICANTLY BUT ONLY SLIGHTLY, IF AT ALL. NOTE: * BEFORE A TRAIT NAME MEANS THAT THE GROUPS DO NOT DIFFER SIGNIFICANTLY ON THIS TRAIT.

1.0 --> 2.0 --> 3.0 --> 4.0 --> 5.0

Trait	Low			High
Warmongering endorsement.	1.7L	2.4C		
*Violence proneness	1.8C 1.9L			
Positive Foreign Policy			3.6(C)	4.2(L)

Value Religion Comprehensively		2.7(L)	3.7(C)	
Religious Fundamentalism		2.0(L) 2.7(C)		
Kindly Religious Beliefs			3.9(C)	4.2(L)
Special Interest Group Favoritism		2.6(L)	3.0(C)	
Meta religion endorsement			3.4(C) 3.8(L)	
*Common Good Democracy endorsement				4.2(C) 4.4(L)
Authoritarianism		2.5(L) 2.9(C)		
Human Rights endorsem.				4.1(C) 4.5(L)
Environmental concern				4.1(C) 4.6(L)
*Extroversion				4.8(L) 5.0(C)
Agreeableness				4.7(C) 5.3(L)
*Conscientiousness				5.2(L) 5.5(C)
*Emotional Stability			4.5(L) 4.7(C)	
Openness			4.8(C)	5.7(L)
In-group Elitism	1.8(L)	2.2(C)		
Common Good Concern			3.0(C) 3.8(L)	
Messianic Nationalism		2.9(L)	3.2(C)	

This has been a long, but important chapter, exploring in detail how to screen candidates for party sponsorship in bids for political office. Next we'll explore system sickness, an illness that has tended to corrupt even the best of elected officials.

CHAPTER 22

PREVENTING CORRUPTION; SYSTEM SICKNESS AND CURES

ONE WAY CITIZENS CAN VOICE THEIR INDIVIDUAL POLITICAL opinions is via letters to the editors of their local newspaper. Consider the letter in Figure 1 that I wrote on Christmas morning, 2012, two weeks after the mass school shooting in Newtown, Mass. It was published in our paper a few days later (1).

FIGURE 1. LETTER TO EDITOR.

"Are Americans morally deceased?

Recently many opinions have been shared about civilian gun violence in America. Opinions swirl about the National Rifle Association, gun manufacturers, armed guards in public schools, armed citizens everywhere and anywhere, gun policies in other nations, civilian gun deaths per year, violent movies, violent video games and mental illness.

Suggestions abound for how to solve the problem of civilians using guns to kill their fellow civilians.

What I don't see are discussions about how political decisions on such topics are made in the United States. It seems to me that as long as political decisions can be heavily influenced by special interest group money flowing through lobbyists to federal legislators, little if anything will change in our violent civilian culture.

The voice of reason is superseded by short-term financial gain. Power corrupts, money gives power, thus, money corrupts. We have freedom of speech. Money is speech. Money flows freely and speaks louder than reason.

Greed breeds excessive borrowing to feed immediate desires. Our nation borrows and spends to satisfy greed. Our states run slot machines to pad state budgets. States agree to union contracts that they cannot realistically afford, with a trillion dollars of unfunded pension obligations.

In the end can there be any outcome for our states and nation other than bankruptcy? Are we already morally bankrupt as a nation? Or, worse, is our nation morally deceased?"

In this letter I am emphasizing the current *system* of national government as a problem. Specifically, the system is one that requires legislators to raise millions of dollars each to fund their next election campaigns. I have heard from politicians familiar with Washington doings that sitting Congresspersons typically spend two days per week on average on the phone raising money from special interest groups for their next campaign. They do this every week they're in office.

The only realistic way that most of them can raise the millions needed for campaigning is to get it from special interest groups. In return for political favors, such groups are happy to provide the money through any of ten thousand or more lobbyists in Washington.

This is a *system* problem, not so much a problem with the individuals elected by the people and sent to Washington. All members of Congress, liberals and conservatives alike, participate in this system. In our government system, they *must*, to survive in office.

Many citizens know this is a system problem, the solution to which, some propose, is to "get the money out of politics".

Consider another system that has problems. Susan, a member of my church Bible study class, told us one Wednesday evening in the fall of 2012 of her tragic loss that week of a good friend and tennis opponent, a local physician, who had committed suicide. A few weeks later a Guest Viewpoint article by Pamela Wible, M.D, a local physician, appeared in our local newspaper (2). She wrote of many physician suicides just during the past year in our community of 130,000, including Susan's friend. Pamela explained that the physician suicide problem is epidemic in the United States, reporting that on average one physician per day commits suicide.

Pamela had spoken at our Rotary Club a year or so prior about her own suicidal thoughts, prompted by intolerable stresses of a medical care system that squeezed all the pleasure out of her practice. She shut it down. She then interviewed 100 of her patients, asking what an ideal medical service would be in their eyes. Her patients wanted their doctors to listen to them, not for just a few hurried minutes, but until the patient had said his or her piece. They wanted other things. Pamela incorporated 90 percent of what she heard in a complete redesign of her practice. She re-opened her practice and she and her patients have been happy with it since. Pamela has gained national attention in the medical industry, even sought out by hospitals for advice about how to redesign medical practices.

At my wife's singing recital in December that same year I visited with the husband of another singer. He heads a local diabetes clinic as a physician's assistant. He said he is going to retire early in a couple of years because medical practice has become so onerous, particularly the very time-consuming service documentation that is required. He also seemed discouraged by the huge national and even international problem diabetes is becoming because people eat too much of the wrong foods.

A couple of weeks later the physician who has his practice next to my office building asked if he could rent more of the offices in my building. He said that with expansion of Medicare 20,000 more citizens in our county would be needing services. But general practitioners were moving *out* of the county at a rate of 10 percent per year. He saw an opportunity and was expanding his practice to add more physicians. He needed more space. I wondered why GPs were leaving the area. Most people like living in our community.

We could conclude from these anecdotes that the medical service industry in the United States may be "sick", as it seems to alienate and sometimes destroy the very professionals who are needed to provide the cures.

How to cure such system sickness? Notice that Dr. Wible started by interviewing the citizens central to the system to learn what they wanted. She took the information seriously and redesigned the medical system to respect the needs of her patients.

This approach could be expanded to include interviews or polls of hundreds or even thousands of citizens, physicians, hospital administrators, employers, insurance company executives and government representatives, and others who currently constitute the medical service industry. The industry could then be redesigned around this information.

The Common Good Political Party could conduct poll research on this topic, at a local level initially. A Chapter or group of Chapters could work with local people and design a revised medical service delivery system as a pilot project. If this was successful, they could offer it to other communities.

The Party project might create a medical service model very different from the current medical care system. It might not include the private insurance industry. It might be a public health care system. It might be a system unique among even current systems around the world. Until it is designed, we can't foresee just what it might look like.

The key to success in such an effort would be carefully listening to all the key players and design a solution that best serves majority opinion, the common good, rather than favoring one special interest group or cluster of groups at the indifference to the majority.

The primary objectives of the system could be defined by polling. These objectives, as defined by citizens, would probably include providing medical services to all citizens at affordable costs, with limits to fit budgets, with caps on profits for any and all providers and limits on lawsuits, careful oversight of drug design and pricing, and careful oversight to minimize incompetent services and business corruption. The defined objective of the system would provide a definition of the common good, as far as medical care is concerned.

SYSTEM SICKNESS MORE BROADLY

System sickness may be defined as self-destructiveness caused by flaws in the system. The flaws may be from changing circumstances, by oversight or by deliberate intent. Typically self-destructiveness in business includes destroying your relationship with your customers or your customers themselves.

A system may fail because of changing circumstances. The U.S. Postal system worked well until the Internet and e-mail took away much of its business.

A system can fail because of oversight, failure to take into consideration probable weaknesses or problems in the design process. Murphy's Law comes to mind: If there's a way for something to go wrong, eventually it will. One probable weakness that can affect many industries is human greed and corruptibility. There's the business adage: "Everything is for sale, for a price".

This might be expanded to "Practically every person can be bought, for a price." For example, in the big commercial banking industry, extremely high salaries and related financial benefits to top executives seemed to induce many top executives to make decisions that would assure their personal profits even at the expense of the stability of the institution for which they worked. Such corruption was prominent in the financial meltdown of 2008, as described by the Federal Commission report.

I heard the head of this commission, Phil Angelides, give a public lecture at the University of Oregon Law School in the fall of 2012. I deliberately sat in the middle of the lecture hall, near the front, so I could ask questions at the end of the lecture. I raised my hand immediately when he was done.

"I have a couple of questions", I said. "Is the United States in the final phase of Empire, as described by Kevin Phillips in his book *American Theocracy*, in which a nation is preoccupied with lending money which eventually doesn't get paid back and the Empire then wanes? And if so, what can we do about it? And related to that question, you have said that top executives in the U.S. financial industry and would-be government regulators were both corrupted by big money. The financial industry executives made poor decisions that led to the financial meltdown in 2008 and government regulators failed to act because financial firms made large contributions to legislator campaigns. My question is this: if both financial corporation executives and government regulators were corrupted by money, and still are, as you say, in spite of your committee report to Congress, who can we depend on to regulate *both* of these groups?"

His answer to the first question was "yes", the United States is in the final stage of Empire. But, hopefully, by understanding that we are in decline we can mitigate its worst side-effects. Regarding the second question, he said that he didn't know, but hoped we can find the moral courage to figure out how to regulate both business and government leaders and prevent their corruption by money.

Phil had made another discouraging revelation. The big commercial banks were unfazed by prosecution of their companies for violating Federal regulations because the corporations could easily afford judgments of even *half a billion dollars*. That amount is only 2 percent of the annual profit for some of these giant corporations. They just pay the fine as another business expense and continue their illegal behavior. Phil said we needed to prosecute not just the companies. We need to prosecute the executives and put them in prison.

So, here we have another example of system sickness, a corrupt system. The money involved is enormous and human nature is corruptible. The combination leads to a version of Murphy's Law: if there's enough money available to corrupt people, corruption will eventually occur.

I see no simple solution to this problem, but hopefully the Common Good Party, motivated more by noble ethics than by money, will try to find one.

The third way a system can become sick is by deliberate, evil design. Hitler designed an evil empire. For a period, many Germans were persuaded to support and promote this empire, perhaps as over-expression of relatively normal human aspirations, as for national pride, a strong economy or to be part of an enthusiastic social movement.

Preventing or "curing" this sort of system sickness can include aggressive conflict to depose the leader or leaders of the system, as via World War II. It can also include preventive measures, such as carefully screening candidates for high political, business and military positions, as via evaluations of psychological traits related to warmongering and other evil actions, as explored in chapters above.

Other sick systems by design, or at least with clear awareness of negative consequences for customers, include the tobacco industry, the street drug industry and the gun industry. Even the commercial food industry is coming under scrutiny for the negative effects of some foods. Tobacco causes cancer, methamphetamine and heroin kill, assault weapons kill innocent victims. Too much sugar in too many foods and drinks is contributing to epidemics in obesity and diabetes in the United States. The violent film and music lyric industries also seem to be designed for profit at the indifference to possible negative motivating impacts on some citizens, such as on persons who commit mass shootings.

In spite of general awareness of negative side-effects on customers, these industries persist in marketing their products; money talks louder than reason.

The Party should be alert to these system problems. The Party should not waste time and energy trying to solve important community problems with simplistic solutions. If a problem is with a system, the solution needs to be a system solution. Either systems must be changed or their scope and influence must be limited.

Some system sickness may be hard to detect, as some systems provide good services along with bad effects. Public employee salaries and benefits via union contracts appear to be an example, as the States of the United States now have 1.4 trillion dollars of unfunded obligations to public employees. The U.S. Postal service is underwater in this regard too. The Social Security Administration, without changes, is predicted to have unsustainable obligations to disabled and retired citizens for similar reasons. As designed, these systems have promised more in benefits than the systems can afford. The same sickness has occurred in many private corporations as well. Many commercial airlines incurred employee pension obligations in the billions and then went bankrupt.

The property damage insurance industry may be another slated for diagnosis as "sick". With climate change, property damage may become so epidemic secondary to catastrophic hurricanes, floods, tornadoes and other "perfect storms" that insurance company assets simply won't be sufficient to cover all the obligations incurred. AIG, an insurer of financial institutions, couldn't cover obligations due to all the big banks that were due to fail in the 2008 meltdown. The government had to bail it out, along with some large banks themselves. But the government itself is in debt to the tune of 16 to 58 trillion dollars, depending on which obligations are included in one's calculations. Even the U.S. Government may someday be unable to afford its obligations as underwriter of last resort.

A specific example of system sickness is manifest in my town, Eugene Oregon, over the four decades I have lived here. My two children went through our public schools. The school services available two and three decades ago have seen considerable deterioration. Due to the financial conditions of teacher union contracts and a limitation on property taxes passed by citizens, junior teachers have been cut, programs have been dropped, schools have been closed and maintenance on buildings has been deferred. Class sizes have increased. The school system is designed in a way that inadvertently undermines the services to its customers, the children.

Even local, state and national infrastructure may be an example of Murphy's Law and system sickness. We have built roads, schools, bridges, railways, public parks, sewer systems and public buildings, all of which will someday have to be replaced when they wear out. But apparently governments failed to budget for this. If governments had saved some revenue each year for infrastructure repair and replacement, we could be putting citizens to work upgrading our older facilities.

Failing to save money for such inevitable renovations suggests poor system design, not of the physical facilities but of the necessary financial underpinnings needed to maintain and replace them. Typically, bonds are used for maintenance and replacement, but government must pay interest as well as principle on bonds.

I was on the board of directors of a Nobel Peace Laureate Project in our town, which involved building a monument in a public park in our city to the two dozen Americans who have won Nobel peace prizes. In the process of getting a building permit we learned that our non-profit organization had to guarantee maintenance services for the park space used, as the park maintenance budget is 4 million dollars in the red.

The Social Security System guarantees payouts to citizens. Systems such as this have to be carefully designed to accommodate changes in numbers of citizens in different age brackets, increasing life-spans over subsequent generations, and changes in costs of living and levels of employment, all of which can have an impact on the long-term viability of the system. And if the money contributed by employees is not protected from borrowing by the government itself from that account, then the entire system is subject to catastrophic failure. Retired citizens can't buy groceries with IOUs.

Another huge system that has inadvertently become "sick" is the fossil fuel power industry. This industry provides much of the power for nations around the world, 86 percent of the power in the United States. But this industry exhausts carbon dioxide and other gasses into the atmosphere, causing global climate change. Scientists now inform us the results could be catastrophic.

A disturbing theme in the book, *The Generals*, cited earlier, is the lack of respect U.S. military officers had for each other and for their civilian overseers in government, and a related theme of unclear, vacillating political philosophy in government as to the purpose of various wars and the ultimate goals to be reached or promoted by war. Generals were criticized by the author for being preoccupied with tactical issues and not broader strategic questions. Government leaders, e.g. the administration, were criticized for having unclear goals beyond simply defeating enemies with military power, such as what to do in Iraq and Afghanistan after military dominance is established.

Perhaps the high and rising suicide rate among Army personnel is an indirect reflection of this. Most soldiers don't innately relish killing enemy persons and require vigorous training to do so. Soldiers who survive combat but lose fellow soldiers often feel survivor guilt. Perhaps soldiers also feel guilt if they have killed enemy soldiers, and especially if they have killed, raped or otherwise destroyed the lives of innocent civilians in combat zones, as has frequently happened since WWII. Perhaps such guilt underlies some of the suicides.

These issues bring to mind the importance of ethics and the common good. We betray ethics at our peril as a nation and as humans. To the extent that we passively trust the agenda of the nation to political and military leaders who appear to be all too prone to looking out for their own careers above the interests of the nation, especially defined in terms of the common good of its citizens, then we run the risk of the common good being increasingly betrayed.

We can hope that the Common Good Party will be guided by sufficiently high moral and ethical principles to promote systems that guard against Murphy's Law, poor system design and the corrupting influence of money and self-interest. And we can hope that the Party will also empower and energize concerned citizens everywhere to take prompt and conscientious action to address problems that current political systems fail to solve.

The next five chapters explore the probable majority opinions of citizens across major dimensions of political discourse. These opinions will hint at the results of polls the Party would conduct and the directions that national politics will go under common good government as it evolves in the decades and centuries to come.

CHAPTER 23

MEASURING WHAT THE PEOPLE WANT
 FROM GOVERNMENT

THE COMMON GOOD PARTY WILL BASE ITS AGENDA ON PERIodic polls of the public to find out general citizen desires for government policies and programs and then polls of party members to determine member preferred specific government policies and programs.

I have used various techniques to measure public opinion and desires. These studies have shown several important trends. The majority of citizens want improvements in many government services. They want government to function within balanced budgets, not making a policy of borrowing much more than it spends. They want a peaceful foreign policy and a decreased emphasis on militarism. They want quality jobs, affordable health care, affordable housing and affordable higher education. They want government to attend to major world problems, such as climate change and global warming.

In addition, based on assessment of many traits related to politics, the majority of citizens endorse human rights, kindly but not fundamentalist religious beliefs, and a proportional rather than contract-driven funding system for public schools. The majority think that slavery is wrong. They feel socially accepted in their communities and prefer government that serves them as members of the community overall rather than as members of special interest groups.

A study of the Occupy movement showed that Occupy members, church members and community college students all, on average, want improved government services in all 24 areas presented in the research questionnaire, as presented in Table 1. You will recall from the earlier discussion of the Occupy study in Chapter 6, above, that the 24 items were generated in a meeting of Occupy committee members, each of whom in turn voiced their most important personal goal for the movement.

The results suggest that the whole community may want the same thing, that the Occupy movement did indeed represent majority public opinion, as it claimed in its slogan of being the 99 percent. The majority may want improvement in a wide range of government services to deal with a variety of important problems, such as civilian violence, climate change, getting the money out of politics, and holding Wall Street responsible for the 2008 financial meltdown.

Because this data is not on a very large sample of citizens and not of a diverse range of communities of citizens, it is not a confident statement of state or national opinion. But, the results are compatible with those of many other studies I have done, totaling hundreds of citizens, so they are probably typical of what studies of larger samples will show.

TABLE 1. MEAN ITEM SCORES FOR DESIRED GOVERNMENT SERVICES. SCORES OF 5 MEAN "STRONGLY AGREE", 4 MEAN "AGREE" AND 3 MEAN "NEUTRAL". THUS, BOTH OCCUPY MEMBERS AND OTHER CITIZENS IN THIS STUDY ESSENTIALLY SUPPORT ALL 24 ITEMS.

66 Occupy members	Other citizens	Scale item:
4.58	4.65	1. It is important that public media (radio, T.V., etc.) be objective and not biased in its reporting.

4.92	4.38	2. The government should hold Wall Street and big bank executives accountable for their roles in causing the financial meltdowns in recent years.
4.77	4.41	3. The government should reinstate and improve regulations of the financial industry to minimize future financial meltdowns.
4.94	4.65	4. As a nation we should strive to get the money out of politics, e.g. reverse the notion that corporations are people and therefore can contribute as much money as they want to candidate campaign accounts.
4.80	4.24	5. Our national government should provide universal health and dental care to all citizens.
4.75	4.26	6. As a nation we need to promote more of a focus on "we", the common good, and less focus on "me", narrow self-interest.
4.81	4.27	7. We need to do more to protect the environment from degradation, as by reducing our use of fossil fuels.
4.73	4.06	8. We should develop a fair and adequate federal tax system that asks wealthier citizens to pay more in return for the opportunities our country has provided them to amass wealth.
4.73	3.76	9. We should do more to empower local communities to have control over how they protect and promote their local lifestyles.

4.73	4.18	10. We need to reexamine the wisdom of outsourcing jobs to other countries to assure that there are family-wage jobs for all of our citizens first.
4.83	4.21	11. We need to do more to provide services to homeless citizens, including housing, counseling, employment opportunities, food and health care.
4.92	4.47	12. We need to do more to prosecute corruption in government itself, even at the level of top positions, such as the Supreme Court.
4.61	3.97	13. Governments need to find ways to fairly define "surplus wealth" and tax it appropriately.
4.77	3.88	14. Communities need to more effectively tap the wisdom of local citizens and help them have the power to express and realize it in community and government service.
4.66	3.94	15. Movements such as the Occupy movement should focus on promoting positive, improved, selfless change in society.
4.70	4.44	16. The movement should take care to channel rage constructively.
4.83	4.12	17. The movement should strive to engage as many citizens as possible, seeking everyone's opinions to find common ground.
4.75	4.21	18. The nation needs to "fix the political system", improving government and political processes to be more effective in addressing problems.
4.89	4.18	19. Our nation needs a more sustained commitment to social justice.

4.78	4.26	20. The (Occupy) movement needs to maintain a positive vision.
4.86	4.59	21. Our nation needs to "teach our children well", improving public and private education.
4.89	4.53	22. The Occupy movement and the nation as a whole should maintain respect for all citizens and their needs.
4.81	3.91	23. The movement and nation should strive to empower all citizens politically, giving them opportunities for constructive actions they can do now.
4.45	3.88	24. We need to oversee, audit and regulate the Federal Reserve to protect the value of the dollar, as from inflation or deflation.

On a sample of 190 Occupy members, homeless folks, community college students and churchgoers, there were 82 strong liberals and 31 strong conservatives. Across all of the 24 items in Table 1 the liberals' mean score was 4.58. For the conservatives it was 4.39. These items were presented for endorsement with a 5 meaning Strongly Agree, 4 meaning Agree, 3 Neutral, 2 Disagree and 1 Strongly Disagree. Thus, mean scores between 4.0 and 5.0 reflect overall agreement with the items. The difference between these means of 4.58 and 4.39 was statistically significant; the liberals were higher in endorsing improved government services. But the strong conservatives, as a group, endorsed the 24 items as areas in which they too want improved government.

Again we see evidence of the closeness of strong liberals and strong conservatives on political agenda items. With a skillfully designed political party we can expect both groups to work together constructively rather than letting their small differences lead to irreconcilable conflicts.

Another aspect of research data when polling in this manner is to compute the proportion of citizens that endorse a particular issue. For example, we can compute the proportion of citizens in the Occupy study who have a mean score on the 24 items that is above 3.5. Scores above 3.5, the mid-point of the Neutral range, reflect overall agreement with the questionnaire items. In this study 92 percent, 174 of the 187 persons had mean scores above 3.5 across the 24 items,.

Thus, if this were the result of a study by the Common Good Party on a large representative sample of citizens in their community, they could conclude with confidence that the citizens wanted improved government services of the sort represented by the 24 items. Their data analysis could check the endorsement percentage for each item separately. If all of the mean item scores were above 3.5 or 3.9, or whatever score the party wants to set as its endorsement standard, then it could include these items in its current party agenda.

Going back to Chapter 20 regarding candidate assessment, the candidates' personal data on the party assessment questionnaire could be included in their candidate profiles. For example, a candidate with a mean item score of 4.8 on the above 24 items would look stronger than a candidate with a score of 3.0.

The items in the Occupy study addressed national political issues. A local Common Good Party chapter would probably start polling on local political issues, such as school budgets and class sizes, public transportation issues, utility bills, salaries and benefits for local city employees, public university tuition levels, bond issues for road maintenance, and property tax levels.

Such issues would be carefully studied in preparation for crafting poll items. On each issue the relevant facts should be written up as introduction for poll takers. Then several poll questions for each topic can be drafted. These can be presented in various ways, such as in "should" statements, e.g. "Our city should increase its public parks budget by 10 percent" and "Such funds should be dedicated exclusively to existing park development and maintenance." Another format might present options from which the citizen can choose, such as:

"Please circle one of the four options below as your preference:

Preamble: The current room tax for hotels, motels and bed and breakfast facilities in our county is currently 5 percent. Half of this income is currently dedicated to developing and maintaining public venues in our county, 90 percent to public county and state parks, museums and performance centers. 10 percent is dedicated to advertising to promote our county as a destination for tourists, conventions and other out-of-state visitors. Because this advertising is estimated to be very productive in increasing tourism to our state and related income to state businesses, the Party recommends an increase in the room tax from 5 to 6 percent and an increase in the share dedicated to advertising from 10 to 13 percent.

Poll item #1. The county room tax should:

- Stay at the current 5 percent rate.

- Increase to 6 percent.

Poll item #2. The proportion of the tax revenue dedicated to advertising should:

- Stay at the current 10 percent rate.

- Increase to 11 percent.

- Increase to 12 percent.

- Increase to 13 percent."

Some issues that the Party may want to address will be controversial and may implicitly challenge current statutes. For example, current policy may specify that local public schools are to be funded exclusively via a State income tax. The party may want to change this to a system whereby poor school districts get a certain percentage supplement from the state, e.g. an additional 10 percent of their prior year school budget, but otherwise local school budgets are to be funded from local property taxes at a rate to be decided by citizens in the community. The party could draft a preamble and then poll questions to solicit public opinion on their one or more proposed school funding systems. If the majority of the public and of party members endorsed a Party proposal, this would then become a facet of the current party agenda.

The Party should not shy away from challenging current government policies and programs via their poll ideas. The Party should consider it a privilege and an exciting opportunity to research, brainstorm, innovate and gather public opinion data. The Party can create any agenda it wants. Agenda items do not automatically become public law. They are simply ideas for changes in public policy that party members as candidates for public office would promote once elected. The Party would hope that their promoted ideas would become part of the agendas of legislative committees and would survive the challenges that all proposed ideas face in legislative processes before becoming law.

Consider another example of polling. I have crafted a poll for measuring what citizens want at four standard levels of government: city, county, state and nation. This poll asks citizens to make two opinion judgments for each item. A sample of items is presented in Table 2.

I loaded this questionnaire on my web site in three sections and had 72 community college students complete it. But, as you can see, it is an attempt to measure two dimensions of opinion on each of many government services. It measures how important a facet is to the citizen and how well government is currently providing that service.

This questionnaire is rather lengthy, covering 72 areas of government service with over 500 separate items or poll responses. The students were able to complete it, giving reliable information. The reliability across the city, county, state and federal levels for

"How important" was very good, at or near .90 for most items. For the four "How well provided" scores, the reliabilities were good, in the .80s.

Table 2. Two by four poll of general government service items.

Please complete the items in numerical order, 1, 2 , 3, 4 and so on.

Use these codes:

<u>How important</u> is the service? ("How important?...)

1	2	3	4	5
Not at all important	Not Important	I don't know	Important	Very important

<u>How well does government</u> provide, encourage or regulate this service? ("How well provided?"...)

1	2	3	4	5
Very Poorly	Poorly	I don't know	Well	Very Well

Now, read each item carefully and circle one number for each of the eight opinions after it:

Government provides services that are free from corruption of government itself (no embezzlement of public funds, no favoritism in awarding contracts, no bribery of government officials, etc.):

City level:

      1 2 3 4 5   1. How important?

      1 2 3 4 5   2. How well provided?

County level:

      1 2 3 4 5   3. How important?

      1 2 3 4 5   4. How well provided?

State level:

    1 2 3 4 5   5. How important?

    1 2 3 4 5   6. How well provided?

Federal level

    1 2 3 4 5   7. How important?

    1 2 3 4 5   8. How well provided?

Government provides services to the common good, serving citizen needs overall, more than special interest groups per se:

Government protects the common good from exploitation by special interest groups that are motivated by financial greed, political dominance, military power or religious fervor.

Government periodically polls citizens on major policy issues to determine what services they want from government (e.g. in terms of taxes, how money much money is spent for various departments, etc.):

Government addresses and resolves important issues in a timely manner:

Government raises sufficient revenue via fair taxes, fees, etc.:

Government does not borrow money excessively to fund services, e.g. via bonds, etc.:

Federal government cooperates with other nations on treaty issues to coordinate space satellites, prevent terrorism, prevent pollution of the atmosphere or oceans, etc.:

Federal level

    1 2 3 4 5   9. How important?

    1 2 3 4 5   10. How well provided?

Federal government cooperates with the United Nations and other nations to promote peace, fair trade, disease control, invasive species control, protection of copy rights and patents, etc.

Federal level

1 2 3 4 5   11. How important?

1 2 3 4 5   12. How well provided?

Federal government cooperates with other nations to prevent international crimes such as drug and sex trafficking, genocides, and other crimes against humanity.

Federal level

1 2 3 4 5   13. How important?

1 2 3 4 5   14. How well provided?

[END OF TABLE 2]

When a questionnaire such as this is presented over a web site, the data from each questionnaire can be saved directly to a file. This data can then be downloaded and processed via a statistical software program. The data can be processed, analyzed and summarized expediently.

The resulting scores showed several interesting things. The opinions were relatively independent of political orientation, liberal or conservative. The correlations between political orientation and the scores was generally insignificant, with a few exceptions. Conservatives tended to think of military and police services as more important. Liberals tend to be more concerned about corruption-free politics. They also are more concerned about government serving the common good, overseeing civilian gun ownership and providing building safety codes.

The fact that political orientations (conservative or liberal) in general did not correlate strongly with opinions about how important political services are, is consistent with my prior findings that liberals and conservatives as groups are relatively close on their attitudes about government services. 92% of the 72 importance scores were above 3.5, the middle of the assessment range. In effect, the majority of these students think that it is important for government to provide a wide range of services. They would not tend to agree with the statement "the less government the better".

In contrast when the students judged how well government was currently performing each of these 72 services, only 11 of the 72 students (15%) gave average ratings across the 72 items above 3.5. In effect, 85% of the students were giving government poor scores overall for providing services. They want improved government services across a wide range of topics.

The students gave government the highest performance ratings for the areas related to collecting enough taxes, regulating radio and television airway frequencies, public transportation, airport services, library services, public recreation, entertainment, museums, military services, water services, building codes, injured worker care and hunting and fishing regulations. They gave government low rankings for avoiding corruption, serving the common good, protecting the common good from exploitation by special interest groups, polling the public on issues of political importance, resolving important issues, borrowing too much money, cooperating with other nations and the United Nations, and favoring special interest groups over the common good.

In summary, the results are satisfying from a research point of view. They show that citizens can give reliable and meaningful information in considerable detail on issues related to government. They know what they think is important and they have reliable opinions about how well government is performing across literally dozens of areas of government service. Government can conduct these kinds of surveys to know exactly what citizens want in terms of government service improvements. Such surveys also provide information as to what government services citizens are satisfied with.

Political parties could also conduct such surveys to know exactly what citizens want so that their party platform can include attention to these services. For example, the Common Good Democracy party could replicate the above study on a large random sample of citizens to obtain information for formulating its initial agenda and platform.

The Party must have the courage to address tough issues and explore solutions to problems that will threaten special interest groups. The reason is that special interest groups impede solutions to many problems and create other problems. For example, the special interest groups that make money by extracting and burning fossil fuels are in effect causing global warming and climate change by adding carbon dioxide to the environment. These groups will be threatened by and try to impede efforts to replace fossil fuels with clean energy. Some teacher unions press for contracts that protect senior teacher salaries and benefits so strongly that junior teachers and non-teacher services to school children, such as counseling, nursing and athletic programs, are eliminated and class sizes are increased.

The Party can conduct polls of citizens and party members to explore possible solutions to such difficult problems. Consider the poll approach I used to explore an alternative school budget system that addresses the issue of excessive teacher union pressure. This is presented as a preamble and then three questionnaire items, as presented in Table 3.

Table 3. Proportional budgeting system questionnaire items.

Consider these two possible types of local public school budgeting systems:

A. Contract-driven budgeting: School budget allocations are dictated by contracts, such as between teacher unions and school boards, such that the salaries and benefits of tenured, long term teachers take priority over all other aspects of the budget (supplies, utilities, buildings, ball fields, club and sport programs, etc.). If budgets are cut, tenured teachers' salaries and budgets are <u>not</u> cut. All <u>other</u> program budgets are reduced and classroom sizes go up. If budgets go up, the first priority is given to increasing teacher salaries and benefits. Then other budget items are considered.

B . Proportional budgeting: A proportion of each school dollar is always protected and used only for a specific portion of the budget. Classroom sizes are constantly at 22 students. Teacher salaries are determined by a formula involving the amount of money available for salaries divided by the number of classes (22 students per class) etc. When budgets decrease, all aspects of the budget are reduced proportionally, but no teachers or programs are eliminated. Classroom sizes stay the same. When budgets increase, all portions of the budget increase proportionally. All programs get more money. Classroom sizes stay the same.

Answer these questions using this code:

1	2	3	4	5
Strongly disagree	Disagree	Neutral	Agree	Strongly agree

1. If I were a public school teacher, I would prefer to work under system B rather than system A.

2. If I were a parent, I would prefer to have my child educated under system B rather than system A.

3. If I were a taxpayer, I would prefer to support system B rather than system A."

The score is the sum of scores across the three items. None are reverse scored.

Persons who endorse the proportional system over the contract-driven system tend to endorse more democratic forms of government, sustainable communities, and the Big 5 traits of Agreeableness and Emotional Stability. They tend *not* to endorse warmongering, social disenfranchisement and military dictatorship forms of government. One study by the author showed that even university students in training to be public school teachers prefer the proportional budgeting system rather than the contract-driven system.

These results suggest that this alternative budgeting system might be preferred by the majority of citizens in a community-wide poll. If the Party replicated this poll and got similar results, this budgeting option would seem to warrant further study by the Party. If the majority of citizens preferred the proportional system, school districts might experiment with various new systems.

For example, they might put teaching out to bid by an independent teaching corporation. The contract would specify the type and number of courses to be taught, the number of students per class, the number of teachers and administrators required, etc. Corporations would have to hire teachers and administrators to staff the program and offer bids to the district. The lowest bid by a reputable corporation would be granted the contract for, say, two or four years.

The Party can use a variety of questionnaire formats to gather public opinion data. The data obtained can be used to craft solutions to community problems in a step-wise fashion, first by gathering public opinion data on initial ideas and later on specific proposals for communities to enact as legislation.

The variety of questionnaire formats and content is virtually limitless, which is some of the great opportunity that modern science and technology offers. And, it can be very interesting and even fun, in my opinion, to use this process to explore possible solutions to community problems. In the long run, the best and longest-lasting solutions will be those compatible with the opinions of the majority of citizens. Thus, testing creative solutions to community problems against public opinion via questionnaires is an efficient way to proceed, and much quicker than waiting for politicians to fight among themselves to pass legislation that may or may not be based on sound research as to its effectiveness or based on whether the majority of citizens will support it.

And, under special interest group democracy, legislators often fear to propose legislation that may threaten a current special interest group, for legislators depend heavily on those groups for campaign contributions and votes. The Party can proceed without such impediments, creatively imagining effective solutions to problems and testing them against public opinion via polls.

There are many very serious problems that citizens must solve if they are to have safe, productive, sustainable communities. These problems range from local problems, such as job opportunities, affordable housing and health care, to national and international problems, such as a stable financial system, a peaceful foreign policy and solutions to global warming and climate change.

Citizen ethics

If communities are going to thrive and survive for many generations to come, citizens must have government that politically empowers them to define and institute effective solutions. Citizens will have to appreciate the importance of social versus personal ethics in this mission. In earlier chapters I addressed the importance of executive ethics. It is also important for all members of the Party to understand that they too must differentiate between personal ethics and social ethics.

Personal ethics relate to what is good and bad, right and wrong for the individual citizen as such. Individual citizens each decide what is good for them, e.g. saving money, eating a balanced diet, exercising, brushing their teeth and getting a good night's sleep.

They must decide what is bad for them, e.g, being obese, smoking tobacco, using street drugs (methamphetamines, heroin, etc.), overcharging on credit cards and criticizing themselves harshly.

Social ethics relate to what is good and bad, right and wrong in one's dealings with other people. Social ethics can be extended more broadly to include one's physical environment. A citizen may decide that his social ethics include, under "good" or "right" behavior, actions such as going to church regularly, obeying community laws, treating family and friends kindly, contributing to charity, volunteering at the public library and as a kids' sport coach and writing letters to the editor to express personal opinions and concerns about community problems. Under "bad" or "wrong" social behavior a citizen may include theft, lying, failing to say 'please' and 'thank you', throwing trash out one's car window and failing to vote in local and national elections.

We are all members of many social groups, from family to friends to acquaintances to town, county, state, nation and even larger groups, e.g. Asians, North Americans, English speakers, Christians, Muslims and the human species. We may identify with only currently living humans. We may identify more broadly with deceased ancestors or peoples as well. We may even identify with future generations, or the concept of them. We may belong to political groups, weakly or strongly, identifying with the Republican political party or with Liberals in general.

How strongly we identify with groups will tend to define our social conscience and thus our ethical perspective. To be an effective member of our town, we must have a conscience or ethical perspective that somehow includes all members of that town. To be an effective member of our state requires a broader conscience and ethical perspective. If we choose to identify only with a subgroup or groups within our state, e.g. only persons of our religion, business group, ethnic group, gender or political orientation, our social ethic will be constrained.

To be an effective member of the Common Good Political party will require sensitivity to this ethical issue and a conscious effort to broaden one's ethical perspective to get beyond a personal ethical perspective to a social ethical perspective. The Party's political agenda in particular will define the "Common Good" and will, in effect, constitute a social ethic. An implicit aspiration of Party members will be to embrace this social ethic. The better a member does this, the more effective he or she is likely to be in the political arena of the Party and in elective office representing the Party agenda.

Conservative political orientation tends to be associated with in-group protectionism. Therefore, it will probably be somewhat more challenging for citizens of conservative than of liberal orientation to constrain their personal ethical perspective and embrace a broader social perspective. It may be harder for a conservative public school teacher to give up the union contract model for a proportional budgeting one. It may be harder for a conservative oil industry executive to endorse investments in non-fossil fuel industries.

Therefore, Party members of conservative stripe should be given special support and praise for embracing the social ethic reflected in the Party political agenda and other policies. All Party members should be praised and appreciated for keeping their personal ethical issues enough to the side to embrace the social ethic required of a political conscience in line with the common good.

As I recommended earlier, the Party should consider developing a party code of ethics, perhaps only a simple one at first, such as that of Rotary International, the four-way test: Is it the truth? Will it build good will and better friendships? Is it in the best interests of all concerned? Will it be beneficial to all concerned? A Rotary motto or slogan, "Service above self," also reflects a social ethic. In short, the Common Good Party will be dedicated to an ethic that is devoted to the common good, as defined objectively by detailed and up-to-date polls of public and party opinion. These polls are the basis for the party agenda and the mission of party members who are successful in running for public office. The voice of the public is thus promoted in the community through government.

A flavor of what to expect Party polls to reveal about majority public opinion is available in the items that make up reliable measures of human political attitudes across the more than ten basic dimensions of political discourse touched on in earlier chapters. The scales for the religious dimension were presented in their entirety in Chapter 5. In the next few chapters I will present two scales for each of these ten dimensions and a few more and offer comments and suggestions about how the Party can build on this information.

Chapter 24

Clues about public opinion
across political dimensions

Religious Beliefs

In Chapter 13 I presented research data based on a study of reliable questionnaire measures of more than sixty political traits. These questionnaire measures appear in a research paper and a manual on my web site (1, 2). They include six scales for each of ten basic dimensions: religious beliefs, social group belonging, government type preferences, gender attitudes, foreign policy, economics, civilian violence management, social group relations, leadership type preferences, and environmental policies.

Additional scales that emerged from this study include measures of political lying and conniving, disease phobia, groupthink, conservative voter attitudes, political fear, self-preservation, xenophobia, general liberal worldview, humanity concern, liberal aestheticism and liberal fairness.

Exploring the content of items from representative scales measuring these several dimensions will give clues to likely public opinion on the many politically relevant issues they touch. I'll present and discuss sample scales for the various dimensions of political discourse. All of the items in every scale correlate positively and substantially with the total score for that scale, meaning that all of the items reflect content true to the scale of which they are a part.

In all of the figures in the next few chapters I present the basic statistics for each scale. These are based on a sample of between about 150 and 190 community college and university students. Keep in mind that these scales are presented in questionnaires in a format that calls for a response ranging from 1 for Strongly Disagree to 5 for Strongly Agree. The statistics for each scale are presented. The mean is the average score for the entire group of research subjects, which included both liberals and conservatives. Thus, the mean of 2.16 for the first scale, Figure 1, indicates that the overall group of subjects completing this questionnaire measure disagreed, on average, with the items in this scale.

The range of scores is from 1 to 4.50. At least one of the 190 or so persons who completed this scale strongly disagreed with all of the items in the scale, getting a score of 1 for every item and thus a mean score of 1 across all the items. At least one person tended to agree or strongly agree with most of the items, as the highest score of all subjects was a 4.50.

The "standard deviation" statistic is presented in the third column of each figure. It is a measure of how scores spread around the mean. Generally, the higher the spread, the more reliable the scale is. Reliability is presented as the next statistic.

The reliability of the scales is presented as the Cronbach alpha coefficient, in this case .95. I think of reliability in the .60 to .70 range as weak but encouraging. .70 to .80 I think of as "adequate". .80 to .90 is good, and .90 or higher is excellent. Reliability is a measure of how well the items in a scale spread people apart. Reliability sets an upper limit on how valid a scale can be. Thus, high reliability facilitates clarifying the validity or meaning or value of a scale as a measure of human behavior.

One of the consistent meanings of traits related to politics is the relationship between a trait and the traits of conservatism and liberalism. This relationship is presented in the next to last column of the statistics for each scale. Finally, the percentage of research subjects who had mean scores of 3.5 or higher is presented, which, along with the scale mean presented in the first column, provides a suggestion of the probable percentage of citizens likely to endorse the trait.

Religious Beliefs

Measures of religious beliefs are presented and discussed in this chapter, and then the other dimensions will be presented in following chapters.

Religious fundamentalism and kindly religious beliefs

Religious fundamentalism expressed in terms of beliefs specifically about government in the United States, is reflected in the 16 items in the Religious Conservatism scale presented in Figure 1.

Notice that the items in this scale reflect a desire for a melding of religion with government, in conflict with the basic tenant of the First Amendment to the U.S. Constitution for a separation of church and state. This Amendment guards against problems that Europeans had witnessed for generations before migrating to North America. The Religious Conservatism scale items also reflect a desire for promoting religion in public school classes, an issue that has arisen periodically in discussions of text book content, especially regarding discussions of biological evolution. Religious fundamentalism tends to be endorsed by a relatively small percentage of citizens, about 6 percent, based on my studies. For this study specifically, 11 percent of students endorsed this content, as given in the last column of Figure 1. Thus, polls of public opinion on endorsement of political policies such as those found in this questionnaire are not likely to reflect majority endorsement.

Figure 1. Religious Conservatism.

Mean	Range	Standard Deviation	Alpha reliability	Correlation with Conservatism, Liberalism	Frequency percentage
2.16	1 - 4.50	0.92	0.95	.57**, -.44**	11%

1. In it is quite proper that key religious writings be inscribed on public buildings.

2. Our nation cannot be strong unless it is favored and blessed by my God.

3. Prayer should be a regular part of meetings of government officials.

4. It would be good if all public school children began their school day with a prayer.

5. It would be good if all public school teachers were members of my preferred religion.

6. It would be good if the basic truths of my religion were taught in public schools, e.g. about God and how the world was created by Him.

7. Artificial contraception and abortion are against the will of God.

8. Government should support legislation that promotes my religious faith.

9. Religious values are of paramount importance in politics and government.

10. The truths of my religious faith should strongly guide government in my community, state and nation.

11. The truths of my religious faith, e.g. about how the earth was created, should be taught in public schools.

12. The values of my religious faith, about family and sexual behavior, should be taught in public schools and promoted in public laws.

13. Government laws should permit no abortions except under very special cases as specified by religious leaders of my faith.

14. Our national Pledge of Allegiance must always have in it the phrase "under God".

15. Our money should always have printed on it "In God We Trust".

16. It is entirely appropriate that the United States Declaration of Independence included the phrase "endowed by their Creator with certain unalienable rights".

The political manifestation of kindly religious beliefs is reflected in the Religious Liberalism scale presented in Figure 2. Notice that this group of beliefs tends to be diametrically opposed to several of those in the fundamentalist scale immediately above. For example, in item 3, we see a direct statement of the belief that religion and government should be kept separate. The beliefs in the Religious Liberalism scale tend to be positively associated with liberalism and negatively associated with conservatism, as reflected in the statistics in the next to last column. Notice the endorsement percentage in the far right column; the majority of citizens are likely to endorse the ideas conveyed in this scale.

FIGURE 2. RELIGIOUS LIBERALISM.

Mean	Range	Standard Deviation	Alpha reliability	Correlation with Conservatism, Liberalism	Frequency percentage
4.13	2.33 - 5.00	.65	.82	-.49**, .46**	83%

1. Different human groups have different and equally valid religions.

2. Basic religious truths change, evolve and improve over the centuries.

3. In general, religion and government should be kept separate.

4. Our government should not favor any one religion over any other.

5. Our government should not favor religiously devout citizens more that citizens who do not believe in religion or God.

6. Citizens of our nation should be free to worship their preferred religion, such as Christianity, Islam, Buddhism or Shintoism, or no religion at all, as long as long as their faith respects civil laws.

7. Prayers and other religious rituals, including religious songs and music, should not be part of public school activities except as cultural or educational experiences.

8. Specific religious beliefs, such as Creationism, the Christian idea of how the world was created by their God in six days, should be taught in public schools only as part of a formal course on several religions, if at all, and only as a religious belief, not as scientific fact.

9. Whether a woman has an abortion is primarily for her and her doctor to decide and should not be governed by other citizens' religious beliefs.

GENERAL COMMENTS ABOUT RELIGIOUS BELIEFS.

As expressed in earlier chapters, it seems that the fundamentalist and kindly religious beliefs orientations appear to have evolved in the human species as aspects of two clusters of traits, one that focuses on protection of the in-group and another that focuses on promoting constructive relationships between the in-group and neighboring out-groups. Related evolutionary theory, as proposed by Randy Thornhill and colleagues posits that the in-group protection trait cluster, which is related to the conservative political worldview and may constitute its original form or manifestation, includes a focus on preserving the local religion and language from change. The fundamentalist orientation also includes the belief that one's own religion is the only true religion.

These two attitudes are likely to reflect resistance to embracing and respecting religions other than one's own.

Indeed, research data on a brief scale of attitudes about "meta-religion" that I designed, suggest that some conservatives tend to oppose religious activities designed to bridge gaps between religions and promote peace and understanding across various religious faiths. In contrast, persons of a liberal orientation are more likely to feel comfortable promoting such cooperative activities across religions. It is expected that the majority of citizens will be reasonably comfortable with promoting cross-religion activities, as the majority of citizens endorse kindly religious beliefs and eschew fundamentalist beliefs.

It is expected that fundamentalist and kindly religious beliefs are likely to be evident in some form in all major religions, as theory posits that they are aspects of species evolution rather than specific to one or another human culture. Regarding the Christian religion, the content of the Old Testament books of the Bible tend to reflect considerable fundamentalist religious thinking, with emphasis on authoritarianism, warmongering and in-group favoritism.

The content of the New Testament books of the Bible reflects kindly religious beliefs primarily. Jesus' message of turning one's cheek, being kind to even to one's enemies and out-group peoples, and his emphasis on love and compassion over selfishness and anger all appear to reflect this kindly religious beliefs orientation. This may help explain the popularity of his teachings. We see in current frequency data that the majority of citizens prefer this kindly religious orientation over the fundamentalist orientation.

There are at least three major types of ultimate authority offered in various world religions:

1. A god seen as a supernatural being, often with human qualities,

2. A human with great wisdom regarding how to live a good

life, and

3. A general spirit, such as a spirit of human goodness and kindness, perhaps the "Holy Ghost" of New Testament Christianity, and perhaps in some degree the karma of Buddhism and other Asian religions.

There are advantages and disadvantages of each of these ultimate authorities. A given citizen may embrace one or another of these, all three, or none of them. Clarifying these types of religious authority can assist in making choices as to which to turn to for personal spiritual guidance. The third type of authority is informed by psychological research on human religious beliefs and is thus directly open to scientific inquiry. It holds potential for addressing international conflict.

A GOD AS ULTIMATE RELIGIOUS AUTHORITY.

A god, or for some religions "God", is often conceived of as a supernatural being with supernatural powers, including the power to help groups or individuals succeed in war or other competitions. Success in war was necessary for survival of primate human groups and thus this concept of God and its related religion presumably served primate groups in their struggle for survival as a species, giving an edge to primate types who could imagine and depend on such a concept. Presumably Homo sapiens had an edge on this over other primate species. God as ultimate authority is often granted other great powers, such as the power to cure illness, grant good fortune, or punish or condemn to endless suffering, as in an afterlife in hell, individuals who have transgressed basic commandments.

One advantage of this type of ultimate authority is that political and religious leaders can use it to reinforce their authority over people they lead. An example is monarchs who have claimed the "divine right" to lead. Religious leaders claiming a god's ordination helps them provide religious advice and leadership with confidence and respect.

Another advantage of this source of authority is that it is universally available to the believer, especially if the believer considers the channels of communication with this god to be direct, as through personal prayer, rather than through an intermediary, such as a religious leader.

A complication of this authority is having a clear and constructive enough image of him/her to enable one to believe strongly and communicate effectively with the god/God, as through prayer. If one has lacked good models of authority in childhood, it may be difficult to create a sufficiently good image of one's god/God for this purpose.

Another complication with god authority is defining the god's detailed characteristics. How is the god conceived? Who does the defining or interprets these characteristics? If we define this supernatural being ourselves, we are limited to the framework of our own wisdom and biases. If we or some authority that we depend on defines our god/God too narrowly, we may unnecessarily limit our own potential to benefit from his/her/its power. If we define God too grandiosely or generously, we may encounter or create the problems of egomania, imagining that God has granted us dominion over nations, such as having the divine right of a king or emperor to rule, as did many European kings and Napoleon, Emperor of France. Hitler thought he was doing the work of the lord.

Another complication of this authority is that God/god is not available to individuals or groups for guaranteed results. Results are said to depend in part on humility, loyalty and obedience, etc. Even with good behavior, there are typically no guarantees of a god's favor. A God who does not guarantee services to faithful followers causes confusion and doubt in followers when suffering persists in spite of requests for help. A classic example in the Hebrew/Christian faiths is the story of Job. He sees his God initially as hiding from him, troubling him, forsaking him, testing him rather than helping him. Job suffers greatly and complains to God. But for a long time his suffering continues, put on Job by God and Satan to test him. In the end, Job is given by God great wealth (camels, oxen, sheep, etc.), a large family of beautiful children and 140 years of life, simply for repenting for doubting God and for maintaining his faith in spite of the prior hardships. Job was fortunate. For some, relief from suffering does not come.

Also, theologians have asked how God could have permitted the atrocities and suffering of WW II. One answer they have offered is that God turned his head, too ashamed or shocked to view what was happening. But a god who looks away from problems rather than helping can be seen as confusing at best and a failure at worst.

Not infrequently, a god is looked upon as granting special rights to his "chosen people", such as the Hebrews considering their God as having granted them the right to the land of Canaan, even though at the time this land was occupied by other tribes. A group that claims their God has given them rights to a particular geographic land is inviting conflict with other groups who claim in various ways the rights to that same land. Present day Israel's conflict with Palestinians comes to mind.

Claiming that one's God or one's form of worship is the most superior, as is the case for the Religious Fundamentalism belief trait, sets a group up for conflict with other human groups that claim theirs is the superior God or perfect form of worship. Muslims fight among themselves over such conflict (Sunni and Shiite). Christians conflict with Muslims. Catholics have conflicted with Protestants.

A WISE HUMAN LEADER AS ULTIMATE RELIGIOUS AUTHORITY.

The second way to conceive of a religious authority is to turn to a divine or highly revered human being and his or her teachings.

Jesus fills this role in Christianity as a divine leader and Buddha as simply a revered but not divine leader in Buddhism. Muhammad founded the Muslim faith of Islam, presenting himself not as a divine being, apparently, but as a wise teacher. Confucius has been a wise leader of this sort for Southeast Asian peoples.

Typically, this mode of authority provides the advantage of detailed prescriptions for how to live a good life. Typically we get much more detail from human religious leaders than from a God. A god's prescriptions may be limited to a few general guidelines, such as the Ten Commandments of the Old Testament. A human leader may detail scores of prescriptions in writings, sermons and other teachings.

This form of religion is not without its complications, as teachings are sometimes interpreted and recorded in complicating ways. For example, we know of Jesus' teachings not from his writings but only from his sermons, and these only through the memories and writings of his disciples. And some of these writings present contradictory interpretations. One disciple says deeds without faith are meaningless; another says faith without deeds is meaningless.

Another complication with this basis of religion is cultural changes over time. Buddha, Jesus, Muhammad and Confucius lived many centuries ago. Their teachings must be interpreted to have relevance to modern societies. Who should have the authority to make these interpretations? Which authority should a given citizen trust in this? How does a citizen make this choice?

A SPIRIT AS ULTIMATE AUTHORITY.

A third way to conceive of one's ultimate religious authority is to think in terms of a general spirit or concept, such as the "Holy Ghost" of Christianity, the concept of karma of Asian religions or the universal spirit of human goodness and kindness in the Kindly Religious Beliefs factor of modern scientific research on human psychological traits. This concept provides its own advantages and challenges. The challenges include definition.

How should this concept be defined? For example, there is little clear definition in the Bible for the Holy Ghost, which appears as a concept only in the New Testament. It is referenced briefly as a source of inspiration to disciples, enabling them to "speak in tongues" and prophesy. It is referred to as coming from God and from Heaven. But Heaven is described as something within citizens. Thus, it is, implicitly, to some degree a social spirit of good ethical inspiration and guidance. Indeed, in the New Revised Standard Version of the Bible, Paul's first letter to the Corinthians, chapter 12, verse 7 reads "To each is given the manifestation of the Spirit for the common good." Paul is encouraging his Corinthian colleagues to express their individual personal talents in the service of others, all others, thus promoting the common good.

Paul lists several of these personal talents or gifts, all of which he considers to be manifestations of the "Spirit for the common good": speaking with wisdom, having and sharing knowledge, having faith in goodness, healing, performing miracles, prophesying, speaking foreign languages, and translating and interpreting languages.

Paul says that all personal talents are gifts given to people by the Holy Spirit, but there are no instructions in the Bible from him or other disciples, as far as I know, as to how to access or gain guidance from this spirit, other than prayer, perhaps. Or, perhaps we must simply discover our own talents and exercise them for the good of our communities.

Psychological research provides information on related citizen beliefs that can flesh out the meaning of the concept "universal spirit of human goodness and kindness". This concept seems to be similar in content to the Holy Ghost as presented in the Bible. Questionnaire items that measure the kindly religious beliefs factor include one definition of god as "the universal spirit of human goodness and kindness". In addition, the principles of the Rotary

Four Way Test correlate positively with this factor. This code consists of four ethical questions for evaluating or "testing" the ethics of one's behaviors: Is it the truth, will it build good will and better friendships, is it in the best interests of all concerned, will it be beneficial to all concerned? A complication of this form of "spirit" is finding relevant answers to such questions in a given case.

An advantage of the human goodness and kindness concept is that it makes much room for science and other sources of wisdom and guidance in addition to religious teachings. People can be kind to each other in many ways, e.g. physicians guided by scientific research and professional training and experience. Teachers and counselors can be kind to their students and clients, guided by professional training, science, literature and personal experience. Parents can be kind to their children by years of thoughtful living and from wisdom gained from their own parents. Friends can be kind to each other based on similar personal experiences. The human kindness concept seems to make room for all of these sources of kindness and support.

Kindly behaviors take many modern day forms that are reminiscent of Paul's concepts of "gifts": healing (by physicians, nurses, psychotherapists, chiropractors and social workers), knowledge (college and primary and high school teachers), prophesy (journalists, economists, political pundits, ministers, rabbis), wisdom (political leaders, novelists, poets, artists, philosophers) and miracle workers (research scientists, engineers, inventors).

Another advantage of the kindly religious beliefs type of authority is that it is available wherever there are kind people present. Church meetings and activities provide members with opportunities to share problems and experiences, to ask for help and give help to each other. Gatherings of kind people in church or other activities, such as service club meetings and projects, provide a venue for this universal spirit of human goodness and kindness to flow to and from citizens.

For most of us, turning to a spouse, intimate partner, other family member or relative or close friend is a first choice when mulling over a personal problem. We tend to choose carefully, avoiding helpers who might blame us for our problems, criticize us, dismiss our problems as unimportant or otherwise fail in the helping role. We choose helpers who empathize, listen patiently to our perceptions and opinions, encourage us, make helpful suggestions and otherwise comfort us with smiles, a hand on our shoulder, a reassuring hug and words of confidence and hope.

To benefit from this kindness, one need only comply with the basic principles of social and group decorum as espoused by the individual or social group. One need not agree to complex creeds or beliefs beyond this to reap the benefits of giving and receiving help. Thus, for persons who have difficulty embracing the concepts of god/God or divine human leader, the human goodness and kindness concept may provide a more palatable spiritual hitching post. For those that embrace a religious framework, Karma or the Holy Ghost can be their parallel conceptual guide.

World travelers, such as Rotarians, who have Rotary clubs they are encouraged to visit when traveling anywhere in the world, have observed that there are friendly people in all nations. To the extent that we can find personal help and kindness from people that we befriend anywhere in the world, we can consider the good that flows to us to be an expression of the universal spirit of human goodness and kindness. As this spirit is likely to come even from people of differing religious faiths, it can indeed be considered universal; Rotarians are of many faiths. And, as such, this universal spirit may be the primary hope for understanding and cooperation across peoples of different religions around the world. In effect, it may have the potential to serve as "a bridge over troubled water", especially between Christians and Muslims and between conflicting Muslim sects in the Middle East.

Note: I refer repeatedly to Rotarians, Rotary International, but there are many organizations that manifest the benevolent, helpful spirit. I use Rotary simply because I am most familiar with it. You can think of other such organizations to get my points.

Thus, to promote cooperation across citizens of different religions, the Common Good Party might thus see fit to promote the universal spirit of human goodness and kindness. For example, congregations of worshippers in different faiths could be encouraged to clarify in what ways their faith manifests a concept akin to "universal spirit of human goodness and kindness". They could be encouraged to meet with representatives of other faiths and exchange ideas, traditions, songs and essays on this theme. They could be encouraged to address this theme periodically in their religious services back in their home countries.

Congregations could be invited to confer with political leaders in their countries to promote expressions of this concept in foreign policy and programs. For example, the Peace Corps of the United States could be promoted as a manifestation of a universal spirit of human goodness and kindness extended to foreign nations. International meetings on issues such as climate change, economic trade and arms control could include invocations that embody and express this theme of universal human goodness and kindness, rather than prayers to specific gods or God.

At a national level, governments could be encouraged to limit government expressions of religion to this concept, to minimize favoritism to specific religious faiths and risking the conflict this might foster. For example, instead of having the President of the United States sworn into office with hand on Bible, "Under God", he or she could be asked to preside in office under a spirit of universal human goodness and kindness.

In conclusion, religious beliefs are a pervasive and important element of human society. Religious beliefs and practices serve as a guide to and comfort for individuals and groups. Religious beliefs influence political attitudes and preferences. To the extent that the universal spirit of human goodness and kindness can be promoted to encourage understanding and cooperation across different religious faiths, it may assist the Common Good Party to promote cooperation across faiths to mitigate the conflict that often flairs between religions that depend heavily on other forms of ultimate religious authority.

<h1 style="text-align:center">Chapter 25</h1>

<h2 style="text-align:center">More citizen attitudes:
social group belonging, gender
issues, foreign policy, government
type preference and economics</h2>

This chapter continues the discussion of research findings that suggest what citizens are likely to endorse regarding polled opinions about government services and function.

Social group belonging.

The social group belonging dimension of political discourse refers to how citizens feel as members of a social community. The theory of psychologists Roy and Judy Eidelson is operationalized in the present author's Social Disenfranchisement scale. Research with this scale supports their hypothesis. A worldview characterized by feelings of injustice, distrust, helplessness, vulnerability and superiority correlates positively and substantially with endorsement of warmongering and other traits associated with conflict between groups. A political manifestation of this orientation is reflected in the Cultural Conservatism scale presented in Figure 1.

The content of this scale reflects especially the superiority facet of the social disenfranchisement dimension, such as in item 2, which emphasizes the belief in the superiority of one's nation. It also reflects a belief in privileged access to more resources, as reflected in item 8. As reflected in the frequency percentage column, the majority of citizens are not expected to endorse these ideas. A friend who read this manuscript asked if this was theory or the result of some administered test. My answer to him was as follows:

The 2 percent figure is a result of a study I did with this trait measure. Only 2 percent of subjects in my study endorsed this concept, i.e. had an average score on it of 3.5 or higher. Data I've gleaned from other larger samples of citizens on various traits such as these runs generally in line with my results. Thus, I assume that a random sample of citizens from around the country would yield similar results on this trait measure, with only a very small portion endorsing it.

My friend also asked what the alpha reliability figure is (for this trait .85.) I explained it earlier in the manuscript, but I'll remind you again what it is. It is a measure of how well the items in the scale or trait measure spread people apart, or how reliable a given person's score is as a measure of this trait. The higher the coefficient, the more reliable the scale. An alpha coefficient of .80 or higher is good. .90 or higher is excellent. Another way of saying this is that a scale with high reliability is one for which all the items in the scale are truly measuring something in common with the other items. Or, a person who endorses one of the items is likely to endorse the others. Another way of explaining this is to say that the items in the scale truly reflect the way some people think.

The fact that only 2 percent think a certain way can be very important if the content of the thinking is important, as it is, for example, in a measure of violence-proneness. If only 2 percent of 400 high school students are violence prone, as measured by a valid test, that means 8 of those students are violence prone. The school would be wise to provide those students counseling services to minimize the risk of a violent act. Similarly, if only 2 percent of 100 Air Force officers were severely mentally ill, as measured by a reliable and valid test of mental illness, then 2 of them would be at risk for failing on the job. If they were persons with responsibility over nuclear missiles or bombs, then it would be important to replace them with other officers.

Mean	Range	Standard Deviation	Alpha reliability	Correlation with Conservatism, Liberalism	Frequency percentage
2.59	1.00 - 3.73	.51	.85	.49**, -.35**	2%

1. Some people, ethnic groups and nations are innately superior in various ways to others.

2. Our nation is the best and should strive to keep its status.

3. Our nation must remain dedicated to a few key, unchanging, basic principles.

4. Our nation can be strong only if certain core laws are conserved and preserved.

5. My preferred political group's judgment on important political matters is virtually always correct.

6. The judgment of other political groups is almost always wrong.

7. My preferred political group knows what is best for our nation and how to get it.

8. Our nation must have access to important natural resources from around the world, and at whatever cost.

9. Government should stay out of the way of big business or help big business succeed.

10. Powerful, large corporations and organizations should have room to operate and grow without interference from government.

11. The rights of big, powerful corporations and organizations are more important than the rights of smaller, weaker ones.

12. If government functions mainly to keep these powerful corporations strong, everyone in the nation will benefit.

13. Might makes right, in business as well as in politics.

14. Everyone should be responsible for his own success in life.

15. In business and politics there are times to be ruthless to get ahead.

16. Loyalty to top political leaders is important for the success of our nation.

17. Citizens who know and follow the right values deserve to be rewarded.

18. Guarding our borders is of utmost importance to maintain national security.

19. Our nation must look out mainly for our current citizens and not encourage immigrants.

20. Every citizen or family is responsible for earning his/her/their own living.

21. Every citizen or family is responsible for paying for his/her/their own health insurance.

22. Every citizen should be responsible for his own transportation and higher education costs.

"Cultural egalitarianism" is measured with the scale presented in Figure 2. It is intended to measure the general opposite of cultural conservatism, as presented above. Figure 2 is a partial presentation of the scale, which has several additional items in its full version. Notice in the correlation column that this scale tends to reflect liberal ideas over conservative ones. It reflects an attitude of social inclusiveness, a general principal in the United States Constitution. This trait measure emphasizes concern for the welfare of all social groups, and even minority groups, and in a wide range of opportunities, ranging from jobs, education and housing to opportunities for social support services, such as Social Security payments and health care. Notice in the frequency percentage column that the majority of citizens are likely to endorse the ideas embodied in this measure.

Mean	Range	Standard Deviation	Alpha reliability	Correlation with Conservatism, Liberalism	Frequency percentage
4.08	1.00 - 5.00	.58	.91	-.42**, .38**	87%

1. "All men are created equal" means to me that all humans should have the same basic rights, as to life, liberty and the pursuit of happiness, jobs, educational opportunities and health care.

2. Our government should be concerned about the welfare of all groups within our nation.

3. Minority groups deserve special assistance to protect their access to jobs, education and housing.

4. Poor people deserve special assistance, such as school lunches and head-start school opportunities for pre-school children.

5. The elderly deserve financial assistance in the form of monthly Social Security payments.

6. Our nation should have an affordable government-sponsored health care program that assures medical care for all citizens.

Gender attitudes

Another important dimension of political discourse is attitudes about gender. These attitudes historically have tended to favor males. This favoritism is reflected in the items in the Masculine Leadership Preference scale presented in Figure 3. While this scale is only nine items long, it provides a very reliable measure of this masculine political worldview. The items in the scale speak for themselves. Item 8 seems to help explain the perhaps evolutionary origins of this trait. We can imagine that this trait helped the human species survive to have males in particular interested in impregnating women in their group to keep the numbers of their clan growing relative to competitive neighboring clans. A minority of citizens is expected to endorse this trait, as reflected in the low Mean and Frequency Percentage figures.

FIGURE 3. MASCULINE LEADERSHIP PREFERENCE (MASCULINE POLITICS)

Mean	Range	Standard Deviation	Alpha reliability	Correlation with Conservatism, Liberalism	Frequency percentage
1.81	1.00 - 3.78	.66	.88	.47**, -.38**	2%

1. Males, especially strong ones, should be highly respected.
2. In general, males make better leaders than do females.
3. In general, men make better business managers than do women.
4. In general, only men should hold top business, political and religious leadership positions.
5. Men should have the last word in family affairs.
6. Women should submit and defer gracefully and respectfully to men.
7. Women who claim to have been raped should have to pay for their own vaginal medical tests to check the truth of their claims.
8. With few, if any, exceptions, there should be no birth control measures or abortions for the women of our group.
9. No special laws should be passed specifically for the welfare or protection of homosexual men or lesbian women.

In contrast to favoring males, the Female Egalitarianism scale presented in Figure 4, reflects a strong respect for females and their voice in political issues, especially those unique to them, such as pregnancy and abortions. The scale also reflects a concern for the rights of children in schooling. It is an extremely reliable measure, with an alpha coefficient of .95, in spite of the fact that it consists of only six items. Thus, it provides a very efficient measure of this attitude.

FIGURE 4. FEMALE EGALITARIANISM.

Mean	Range	Standard Deviation	Alpha reliability	Correlation with Conservatism, Liberalism	Frequency percentage
4.48	1.00 - 5.00	.63	.95	-.31**, .26**	94%

1. Women should have primary say in how many children they bear.
2. Women should have primary say in their access to various forms of birth control of their choice.
3. Women should have primary say in whether they have access to abortion of pregnancies that have been forced upon them.
4. Human sexual reproduction biology and related issues should be taught in appropriate ways to children of all ages in public schools.
5. Women should have equal say with men on legislation that directly affects women per se, such as abortion laws.
6. Girls and women should have the same opportunities and support to attend elementary, high school and college that boys and men have.

FOREIGN POLICY

Foreign policy can range from an aggressive, militaristic, dominant attitude to a peaceful, helpful, cooperative attitude. The militaristic attitude is represented in the "Militaristic Philosophy" scale presented in Figure 5. Keep in mind that all of the items withstood the test of correlation with the total score; they are all meaningful elements of this trait. The content of the traits speaks for itself. Note items 12 and 18 in the context of concerns about civilian mass homicides with assault weapons, and the items about sports and Scouting as preparation for military service. Items 19 and 20 are consistent with the evolutionary and species survival theory underlying this and related traits in the in-group protection cluster of traits discussed in Chapter 12.

FIGURE 5. MILITARISTIC PHILOSOPHY

Mean	Range	Standard Deviation	Alpha reliability	Correlation with Conservatism, Liberalism	Frequency percentage
2.11	1.00 - 4.10	.66	.92	.49**, -.28**	8%

1. I believe in survival of the fittest...that the strongest are destined to survive while weaker individuals don't.
2. I believe in "an eye for an eye", that our nation should always seek revenge when offended.
3. I want great power and strength for our nation.
4. I feel scared and vulnerable unless our nation is strong and powerful.
5. I think it was quite proper to drop atomic bombs on Japan in World War II.
6. Hitler's orders to totally destroy towns and civilians as acts of revenge were quite reasonable.
7. I support the vigorous use of propaganda, lying and demonizing foreigners to incite our civilians to war against them.
8. I love to read and think about military things.
9. I have been fascinated with military things since childhood.

10. War is necessary and desirable to keep a nation united, focused and fully employed.

11. I think civilian vehicles that look like military ones, like the Jeep or Humvee, are really neat.

12. Our citizens should have access to whatever military small arms they wish to own.

13. I like to read letters to the editor and editorials that support and encourage military actions by our nation.

14. All physically and mentally fit teens and adults between ages 18 and 32 in our country should be active or reserve members of the military or of the National Guard.

15. It is a good to promote camouflage clothing, toy guns and violent video games for children to help prepare them for military combat.

16. It is good to promote Boy and Girl Scout programs for children to help prepare them for military combat as adults.

17. It is good to promote competitive, aggressive team sports to help prepare young citizens for possible military combat as adults.

18. It gives me a feeling of power and safety to think of owning handguns and rifles.

19. If I were an ant in a colony I would prefer to be a warrior rather than a food gatherer.

20. If I were a chimpanzee I would rather fight neighboring chimps than gather food.

The Peace Policy scale, Figure 6, provides a very reliable measure of the opposite of a militaristic foreign policy. Based on the mean above 3.5 (first column) and the frequency percentage in the far right column we can anticipate that the majority of citizens will support this foreign policy. Notice that many of the items can translate directly into specific government policy, such as items 1, 6, 11 and 16. Notice too that Peace Policy doesn't mean total abdication of military strength. It includes maintaining strength for defensive purposes, as reflected in item 18. In retrospect, I see that there are items in this scale that address civilian violence management. As such, these items (11 and several thereafter) would perhaps be better in another scale.

FIGURE 6. PEACE POLICY SCALE.

Mean	Range	Standard Deviation	Alpha reliability	Correlation with Conservatism, Liberalism	Frequency percentage
3.78	1.00 - 5.00	.62	.91	-.44**, .51**	56%

1. In the U.S., only Congress, not the President, should declare war.
2. Our government should carefully weigh alternatives before declaring war.
3. We should try all diplomatic efforts before we declare war on another nation.
4. When in a war in another country that we seem unable to win promptly with military action, as for the U.S. in Vietnam or Iraq, we should get out quickly.
5. A person does not need military leadership experience to be well qualified for the office of President of our nation.
6. We should decrease our national military budget.
7. We should dismantle and reduce our major military weapons, such as atomic warheads.
8. We should support United Nations programs to quickly stop civil wars and genocides.
9. Anti-war protesting in public places is a patriotic service to our nation.
10. We should promote disarmament treaties with other nations.

11. We should reduce marketing and use of violent video games and movies, especially by children.

12. We should promote diagnosis and treatment of violent behavior in children and teenagers.

13. We should promote media coverage of the less socially desirable aspects of wars we wage, such as coffins of our dead soldiers, casualty statistics and stories of veterans who are permanently disabled.

14. If our government engages in secret war-promoting activities, we should expose and report it to the public.

15. We should spend as much for violence prevention and treatment of violent criminals as for locking them up.

16. We should outlaw handgun and military weapon ownership by civilians.

17. We should closely monitor police department activities to minimize misuse of their authority for cruelty to citizens.

18. We should maintain enough military preparedness to defend our nation if and as necessary.

19. Our government should not use our military to participate in other nations' affairs behind the scenes for overthrowing and replacing governments.

GOVERNMENT TYPE PREFERENCE

Citizens can be polled on what type of government they prefer. Government types range widely, from virtually no government to dictatorships, monarchies and various forms of democracies, and blends of these. Government in the United States at present (2013) can be considered a form of democracy that serves citizens primarily as members of special interest groups. We might consider this a form of "Power politics government". This form of government is reflected in the scale presented in Figure 7. This scale is rather reliable, tends to correlate positively with conservatism and tends to be endorsed by a minority of citizens. The content of the items directly reflect attitudes debated repeatedly in U.S. media, especially the power of money to control national politics.

While none of the students in the study on which this scale was used endorsed this trait, that doesn't mean the trait is meaningless. The trait is quite reliable (.88 Alpha). It spreads people apart. In a larger sample of citizens, perhaps one half of one percent, e.g. 1 out of 200 persons might endorse this trait. If the Common Good Political party had a member that wanted to run for political office, but had a score of 3.5 or higher on this trait, he or she would probably not be considered a good candidate, for the content of the items in the scale are not in the interests of the common good, the majority of citizens.

FIGURE 7. POWER POLITICS GOVERNMENT

Mean	Range	Standard Deviation	Alpha reliability	Correlation with Conservatism, Liberalism	Frequency percentage
1.77	1.00 - 3.30	.62	.88	.31*, -.26**	0%

1. Government should serve the special interest groups that have the most money.

2. I prefer a political party that represents primarily the interests of business managers, owners, and stockholders.

3. I trust lobbyists (persons who represent special interest groups and give money to legislators in return for passing legislation favoring their groups).

4. I trust special interest groups that contribute money to legislators' election campaign funds.

5. I prefer political candidates who will do what their major campaign money contributors want them to do, whether that is in the best interest of the nation as a whole or not.

6. Wealthy corporations and other such groups should be free to influence legislators via lobbyist money.

7. Wealthy citizens and groups should be free to contribute as much money as they want to campaigns for elective office.

8. Elected officials should vote on legislation the way their biggest campaign contributors want them to.

9. Government should serve large, powerful corporations, mainly by staying out of their way.

10. I am comfortable with government making big loans to large corporations, such as banks and auto manufacturers that get into financial trouble.

Government that serves citizens as members of the community overall rather than as members of special interest groups is measured quite reliably with the brief, 6-item scale presented in Figure 8. This scale correlates positively with liberalism and negatively with conservatism and is likely to be endorsed by the majority of citizens, as reflected in the mean of 4.28 and frequency percentage of 88. This scale might appeal to the Common Good Party as a standard feature in questionnaires it uses to accept members into the party and to screen candidates for elective office. The party would want these persons to have high scores on this scale. The majority of citizens are expected to.

Figure 8. Common Good Democracy Endorsement scale

Mean	Range	Standard Deviation	Alpha reliability	Correlation with Conservatism, Liberalism	Frequency percentage
4.28	1.00 - 5.00	.72	.91	-.39**, .28**	88%

1. Elected officials should run the government to serve the current and long-term best interests of the community overall, including sustainable programs such as conserva-

tion of resources and control of pollution and global warming. No one special interest group or groups are favored.

2. Elected officials should run the government to include sustainable programs such as conservation of resources and control of pollution and global warming.

3. Elected officials should run the government so that no one special interest group or groups are favored over others.

4. Government should have policies that promote a world safe for lower species.

5. Government should have policies that promote a world safe for future generations of humans and lower species.

6. Elected officials should run the government to serve the current and long-term best interests of the community overall.

ECONOMICS

Citizen attitudes about government economics range widely, judging from discourse in the media, including articles by economists and the man and woman on the street. These attitudes seem to range from retention of wealth by the wealthy to sharing opportunity to the less economically privileged in society. This is an issue of political importance perhaps as old as human civilization. For example, 2000 years ago Jesus frequently preached on the importance of wealthy citizens sharing with the poor.

One end of this debate is reflected in the attitudes measured in the Economic Conservatism scale presented in Figure 9. The items speak for themselves. This brief scale is quite reliable and correlates significantly and positively with conservatism and negatively with liberalism. It is likely to be endorsed by only a minority of citizens, based on the available mean and frequency data.

FIGURE 9. ECONOMIC CONSERVATISM.

Mean	Range	Standard Deviation	Alpha reliability	Correlation with Conservatism, Liberalism	Frequency percentage
2.01	1.00 - 4.00	.69	.85	.54**, -.40**	2%

1. Taxes on wealthy people should be kept as low as possible.

2. There should be no minimum wage; employers should be free to hire the cheapest laborers who are available and willing to work.

3. Businesses should be free to import products made by the cheapest labor anywhere in the world, regardless of working conditions in foreign factories.

4. Military budgets should be increased.

5. Our military budget should be kept high enough to supply our nation with the best, most powerful weapons and strongest forces in the world.

6. Federal Reserve interest rates should be kept low, to make it easy for big business to borrow money.

7. The Federal government should bail out big corporations that might otherwise go bankrupt.

8. Wealthy people should be permitted to pass on all their wealth to their offspring without paying estate taxes.

The "Liberal Economics" scale presented in Figure 10 reflects another dimension of attitudes about political financial issues. This scale correlates negatively with conservatism and positively with liberalism. Notice that the scores for the sample of citizens upon which the presented statistics are computed ranged to both extremes (from 1.00 to 5.00); at least one person strongly disagreed with all 8 items in the scale, and at least one strongly agreed with all 8 items. This wide range and the good reliability of .85 are signs of a promising scale.

Notice also that the items in this scale are relatively lengthy, providing detailed policy statements. The Common Good Party can use detailed statements of this nature to measure public support levels for specific government policies and programs it conceives through issue research.

The statistics in Figure 10 suggest that the majority of citizens will support "Liberal Economics" of the sort depicted in this scale. In retrospect, item 3 seems to be somewhat poorly written. It could be improved, perhaps by breaking it into two separate items or by rewording it. Care must be exercised in drafting questionnaire items.

FIGURE 10. LIBERAL ECONOMICS SCALE

Mean	Range	Standard Deviation	Alpha reliability	Correlation with Conservatism, Liberalism	Frequency percentage
3.76	1.00 - 5.00	.59	.85	-.20**, .40**	70%

1. Progressive income taxes are reasonable, with the wealthy paying more than the less wealthy.

2. Sales taxes are good because they discourage spending and consumption, which can help protect the environment from over use of resources.

3. Government serves many important functions, including redistribution of wealth from some sources to others, including money for public services such as roads, schools, safety programs, disease control, national defense, educational funding and management of national parks and natural resources (oil, ores, etc.) on public lands.

4. One of the most important functions of government is redistributing wealth such that children and handicapped or elderly adults who cannot work can still get basic services

they need.

5. Government should promote programs to assure adequate jobs for all able-bodied citizens who can work.

6. Government should promote and/or fund injured worker programs, unemployment benefits, protected retirement pension funds and Social Security for those who need it.

7. Government should design, fund and administer a national health care program for those who can't afford private care.

8. Government guaranteed student loans and housing loans are desirable.

Civilian violence management

The counterpart of foreign policy might be considered "civilian violence management". Some policies support or facilitate civilian violence, while other policies seek to contain or restrain it. Policies that seem to *facilitate* violence are reflected in the Violence Enabling scale presented in Figure 11. This is a rather reliable scale (Alpha of .89) that correlates positively with conservatism and negatively with liberalism and is endorsed by a minority of citizens.

Figure 11. Violence enabling.

Mean	Range	Standard Deviation	Alpha reliability	Correlation with Conservatism, Liberalism	Frequency percentage
2.61	1.00 - 4.20	.68	.89	.48**, -.31**	11%

1. I support the National Rifle Association's interest in citizen access to firearms.

2. Adult citizens should be allowed to own rifles and shotguns.

3. Adult citizens should be allowed to own pistols.

4. Citizens should be allowed to hunt game birds and rabbits.

5. Citizens should be allowed to own military handguns, including automatic rifles.

6. Children should be allowed to own and shoot air guns (e.g. BB guns).

7. We should build more prisons rather than provide more rehabilitation counseling and education to criminals.

8. We should put more money into police forces than into school counseling for violence-prone children.

9. We should spend more to research new military weapons than to research the causes of youth violence.

10. We should execute criminals convicted of rape or murder.

11. We should let children play violent video games to help prepare them for possible future military combat.

12. We should promote violent sports like football and boxing to help prepare children for military combat.

13. We should support Boy and Girl Scout programs to help prepare youngsters for possible future military combat.

14. We should encourage citizen access to movies and television programs about war to keep them ready for war.

Note: My manuscript editor raised a question about item 12, apparently challenging the reference to football as a violent sport. Citizens can have different opinions about whether football is or isn't a violent sport. This questionnaire item is phrased in a manner to elicit endorsement of football as a violent sport, along with the notion that violent sports help prepare citizens for combat. The item works as a questionnaire item because data shows that it correlates with the other items in the scale and positively with the total score for this scale. Thus, this phrasing serves our purpose in measuring this violence-promotion attitude. All the items in all of my scales have passed this "item analysis" test. Items that did not pass were to be excluded. As it turned out, all of the items in all of the scales in this study of about 64 traits survived item analysis of this nature.

Violence *prevention* attitudes, and safety promotion, are measured with the scale presented in Figure 12. This is a very reliable scale that appears to reflect majority citizen opinion, with a mean of 4.00 and frequency percentage of 86% in the sample of community college and university students used for the present data. Notice that several of the items in the scale are directly related to community policies and regulations, e.g. items 7, 10 and 11 about dogs on leashes and helmet use.

FIGURE 12. VIOLENCE PREVENTION/SAFETY PROMOTION.

Mean	Range	Standard Deviation	Alpha reliability	Correlation with Conservatism, Liberalism	Frequency percentage
4.00	1.00 - 5.00	.55	.90	-.31**, .30**	86%

1. I support efforts to ban handguns for civilians.
2. I support civil rights efforts to protect minorities from police abuse.
3. I think it is shameful that citizens of our country have lynched minority group members in times past.
4. I believe we should remind parents to be kind and polite toward officials who referee youth sporting events, such as soccer and football.
5. Especially in kids' sports, good sportsmanship is more important than winning.
6. Parents should not yell angry insults at players or referees during youth sporting events in which their children are playing.

7. Dogs walking with their owners on city streets should be on a leash for safety of others.

8. Regarding personal auto use, we should do more to reduce speeding and running red lights.

9. We should do more to improve safety for bicycle riders on our streets.

10. Persons riding bicycles and motorcycles should be required to wear helmets.

11. Persons who downhill snow ski should be required to wear helmets.

12. We should do more research to understand and prevent civilian crimes such as assault and murder.

13. We should do more to prevent violent crimes by providing treatment and other rehabilitation programs for offenders.

14. We should do more to teach teenagers how to be kind and peaceful spouses and parents in adulthood.

15. Alcohol use in public sporting events should be prohibited if necessary to reduce fan violence.

16. We should do more research to understand the causes of child abuse.

17. We should do more to prevent child abuse in our families.

18. We should do more to prevent spousal abuse in our families.

19. We should do more to prevent violence among inner city minority youth groups.

This discussion of questionnaire measures of public opinion on political matters will be continued in the next chapter.

CHAPTER 26

SOCIAL GROUP RELATIONS, LEADERSHIP TYPE PREFERENCES AND ENVIRONMENT ATTITUDES

"…A REMARKABLE SURVEY WAS MADE PUBLIC LAST SUMMER THAT clearly shows a significant majority of people in Eugene [Or.] connect the dots between climate change, human-caused damage to the environment and our own resource-intensive lifestyles. A majority recognize an urgent need to go green and would like to know more about choices for doing so." (1).

This report appeared in the Guest Viewpoint section of our local newspaper, demonstrating how surveys of the public can yield information to guide community action on politically-relevant issues. Its topic is environment concern. But first, consider two other areas of importance.

SOCIAL GROUP RELATIONS.

Politics involves relationships between groups. These relationships can be characterized by competition, as between majority and minority ethnic or religious groups or between economic groups, such as labor versus management or wealthy versus poor. Or, group relationships can be characterized by cooperation.

A form of the competitive style is represented by the In-group Favoritism scale presented in Figure 1. This very reliable scale correlates substantially and positively with conservatism and negatively with liberalism. This perspective is likely to be endorsed by only a minority of citizens, given the endorsement frequency of only 1% in the study data. Notice that item #1 expresses a political party characteristic diametrically opposed to that proposed for the Common Good Party. Notice also the favoritism of select colleges, universities, cities, churches and corporation executives.

FIGURE 1. IN-GROUP FAVORITISM/ OUT-GROUP CONTROL.

Mean	Range	Standard Deviation	Alpha reliability	Correlation with Conservatism, Liberalism	Frequency percentage
1.94	1.00 - 3.64	.69	.90	.53**, -.32**	1%

1. The platform of my favored political party should be determined by an elite group of party leaders.
2. The core leaders of our party should dictate policy for our nation through elected officials loyal to the party.
3. Ideally, gays and lesbians should not be allowed in the military.
4. Ideally, physicians who favor abortions should not be permitted to practice in our nation.
5. Cities that are faithful to our party ideals should be rewarded with military bases and other favors by elected officials from our party.
6. Colleges and universities that permit ROTC (Reserve Officer Training Corps) and military recruiters on their campuses should be given first consideration in research grants.
7. Churches that support our political party should be given tax exempt status even though they preach support for our candidates and legislation.
8. It is more important to protect the financial security of large corporate executives and other powerful leaders than to assure jobs for laborers.
9. It does not make sense to provide student loans to people who cannot afford them because they probably won't pay

them back.

10. Local retail business owners should be free to buy products made by workers in other countries if the owners can make more profit doing so.

11. It doesn't matter much that some workers lose their jobs in hard times, as long as employers can keep their businesses going.

Another example of a dominant, group-controlling political philosophy is represented by the Power Oligarchy scale presented in Figure 2. This brief but very reliable scale also correlates positively with conservatism. It is endorsed by only 1% of subjects in this sample. It reflects prejudice against certain groups, such as ones that the in-group tries to keep from the polls, uses as military members or simply considers weak or poor.

FIGURE 2. POWER OLIGARCHY.

Mean	Range	Standard Deviation	Alpha reliability	Correlation with Conservatism, Liberalism	Frequency percentage
1.68	1.00 - 3.90	.66	.94	.40**, -.15	1%

1. My favored political party should dominate state and national politics to the exclusion of other parties, if possible.

2. When in political power, elected representatives of our party should strive to give preference in government contracts to businesses faithful to the party.

3. Our party should do what it can to minimize voter registration of members of groups we disfavor.

4. Our party should do whatever is necessary to win elections for party members.

5. Our party should limit its core membership to people of a preferred ethnic and moral type.

6. Our party should quietly but effectively strive to keep members of certain ethnic and minority groups in their current inferior place.

7. Lower class people failing to get to polls to vote for national leaders is not that bad, because they often vote for the less appropriate candidates.

8. It is reasonable to have our lower-class citizens fight and die in our wars, because higher-class people are better suited for other things.

9. Because it's nature's way that the stronger survive, it doesn't matter that many poor people can't afford health care.

10. It is more important that government serve the powerful than the weak in society, for the powerful have what it takes to keep our nation strong.

A very different political group relations philosophy is reflected in the Anti-oligarchy policy scale presented in Figure 3. This very reliable scale correlates positively with liberalism and negatively with conservatism. It is likely to be endorsed by a majority of citizens, considering the endorsement frequency of 87% in the study sample. Notice that this scale includes in item 4 a specific endorsement of the central philosophy underlying the Common Good Party.

FIGURE 3. ANTI-OLIGARCHY POLICY.

Mean	Range	Standard Deviation	Alpha reliability	Correlation with Conservatism, Liberalism	Frequency percentage
4.24	1.00 - 5.00	.70	.95	-.23**, .33**	87%

1. Government should enforce anti-trust laws to prohibit large corporations from dominating society to the detriment of the general public.

2. Government should not be manipulated by big business to

the detriment of the public.

3. Government should not be controlled or run by families and relatives of leaders just because they are related.

4. Government legislation should be driven more by principles of public good that by the narrow interests of small special interest groups.

5. We should remember, appreciate and promote our country's traditions of opportunities for persons of lower social class and wealth to rise to positions of prominence, leadership and importance by hard work and persistence.

6. We should discourage political power maintained by economic favoritism given to political party loyal supporters.

7. We should make sure that government oversight committees have the power and support they need to investigate and report political wrongdoing by elected officials, regardless of political party affiliation.

8. We should be on the alert for abuse of political power and exercise the power of impeachment of even the President, when necessary.

9. We should be careful to respect the balance of powers provisions of our national government constitution, to assure that no one branch of government becomes too powerful and unaccountable to the public.

10. Each branch of government, legislative, judicial and executive, should carefully assume its unique responsibilities and not give them to another branch.

LEADERSHIP TYPE PREFERENCES

Leadership can reside in authoritarian leaders to make the decisions or more broadly in elected representatives of the people. When the elected representatives' decisions are contaminated or corrupted by special interest group money for campaigns or more crass forms of bribery, the best interests of the people are betrayed. Authoritarian leaders are often dangerous, as in the case of many military dictators. Occasionally an authoritarian leader is uniquely noble, having the wisdom, character and will to call citizens to rise to the "higher angels of their natures", as Lincoln has been revered for doing.

One form of leadership dependence has been studied as "authoritarianism". The Authoritarianism scale presented in Figure 4 provides a measure of this trait. Note that it correlates positively with conservatism and negatively with liberalism. The content of the items reveal that this form of authoritarianism can be dangerous, and indeed this scale correlates positively and substantially with warmongering endorsement. This trait suggests a characteristic of dependent persons. It is endorsed by a minority of citizens, based on studies I have done, and as reflected in the 4% frequency in the study cited for this chapter.

FIGURE 4. AUTHORITARIANISM. (THE ITEMS IN THIS SCALE ARE TAKEN FROM A LONGER SCALE DEVELOPED BY THE AUTHOR. (2)

Mean	Range	Standard Deviation	Alpha reliability	Correlation with Conservatism, Liberalism	Frequency percentage
2.33	1.00 - 4.20	.69	.86	.51**, -.13	4%

1. In conversations with others, I prefer the clear guidelines of rules and doctrine to the uncertainties of personal opinions.

2. I feel reassured by parades of soldiers and induction ceremonies of Presidents or other national leaders.

3. I am a member of a group that is almost all good and righteous.

4. Persons should learn to depend on rules given by authorities more than trust their own judgments.

5. We should not question persons in positions of authority

but rather take them at their word.

6. Society will completely fall apart if everyone does not know and obey laws and regulations.

7. For handling everyday problems I trust religious authority more than I trust my own judgments.

8. On foreign policy, I trust the top political leader of my country (e.g. the President) more than my own opinions.

9. I usually feel reassured by major public speeches by top government leaders, such as Presidents.

10. I believe that our political leaders are wiser than those of other nations.

The scale in Figure 5 is an attempt to measure leadership residing in the people. While this scale is fairly reliable, its content could be improved, as several of its items are not directly related to citizen leadership. The best items are 1, 2 and 4. This scale is endorsed by the majority of citizens (83%) in the study upon which the statistics provided are computed. The scale correlates positively with liberalism and negatively with conservatism.

FIGURE 5. CITIZEN AUTHORITY.

Mean	Range	Standard Deviation	Alpha reliability	Correlation with Conservatism, Liberalism	Frequency percentage
4.02	1.00 - 5.00	.71	.84	-.36**, .33**	83%

1. We citizens should be less focused on unquestioning acceptance of political leaders' decisions and be more concerned with the government services needed by our citizens.

2. Our government should conduct carefully designed polls to determine how citizens want government to run and incorporate the findings into government policy.

3. Our government should create a stable, fair tax system that

is sufficient to fund government programs without constant borrowing against the future or promises to lower taxes unrealistically just to win votes in elections.

4. Our government should fund research on the development and maintenance of sustainable communities, to include determining the carrying capacity of each county and state (the number of people that can be supported by the available energy, fresh water, jobs and resources in the area).

5. Our government should fund research to improve government itself, e.g. finding ways to reduce the influence of special interest group money on legislative decisions and assuring fair elections

Environment attitudes

Environment attitudes range from great indifference to the environment, using up natural resources for immediate value on the one hand. On the other hand is a desire to protect the environment from pollution, global warming, etc. The very reliable 10-item scale in Figure 6 provides a measure of the "indifference, use-it up" attitude. It correlates positively with conservatism and negatively with liberalism and is supported by only 4 percent of the 151 students in this sample.

Figure 6. Personal immediate natural resource use.

Mean	Range	Standard Deviation	Alpha reliability	Correlation with Conservatism, Liberalism	Frequency percentage
1.84	1.00 - 3.90	.78	.95	.51**, -.36**	4%

1. I am not concerned about global warming.

2. I do not worry about some species going extinct.

3. Cutting down forests for farmland in South America does not concern me.

4. I am not interested in making sure salmon fisheries are preserved in the Northwest states of the U.S.

5. I do not worry about overpopulation of the earth.

6. Melting glaciers and polar ice caps does not seem important to me.

7. Air pollution does not worry me.

8. I see nothing wrong with using gasoline and Diesel oil to power our vehicles.

9. I see nothing wrong with burning coal in electrical generating plants.

10. I am not concerned about how many people there are in the world.

The very reliable 9-item scale presented in Figure 7 provides a brief measure of concern for the environment and specifically in terms of desired government policy to protect the environment, broadly speaking, from contaminated foods and drugs marketed to the public. It includes concern for rivers, forests and the atmosphere. The statistics for this very reliable scale suggest that the majority of citizens (89% in this study) are deeply concerned about the environment, consistent with data from international polls of public opinion. For example, "A WorldPublicOpinion. org (WPO) poll for the World Bank found majorities in all sixteen countries polled saying that at the conference their country should "be willing to commit to limiting its greenhouse gas emissions as part of such an agreement"—on average 87%, including 82% of Americans." (3)

FIGURE 7. GREEN/CLEAN/SAFE POLITICS SCALE.

Mean	Range	Standard Deviation	Alpha reliability	Correlation with Conservatism, Liberalism	Frequency percentage
4.26	1.00 - 5.00	.67	.94	-.29**, .42**	89%

1. Our national forests should be protected from excessive cutting so there is an endless crop of harvestable trees.

2. Our wetlands should be protected to assure adequate ground water for wells and habitat for waterfowl, fish, etc.

3. Many of our rivers should be restored to dam-free condition to aid in the rejuvenation of wild fisheries, especially salmon fisheries.

4. Government should establish and enforce effective clean air standards to protect humans from respiratory diseases, such as asthma.

5. Government should invest in and provide industry incentives to find alternatives to fossil fuels to reduce greenhouse gasses and global warming.

6. Government should establish and enforce adequate standards to minimize harmful discharge of sewer and industrial waste products into our streams and rivers.

7. Government should establish and enforce policies for protecting the environment from toxic waste and other damage to the environment resulting from coal and other mineral mining.

8. Government should establish and enforce effective standards for foods, toys and other products to assure that they are safe for public consumption and use.

9. Government should establish and enforce adequate safety standards for medicines, pharmaceuticals and other medical procedures.

Thus, we have seen in the last three chapters how citizens view issues across ten major dimensions of political discourse. In the next chapter, we'll explore how they view several somewhat esoteric dimensions of politics.

CHAPTER 27

MORE CITIZEN ATTITUDES: CLUES
FROM TEN ADDITIONAL SCALES

ADDITIONAL CLUES AS TO PUBLIC OPINION ON POLITICAL IS-sues are available via several additional scales that result from two clusters of miscellaneous items that were included in the study that generated the many scales presented in the immediately preceding chapters. These miscellaneous items were ones that I sensed might differentiate the liberal and conservative worldviews from each other but didn't fall into the 10 dimensions of political discourse used for organizing the majority of scales, or I suspected that they might augment one or another of the scales in those dimensions. Factor analysis revealed several reliable scales.

CONSERVATIVE VOTER ATTITUDES

The content of this scale, presented in Figure 1, includes items about managing voting, disease phobia, subservience to leaders, and dominating other nations, suggesting that it reflects broad, core conservative worldview content. As such, it might be useful in international studies as a tool to identify conservatives (if the term "conservative" may not be easily translated). It correlates positively with conservatism and negatively with liberalism. While the content of this scale is not flattering to conservatives, keep in mind that the mean score is quite low (1.68), meaning that most persons who see themselves as conservatives will tend to disagree with the statements in this scale, though less strongly than liberals will. The scale might be considered an underlying conservative worldview that is "politically incorrect", in the sense that it would not be openly expressed to the voting public, so as not to alienate independent or liberal voters unnecessarily. This illustrates an interesting value of creating such questionnaires; they enable one to learn about traits that may be suspected but are not easily accessible for confirmation by reading public media or by listening to informal political conversations between citizens.

FIGURE 1. GENERAL CONSERVATIVE ATTITUDES.

Mean	Range	Standard Deviation	Alpha reliability	Correlation with Conservatism, Liberalism	Frequency percentage
1.68	1.00 – 4.08	.63	.93	.35**,-.19*	2%

1. What my leaders tell me is the truth *is* the truth.

2. People in other states are more likely to carry infectious diseases than people in my state. People in other towns or cities are more likely to carry infectious diseases that people in my town or city.

3. It is smart for my preferred political leaders to lie and cheat if necessary to win elections and hang onto political power.

4. It is wise strategy for leaders of my preferred political party to keep those citizens away from the polls who might vote against us.

5. It is okay for my political candidates to run down and discredit their opponents during campaigns for office.

6. I like movies about keeping other nations in their place by defeating them in war.

7. In business, as in sports, profit and winning is more important than sportsmanship or fairness.

8. In political campaigns, winning justifies lying and conniving.

9. In political campaigns, belittling your opponent, even with

lying, is justified if it will help you win.

10. In times of war, it is worthwhile to use propaganda to demonize enemies.

11. Even in times of peace, it is more important to dominate other nations than to make friends with them.

Fundamentalist religious beliefs

The content of the 10 items in this very reliable scale is all clearly religious in focus, with a Biblically literal, fundamentalist flavor. Preferences for dependence on authoritarian religious leaders and eschewing science are also present. Also, some of this content is personal enough that it would not often be openly expressed.

Figure 2. Religious fundamentalism scale.

Mean	Range	Standard Deviation	Alpha reliability	Correlation with Conservatism, Liberalism	Frequency percentage
2.36	1.00-4.60	.98	.94	.55**, -.39**	15%

1. For me, God is important primarily as a protector.

2. I believe Heaven is somewhere other than on earth.

3. I believe that I will go there and live forever when I die.

4. I trust God to take care of those things about which I tend not to worry.

5. Being part of a tightly united group of people of faith is very important to me.

6. I prefer to be part of a group of people who all believe in the same things and worship the same way.

7. What my leaders tell me is the truth *is* the truth.

8. Spiritual truth is more important than scientific truth.

9. When there's a conflict between scientific facts and my reli-

gious beliefs, I prefer to ignore the scientific facts.

10. If scientists come up with facts that are contrary to my religious beliefs, I expect my religious leaders to explain why the claims of the scientists are false.

Political Fear.

This scale appears to measure what might be termed "political fear", which extends from fear of losing personal wealth to fear of international threats. It is associated positively and rather substantially with conservatism and negatively with liberalism.

Figure 3. Political fear scale.

Mean	Range	Standard Deviation	Alpha reliability	Correlation with Conservatism, Liberalism	Frequency percentage
2.50	1.00-4.29	.80	.84	.52**, -.19*	11%

1. I worry about terrorist attacks.

2. I worry about diseases coming into our area from foreign places.

3. I worry about military attacks against our nation.

4. I worry about high taxes that could take away my wealth.

5. In international matters I am motivated more by fear than by hope.

6. There may be times when we may need to take military action to keep groups of diseased people from invading our country.

7. In successful business, outwitting competition is a primary objective.

Self-preservation.

This scale appears to measure what might be termed "self-preservation", as it reflects indifference to other people, past, present or future, and a focus instead on living in the present and using resources as needed to secure one's own present survival. It correlates positively with conservatism and negatively with liberalism. The self-preservation, "survivalist" focus is reminiscent of the theorized evolutionary origins of the conservative and liberal worldviews, as discussed in earlier chapters.

FIGURE 4. SELF-PRESERVATION SCALE.

Mean	Range	Standard Deviation	Alpha reliability	Correlation with Conservatism, Liberalism	Frequency percentage
2.03	1.00-4.00	.69	.84	.33**, -.25**	3%

1. I tend not to worry about poor or unfortunate people unrelated to me.
2. I tend not to worry about the welfare of future generations.
3. I tend not to worry about poor or unfortunate people in foreign lands.
4. I tend not to think much about the past or about history.
5. A primary goal for me is to look out first for my own best interests rather than for other people.
6. It makes more sense to me to use natural resources like oil and iron ore to build security and wealth now than to worry about the environment.

XENOPHOBIA/DISEASE PHOBIA.

This scale appears to be a combination of fear of both foreigners and of diseases from foreigners. It correlates positively with conservatism.

FIGURE 5. XENOPHOBIA/DISEASE PHOBIA SCALE.

Mean	Range	Standard Deviation	Alpha reliability	Correlation with Conservatism, Liberalism	Frequency percentage
1.84	1.00-5.00	.81	.87	.32**, -.19*	3%

1. People of different language, skin color or nationality are more likely to carry disease than people like me.
2. Such people are more likely to be terrorists than I am.
3. Such people are more likely to be dangerous than I am.
4. People living in foreign lands are more likely to carry infectious diseases than people in our nation.

GENERAL LIBERAL POLITICAL WORLDVIEW

The items in this scale reflect a wide variety of attitudes associated with liberalism in prior studies mentioned above. Thus, it appears to be a measure of the liberal political worldview in general. It is brief and very reliable, providing a convenient research measure. For example, it could be used in international studies to identify liberals, when the term "liberal" per se might have different meanings.

FIGURE. 6. GENERAL LIBERAL WORLDVIEW SCALE.

Mean	Range	Standard Deviation	Alpha reliability	Correlation with Conservatism, Liberalism	Frequency percentage
4.07	1.00-5.00	.66	.92	-.32**, .32**	83%

1. I worry about the welfare of future generations.
2. I feel a sense of obligation to protect the environment for other species and for future generations of humans.
3. I enjoy traveling, visiting with strangers and learning about people different from myself.

4. I would enjoy traveling to foreign lands.

5. I believe scientists have much to teach us about how to improve our nation.

6. I think government should fund research to figure out how to improve our nation and our government.

7. I sometimes think about how our community and government could be much better.

8. My opinions and ideas about improving our nation are as important as those of our leaders.

9. I prefer to decide for myself what is best for our nation, rather than simply trusting our leaders to decide.

10. I am more inclined to trust rather than fear a stranger from a foreign land

11. I like stories and movies about exploring and discovery.

HUMANITY CONCERN

This scale reflects concern for the future welfare of the planet as well as for current concerns for humans everywhere. It has content that is reminiscent the Identification with All Humanity scale of Sam McFarland. (Sam is at Western Kentucky U.).

FIGURE 7. HUMANITY CONCERN SCALE.

Mean	Range	Standard Deviation	Alpha reliability	Correlation with Conservatism, Liberalism	Frequency percentage
3.87	1.00-5.00	.73	.89	-.22**, .26**	69%

1. It is hard for me to be completely happy as long as there are millions of starving and homeless people in other nations.

2. I feel deep concern for the less fortunate citizens of my own nation.

3. I care about people different from us who live in foreign lands.

4. I feel a sense of obligation to help people in foreign lands who are less fortunate than we are.

5. I worry about the welfare of future generations.

6. I feel a sense of obligation to protect the environment for other species and for future generations of humans.

7. I am more interested in helping other nations fight disease than in avoiding contact with those nations.

LIBERAL AESTHETICISM

This scale has good reliability and seems to reflect liberal values of concern for human welfare. This scale is only weakly associated with liberalism, but it is endorsed by the majority of subjects in the research study and thus suggestive of public opinion.

FIGURE 8. LIBERAL AESTHETICISM SCALE.

Mean	Range	Standard Deviation	Alpha reliability	Correlation with Conservatism, Liberalism	Frequency percentage
4.03	1.00-5.00	.87	.87	-.15, .22**	85%

1. I like music about overcoming hardship and suffering.

2. I like stories and movies about overcoming injustice and being compassionate.

3. I like stories and movies about exploring and discovery.

4. I like movies about helping unfortunate, helpless people to succeed.

5. I like movies about overcoming oppressive political leaders.

6. I like movies about cooperation, love and kindness.

This scale seems to be one of fairness in business and politics. It is termed "liberal" fairness because of its positive correlation with liberalism and negative correlation with conservatism, though these relationships are not very strong. It is endorsed by the majority of persons in the research study from which the statistics come.

FIGURE 9. LIBERAL FAIRNESS SCALE.

Mean	Range	Standard Deviation	Alpha reliability	Correlation with Conservatism, Liberalism	Frequency percentage
4.11	1.00-5.00	.68	.86	-.22**, +.21*	85%

1. In business, it is more important to cooperate, build trusting relationships and be fair rather than to compete, dominate and win however you can.

2. In business providing excellent customer service is more important than improving profit.

3. Good sportsmanship is as important, or more important, than beating your opponent in sports.

4. Candidates for political office should not degrade their opponents to make them look bad.

5. All citizens of voting age should be helped to vote, even if it is for candidates of a political party different from my own preference.

Lying and Conniving Scale

This scale measures endorsement of political lying and conniving, as reflected in the items. It is associated positively with conservatism. The majority of citizens are unlikely to support this trait, based on the statistics provided.

Mean	Range	Standard Deviation	Alpha reliability	Correlation with Conservatism, Liberalism	Frequency percentage
2.14	1.00 to 4.3	.57	.91	.36**, -.18	2%

1. It is smart for my preferred political leaders to lie and cheat if necessary to win elections and hang onto political power.

2. It is wise strategy for leaders of my preferred political party to keep those citizens away from the polls who might vote against us.

3. It is okay for my political candidates to run down and discredit their opponents during campaigns for office.

4. In political campaigns, winning justifies lying and conniving.

5. In political campaigns, belittling your opponent, even with lying, is justified if it will help you win.

6. In times of war, it is worthwhile to use propaganda to demonize enemies.

7. Even in times of peace, it is more important to dominate other nations than to make friends with them.

Chapter 28

Party Platform in a Nutshell

W E CAN IMAGINE WHAT THE COMMON GOOD PARTY PLAT-
form or political agenda might look like by summarizing
the import of the public opinion estimates reviewed in the questionnaires presented in the last four chapters. I'll phrase these
comments as the beliefs of "we", the hypothetical members of the
Party. Keep in mind that what the Party decides will be up to the
Party; my comments are only offered as an example of how questionnaire data can be translated into policy.

Religion. We tend not to endorse fundamentalist religious
policies regarding government. Government and church should,
in this regard, be kept separate. Religion as a general topic can
be taught in public schools but no one religion to the exclusion
of others. Nor should pubic school activities include prayers or
other formal religious rituals. Public schools should present facts,
not promote specific religious or political philosophies per se.
Thus, our party endorses the teaching in public school curricula
of facts but not of preferred or recommended government policies on topics such as abortion, same-sex marriage, evolution and
the origin of the earth, and the appropriateness of medical care
versus only prayer as response to illness. We endorse citizen rights
to practice any religious beliefs they choose, as long as their practices conform to public laws regarding civility, etc. We do not endorse religious practices that advocate violence against others as
an expression of religious principles. We support the idea that no
one religion or group of religions should be favored over others
in government policies. We support the minimizing of references
to religious deities in public songs, pledges and documents. For
example, we recommend that the President be sworn in not with

hand on Bible but with a pledge to serve under the universal spirit of human goodness and kindness.

Social group belonging. We endorse equality and respect between social groups, with everyone having a place in the "family" of national citizenry. We also prefer not to think of our nation as better than other nations or more privileged or more to be feared. We promote trading for what we need from other nations rather than intimidating or dominating them with militarism or other methods. We do not think corporations should have "personhood" when it comes to contributing money to elected officials' campaigns for office, for this amounts to bribery and transgresses the principle of one vote per person. Financial groups or special interest groups should not usurp political power to the detriment of the common good. Citizens and corporations should consider making money in our nation not a "right" but rather a privilege, with corresponding obligations in return to pay taxes, provide jobs, treat all employees with respect, and respect the interests of the community and the nation. The common good supersedes the interests of corporations. The common good includes respect for the interests of minority groups, including those of ethnic background, age, gender, health status, intelligence, education and physical strength. Government should promote policies that assure jobs for all citizens, with reasonable limits set on imports proportional to levels of local unemployment. Our citizens have the right to pay higher prices for locally made goods and services in return for available jobs for all citizens. The profits of business owners who might make more by importing cheaper goods are of less importance than providing jobs for our citizens. We encourage efforts to help all citizens feel wanted, needed and appreciated and not isolated, excluded and alienated. Jobs give lives meaning and are therefore of central importance.

Gender attitudes. The Common Good Party platform holds that men should not exploit or abuse women in any ways and especially not sexually or in employment. Women should have direct say in how many children they bear, in abortion of pregnancies forced upon them via rape and their access to appropriate medical services for issues related to pregnancy and childbearing. Girls and women should have opportunities equal to those of boys and men in education, jobs, salaries and promotions, based on aptitude and merit.

Foreign policy. We believe in a basically peaceful foreign policy and a military capacity designed for defense, not offensive meddling in other nations' affairs. We advocate a reduction in our nation's military presence in scores of other nations at present and a reduction in military spending in general. We endorse instead an emphasis on peace-promoting policies and programs with other nations.

Government type preference. The Common Good Party believes that national government should serve the common good, broadly defined, rather than special interest groups per se. The common good includes the welfare of current citizens, lower species and the environment, in the present and for the future.

Economics. (Note: Almost all of the following text consists of the items in the trait scale that correlates positively with liberalism in Chapter 24, above. This demonstrates how poll questionnaires can consist of specific desired government policies.) The Common Good Party believes that progressive income taxes are reasonable, with the wealthy paying more than the less wealthy. Sales taxes are good because they discourage spending and consumption, which can help protect the environment from over use of resources. Government serves many important functions, including "redistribution of wealth" from some sources to others, including money for public services such as roads, schools, safety programs, disease control, national defense, educational funding and management of national parks and natural resources (oil, ores, etc.) on public lands. An important function of government is redistributing wealth such that children and handicapped or elderly adults who cannot work can still get basic services they need. Government should promote programs to assure adequate jobs for all able-bodied citizens who can work. Government should promote and/or fund injured worker programs, unemployment benefits, protected retirement pension funds and Social Security for those who need it. Government should design, fund and administer a national health care program for those who can't afford private care. Government-guaranteed student loans and housing loans are desirable. Government should strive to function within a balanced budget, paying off the national debt and restraining spending thereafter as necessary to live within our means.

Civilian violence management. We endorse policies that discourage violence, especially violence with deadly weapons and especially with guns. Specifically, we endorse prohibition on military weapon ownership by civilians, especially rapid-fire weapons. We encourage research on violence prevention and implementation of evidence-based policies and programs to reduce violence in children as well as adults. We endorse evidence-based policies and programs for reducing child abuse and spousal abuse. We endorse local community control over the marketing in their community of violent video games, television programs, music lyrics and movies, if evidence documents that these reinforce civilian violence.

Social group relations. We believe in cooperation between groups rather than competition and exploitation of some groups over others. We believe that the citizens of communities, states and the nation, and even of the world, are not just markets for business to sell to or special interest groups to manipulate, dominate, exclude or otherwise exploit. We believe that citizens as members of various groups, including their community as a group, have rights to a voice in how their communities are managed and that this voice is not to be superseded by other forces that betray the common good.

Regarding government, our beliefs on this topic are well-represented by the items in the Anti-oligarchy questionnaire, as presented in Figure 1.

FIGURE 1. ANTI-OLIGARCHY SCALE:

1. Government should enforce anti-trust laws to prohibit large corporations from dominating society to the detriment of the general public.

2. Government should not be manipulated by big business to the detriment of the public.

3. Government should not be controlled or run by families and relatives of leaders just because they are related.

4. Government legislation should be driven more by principles of public good that by the narrow interests of small special interest groups.

5. We should remember, appreciate and promote our country's traditions of opportunities for persons of lower social class and wealth to rise to positions of prominence, leadership and importance by hard work and persistence.

6. We should discourage political power maintained by economic favoritism given to political party loyal supporters.

7. We should make sure that government oversight committees have the power and support they need to investigate and report political wrongdoing by elected officials, regardless of political party affiliation.

8. We should be on the alert for abuse of political power and exercise the power of impeachment of even the President, when necessary.

9. We should be careful to respect the balance of powers provisions of our national government constitution, to assure that no one branch of government becomes too powerful

and unaccountable to the public.

10. Each branch of government, legislative, judicial and executive, should carefully assume its unique responsibilities and not give them to another branch.

Leadership type preferences. We believe that the ultimate authority of government leadership is the will of the people, as carefully measured with reliable and valid polls of citizen opinions on the issues that government addresses. This will, so defined, constitutes the common good. Leadership should serve the common good. Government should support and encourage research to maximize this goal and be constantly on the alert for erosion of leadership that betrays this, either intentionally or inadvertently.

Environment attitudes. We believe in protecting the environment, comprehensively defined, both for our own sake and for the sake of other species and future generations of life on our planet. This obligates us, through our local, state and national governments, to limit population, and to limit waste, and to clean and decontaminate solid, liquid and gaseous waste before releasing it back into the environment. This is a huge responsibility that must be assumed by us collectively, via our governments, and immediately. It cannot be postponed or disregarded or sacrificed to short-term special interest group agendas.

Principled political campaigning. We believe that in political campaigns candidates should not lie. Citizens should not be discouraged from voting. All citizens' political opinions and preferences are to be honored and heard. Majority opinion and preferences constitute the common good and should carry elections for government leaders and on policy issues. We believe that in sports and in business good sportsmanship and honesty should not be sacrificed to winning and competing.

Sectarian basis for unity. We believe that national unity should be promoted by polling to define the common good, not by universal adherence to one or another religious faith. We do not believe that all citizens have to think the same way or agree with a leader's ideas but that majority opinion of informed, concerned citizens should establish government policies.

Worry and fear management. We believe that worry and fear should prompt careful assessment of potential problems but that action in response should be reasoned, informed and consonant with the common good as defined by polls of citizens. This principle is especially important when it comes to military response to problems.

Self-preservation. While self-preservation is a natural response to ultimate, moral threats, as a community of citizens we do not endorse self-preservation behaviors that clearly and deliberately jeopardize the common good. Citizens with self-preservation thoughts, impulses and plans are encouraged to discuss them with party members or other appropriate persons to assure that they refrain from behaviors that might jeopardize the common good and find alternate courses of action.

Fears of disease and foreigners. We encourage persons with fears of disease, terrorism and foreigners to seek information and guidance to put these fears in perspective and defer to response options that are compatible with the common good.

Progressive ideas. We believe in open-mindedness and encourage independent thinking by citizens and scientific research to constantly seek creative, new improvements to solving community problems and to improving government itself.

Universal concern. We endorse universal concern for all humanity and for the planet and all its life forms and for the environment upon which we all depend for survival.

Pro-social aestheticism. We endorse art and entertainment forms that promote constructive, loving, kind, helpful and cooperative human behavior and discourage forms that promote violence, hatred, prejudice, cruelty and conflict.

Fairness. In business, industry, education and government we advocate fairness, honesty, transparency and cooperation over conniving, deception, dishonesty and competition.

Note: When extrapolating from questionnaires to write a party agenda it is important to refrain from going too far from the questionnaire content. The principle is to serve the common good as defined by the polls, not simply as implied by poll content. Concepts implied by polls can and should be used as inspiration for future poll content. Often, such implied content will indeed prove to yield additional information about majority public opinion. But, until this is confirmed in a subsequent poll, restraint in crafting agenda statements is advised in the interest of integrity.

And so, we have in this chapter a model of the agenda of the Common Good Party. For this agenda to have meaning and value, the Party, or some other institution must adopt it.

Chapter 29

Dreaming

I HAVE PRESENTED A WIDE RANGE OF DIMENSIONS OF POLITICAL discourse, from religious beliefs, gender attitudes and group relations to foreign policy, economics and environmental concerns. Each of these areas can be measured reliably as psychological traits using questionnaires. These questionnaires consist primarily of statements of beliefs and attitudes of citizens.

You may see other areas of politics that I haven't covered. Or areas of community living that aren't a typical political issue but could be. For example, you might think it is important that any community that has a public memorial to war ought to have at least one to peace. Or, you might think that the citizens of a community should have the right to limit what sorts of movies or television programs are marketed in their community, and even what Internet content is transmitted.

Any issue such as these can be treated as an issue of political concern and of legislation to define the characteristics of a community. The general principles of questionnaire construction, you will recall, are making statements that are clear and typical of how a citizen might think, that include just one idea each and that can be agreed with or disagreed with. To create a reliable measure, it is also important to include several statements on each topic, coming at it from different perspectives and covering the various facets of the concept in question.

For example, the issues addressed above could generate questionnaire or polling statements such as:

"Our community should have at least one pubic park monument to celebrate or promote International peace.

Any community that has a monument to war ought to have at

least one monument to peace.

Citizens in our state should have the right to limit what sorts of movies or television programs are marketed in their community.

I disapprove of some types of movies that are shown in our local movie theaters, television programs or over the Internet."

I think of communities as human creations. This creation can be a cumulative process over many years or decades of decisions by different citizens, as either individuals or groups. Or, communities can be designed in a single stage by planners and engineers, architects and crafts persons. Or, they can be designed by citizens who create a vision for a better community and create the legislation to make it happen.

The first stage of such a design is imagination, perhaps inspired by visiting other communities, or reading about them, or viewing photographs and drawings, or just daydreaming. Or ideas might be triggered by reading newspaper, magazine, scientific journal or Internet articles, such as the one titled "Thousands of chemicals pose risks to health" in our Sunday newspaper (1). This article reports that 200 man-made chemicals were found in the blood of 10 newborn American babies in the United States. These were chemicals possibly contributing to health problems such as heart disease, diabetes, asthma, autism, obesity and learning disorders.

My own brush with lymphoma this past year, a disease of the white blood cells, can be triggered by benzene, which is found in gasoline(2,3). Benzene is particularly high in gasoline in the Northwestern states where I live. "Benzene is one of the primary air pollutants contributing to cancer risk in Oregon. Oregon has some of the highest levels of benzene in the United States."

In the first step of dreaming up features of an ideal community, anything goes. No criticism or self-censure. This is a principle of brain-storming sessions. Let your imagination run free. As long as you can put an idea into a statement that is clear and unambiguous enough for citizens to agree or disagree with, the idea can be tested in the crucible of public opinion research. If the majority of citizens sampled and tested with a questionnaire agree with an idea, and with similar ideas on the same topic, the topic is worth serious consideration for adding to one's ideal community wish-list.

So, as an example for you to copy, let me share with you some of my dreams for an ideal community. Keep in mind that what is ideal for one area of a state or nation will be different for another. My "ideal community" is for Eugene, Oregon, where I have lived for the past 40 years. There's much I like and love about this community, but it has much room for improvement.

I am concerned about fossil fuel burning and its contribution to global warming. In Eugene we get all of our gasoline through one pipeline coming down from Portland. The Wall Street Journal reports that in 2012 United States oil production grew more than in any year since 1859 (4). From this it seems there is no serious intention by our oil industry to back off on burning fossil fuels.

One idea I've had is for our community to take the lead, in Oregon at least, in reducing our dependence on all fossil fuels. We could reduce the flow through the pipe from Portland by ten percent per year until we don't bring any gasoline at all into our community. The pressure for finding alternative non-polluting fuels would be terrific, of course, but necessity is the mother of invention. I can imagine more bicycles and redesigned residential and commercial neighborhoods so folks can walk to and from their jobs, stores, entertainment venues…all sorts of secondary changes. I can imagine Oregon State University and the University of Oregon developing alternative energy research programs with intense focus and activity.

As is true for many of us, I depend heavily on gasoline at present and would have to make serious adjustments. I drive a gas-hog GMC Suburban. It's an '86 and dented, but runs well and enables me to pull my sailboat out to the reservoir in the spring and back in the fall. It enables me to haul our substantial yard, garden and hedge trimmings to a mulching company every few weeks. It enables me to pull trailer loads of oak firewood and occasional building supplies to our cabin 80 miles up in the Cascades. It is cherry red, "Big Red".

Our house in town is surrounded by laurel hedges up to 14 feet high that require heavy trimming at least once a year. I use a gasoline powered trimmer. I use a gasoline powered lawn mower to cut our grass and vacuum up several batches of leaves in the fall. I use a gas chainsaw to cut firewood. We have an outboard motor on the sailboat in case the wind dies when we're out in the middle.

I can walk to and from my office, but that takes 25 minutes each way. My weekly Rotary Club and Eugene Executive Association meetings are 1 and 4 miles from my office and home. Doing without any gasoline would require considerable change in my life-style. But I'd be willing to do it as part of a universal community commitment to eliminate fossil fuel use to save the planet.

I can also imagine our community having the right to decide what products and services are marketed here and a resulting significant reduction in the sale of handguns, violent video games and movies, soft drinks and foods that are high in refined sugars, tobacco products and pornography. The Wall Street Journal also recently reports that the soft drink giants are hurting for business. Americans are backing off on these drinks, probably because they're learning of their suspected contributions to obesity, diabetes, etc.

I've wondered if we should require banks that write home mortgages to keep the mortgages locally, rather than packaging them and selling them to investors through big commercial banks back east. I'd need to know more about this before I'd commit to the requirement, but it might make sense and might reduce the likelihood of another financial meltdown like the one in 2008 when packages of these mortgages dropped precipitously when housing prices slumped.

I can imagine that someday the Federal government will require large commercial banks, the ones that are "too big to fail", and too big to manage and too big to regulate, to have pre-approved plans for how they do business, including what products they buy and sell. I can imagine also that their top executives will have to pass extensive screening evaluations that measure their executive ethics and other attitudes relevant to greed, excessive risk-taking and groupthink.

I worry about fresh water supplies. We are blessed in Eugene with a source of very clean mountain river water, but our source is vulnerable. It comes from only one river. If that river were disrupted, as by an earthquake, we'd be in big trouble. With our population constantly growing, the need for a steady and secure water supply grows. I dream of a backup system of water and a steady, non-growing population for our community so we don't need so much water. In 2013 our rainfall locally was so low we couldn't put our sailboats in the local reservoir, for the first time in the 42 years I've lived here.

I dream of no more expansion of industrial and residential development on forest and farmland. We have some of the best farmland and Douglas fir timber land in the world in the Willamette Valley and adjacent Cascade Mountains. We need to preserve and protect it as such.

We have invasive species problems in our rivers and marshes. I dream of total control over these problems to protect our local ecosystems. Our lodge pole pine forests are succumbing to pine beetles, which survive the winters more easily now because of warmer winters…secondary to global warming, apparently. The pines die and then, when hit by lightning, burn fiercely, threatening summer homes and lodges in the forest areas. There was quite a pine fire just a couple of miles from our cabin a few years ago.

I dream too of total elimination of fossil fuel use, everywhere, as it warms the planet. As a kid, the lake in my home town back in Illinois froze over hard for several months every winter. It was groomed and plowed nightly by the park district and provided wonderful ice skating for the whole community. It even had lights at night. It had a boat house that in the winter had baskets in which you could store your shoes while you skated. They had amateur speed skating races on Saturday mornings. The state speed skating championships were held there some winters.

23 years ago our town here in Eugene built a wonderful ice arena. Along with others I helped create a speed skating club. We did short-track racing. We joined the national association of clubs. The executive secretary happened to live in my childhood hometown back in Illinois, Glen Ellyn. I spoke to her on the phone on club business and asked about Lake Ellyn. She said it no longer froze over enough in winter to skate on, apparently because of the warming climate. They'd had to build two indoor rinks like ours. Presumably they use electricity created by coal-fired plants to refrigerate the ice and warm the building, further dooming ice skating on the lake.

I can imagine a world without internal combustion engines in personal vehicles, or only ones that burn hydrogen, the exhaust from which is simply water in the form of steam. Before that, I can imagine trains and busses burning only hydrogen; they have the size to carry the heavy, high-pressure fuel tanks needed to keep hydrogen in liquid form.

I can imagine hydrogen made from water in the highly sunny nations of the world, capitalizing on solar energy to break water molecules into hydrogen and oxygen. The sunny nations would enjoy the economic prosperity previously enjoyed by the oil-producing areas of the world. Fossil fuels would no longer be burned. Oil would be used only for non-combustion products, such as lubricants, plastics, nylon, latex and paints.

I recall the theory discussed in Kevin Phillips' book, *American*

Theocracy, that empires have arisen often in nations that discover and develop a new source of energy, such as wind powering the Dutch seafaring empire, coal powering the British Empire and oil and atomic energy powering the United States Empire. I can imagine that the next empire might be based on hydrogen combustion, with the hydrogen produced by solar energy.

In light of the article cited above about babies with 200 synthetic chemicals in their bodies, absorbed from their mothers' wombs, I dream of rigorous government research and control of any chemicals that can easily pass into humans and jeopardize their health, in food products, as pesticides, as container linings, frying pan coatings, paints, gasoline, and solvents, such as turpentine and paint brush cleaners. And more immediately I dream of elimination of pesticides that kill honey bees, which are necessary to pollinate our food crops.

We've had some very large construction projects in our community, including a factory for Hyundai Semiconductor years ago and a giant, 200 million dollar basketball arena for the U. of Oregon, and currently a giant student housing complex covering 5 acres in the downtown area. All of these were designed and built by companies from outside the state, as I recall, even though our unemployment among construction trades here is very high.

In an ideal Eugene, I can imagine such projects being designed and built only by local designers and crafts-persons, only local contractors. I can imagine the boost to the local community of these workers' income cycling through the economy. I can imagine those persons feeling pride for decades over their accomplishments, showing their grandchildren the buildings they helped create. And I can imagine the rent paid by university student tenants going into the bank accounts of local investors instead of out-of-state investors.

In the ideal community, there would be solutions for some interesting conundrums. The better a community is, the more people it attracts to live there. How can a community that excels in services to the needy keep from being overwhelmed by people moving there for the benefits, e.g. homeless, unemployable folks? Or, as in our case at present, how can a community that is so pressed for jail beds that it lets criminals out after just a few days protect citizens from burglars and thieves that take advantage of minimal punishments?

A partial answer to the first problem might be sharing quality service techniques with neighboring communities so they can take good care of their own needy citizens. A partial answer to the second problem might be some sort of proportional budgeting system, where each department of government gets its share of the budget and all take hits when budgets wane and all benefit proportionally when budgets wax. This may mean that all public employees' salaries would also wane in hard times, so that none has to be laid off or no departments, such as public safety, have to be pared down to marginally functional levels. This may seem a radical departure from current policies, but ideal, sustainable communities may have to be managed in unexpected ways. And at the dream stage, the brain-storming stage, remember, anything goes. These are just ideas.

Another thing I'd like to see in an ideal community is a secure place for everyone, weak and strong, smart and dumb, extrovert and introvert, healthy and ill, ethnic minority as well as ethnic majority. In my work as a clinical psychologist I have been dismayed to see how uncomfortable my community seems to be with persons of below average intelligence. Half of any sizable community will have as many citizens who are below average as above average.

In Lake Woebegone, as lovingly depicted by Garrison Keillor (5) , all the children are above average. This would be the case in a fanciful ideal community, but only in a fanciful one. Most of the children I have evaluated for the Social Security Administration over several decades who come to the evaluation with histories of "attention deficit disorder" have simply been low on intelligence, sometimes in the borderline range (I.Q. between 70 and 79) and some in the mild retardation range, 55 to 69.

Years ago, a middle-aged man whom I had seen previously for counseling called to ask if I would be willing to evaluate his young adult daughter to help determine how she could enter the local university to get schooling so she could "make something of herself". I was happy to see her. She had graduated from high school, but instead of going to college, as her neurologist older brother had, she traveled around the country, supporting herself by waiting table. She was currently back in town, waiting table at a local restaurant and doing well at it. She was happy. She had no strong interest in college studies.

I suspected modest intelligence and gave her a standard I.Q. test. Her score was 85, in the low average range, at about the 15th percentile compared to other women her age. I also measured her Big Five personality traits. She had strong scores on them, especially on Agreeableness and Extroversion. I told her father that she was doing exactly what was appropriate for her, given her level of intelligence and her strong personality scores. Waitressing was just right. It was something that she was smart enough to do and that capitalized on her nice disposition. She was appreciated by her customers and made good tips. She was not smart enough to succeed in college or university coursework of substance. Her father was understanding and appreciative of the perspective this information provided.

My research on violence-proneness further highlights the importance of understanding and accepting the wide range of variation in human nature, and of providing a place for everyone in the community and providing services to those whose traits pose potential problems. There are many traits that put citizens at risk for criminal behavior in general and violence in particular. As you may recall, the traits measured by my 58-item questionnaires for teens and adults include feeling like a school or career failure, rigid thinking, not feeling guilt for wrong-doing, having unresolved anger, enjoying hostile activities, not being interested in counseling for personal problems, being unwilling to help stop violence, feeling socially rejected, and endorsing homicide as a reasonable solution to personal problems.

Scores on this questionnaire correlate positively and significantly with depression, anxiety and criminal record. They correlate negatively with the Big Five traits of Conscientiousness and Agreeableness. The questionnaire takes only 10 minutes to complete. Persons with elevated scores on such an instrument can be provided counseling services to nip problems in the bud. I imagine that in an ideal community, children and adults who are at risk for problems of this sort would be accepted for who they are and provided guidance and help, not just kicked out of school, fired from a job or incarcerated for misbehavior. For school children, such a policy might require a proportional budgeting system, so counselors aren't eliminated from staff when budgets wane.

In general, I like the idea of a system that protects all valuable programs in public schools, no matter what the budget is or how it may wax and wane. Thus, in the ideal community I'd hope to see this or some similar mechanism to assure a steady, balanced, automatically readjusting program of services to school children.

I'd also like the community to protect and provide jobs for citizens of all aptitude and ability levels and provide training to assure the needed skills. This is another conundrum issue. Technology advances provide valuable and less expensive goods and services, but paradoxically displace workers. And unfortunately not all displaced workers have the intelligence to be retrained in the newly created high tech jobs. An automobile production line welder may not be able to run a computer-driven robot that takes his place on an assembly line. And some moderately paying jobs are replaced with only low paying jobs, or none at all.

Similarly, a big national corporation may provide some savings in constructing exotic facilities, such as 200-million-dollar basketball arenas, but bypass qualified local workers. A person with average intelligence who could learn and succeed in a semiskilled trade as a carpenter, plumber or electrician in our community will have limited opportunities if we award too many contracts to out-of-state contractors with lobbyist and government connections.

Citizens with average or low-average intelligence who could be successful factory workers may have no place in a community that imports all its clothing, tools, carpets, furniture and food products from other nations with lower wages and standards of living. In an ideal community, imports may have to be limited enough to assure that all local citizens have meaningful employment.

I once included in a questionnaire study items that revealed that the majority of citizens in the study endorsed the idea of paying 20% more for goods and services if it meant that local citizens would have family-wage jobs. In an ideal community, citizens would have this option, in my thinking. They would also have opportunities to qualify for and work at jobs that use their best aptitudes and talents. And as a result, they could pay taxes to help support government services, including roads, parks and health care.

In essence, communities should be more than simply markets to be exploited. They should be living environments that carefully look after the citizens who live in them. And that empower their citizens to take an active, responsible and comprehensive role in assuring the sustainable quality of their communities.

Finally, ideal communities will be protected from direct or indirect tyranny by minority special interest groups, such as the oil industry or hand gun industry in the United States. A careful reading of the history of the U.S. Constitution reveals that the second amendment ("A well regulated Militia, being necessary to the security of a free State, the right of the people to keep and bear Arms, shall not be infringed") was created at the insistence of southern state slave owners. They controlled slaves with armed militias of white men. They did not want the federal government to be the only military power, one that could abstain from intimidating slaves to stay in line. The second amendment guaranteed these southern states that they could maintain their armed militias under state control.

Armed militias for slave control are irrelevant in the United States at present, so it would seem timely to change or even repeal the second amendment. An amendment that prohibits government from making laws, such as the second amendment prohibition of government to make laws preventing citizen gun ownership ("shall not be infringed"), seems bizarre. Government is citizens making joint decisions and managing their affairs jointly.

In my opinion it would be oxymoronic for citizens, as the government, to prohibit themselves from acting as the government. Government "infringes" on citizen's tendencies to rob, steal, embezzle, rape, assault, lynch and murder. Government can infringe on any citizen tendency that is deemed detrimental to the welfare of other citizens or their property or their collective property or welfare as a community.

A 6-year-old child might argue that he needs the kitchen paring knife in his pocket because he might need it to defend himself against a neighborhood dog. A responsible parent would overrule this argument on the grounds that it is more likely that the child would hurt himself or a friend with the knife. Citizens, as a government, can similarly argue that private citizen gun ownership is more likely to result in homicides and suicides than self-defense events, and that therefore citizen gun ownership is prohibited. Citizens can also point out that even self-defense can go terribly wrong, as it did for Oscar Pistorius, who shot his girlfriend to death when firing four shots through the bathroom door where he heard a sound and suspected an intruder in the middle of the night. At least that was his explanation of what others thought was premeditated murder in a couple who had a record of domestic conflict.

In ideal communities, majority opinion of informed, concerned citizens will be trusted to establish government policies and programs, with changes in even state constitutions and the national Constitution, as the majority of concerned, informed citizens choose.

As I was writing this chapter, which was about a month after the mass shooting in the preschool in Connecticut, I decided to sell all of my own guns. I hadn't used them for years. I had about 10…shotguns, rifles and a pistol. I didn't think I needed them to protect myself from anyone or that the value in that was greater than the danger of misuse. We have a city police department and a National Guard at the state level. Our federal armed forces are more than enough for protection at the national level, in my thinking.

I shuddered that same week when I heard a comment from a young man on whom I was doing a comprehensive psychological evaluation for a local attorney, who was to represent the fellow before a judge in a Social Security hearing. The fellow had been in jail about 10 times. During the interview he told me that if he wasn't a felon, from a prior gun charge, he'd carry a gun all the time when out in public.

Why? "To protect myself and my family. Because of all the shootings I read about, the homicides and stuff", he explained. Later I scored his tests and saw that they confirmed his interview comments about feeling very paranoid all the time. I imagined that paranoid persons may shoot first and ask questions later. He had very high scores on several facets of the At Risk for Violence test, including Homicide Endorsement. His score on the Paranoia scale in my Anxiety and Worry test was also very high.

After Common Good Party members brainstorm ideas, they will write questionnaire items to measure public opinion with a poll. Consider the item examples in Table 1 for the several topics touched on above. This questionnaire does not have many items on each topic, so if it turns out to be a reliable measure, it would only be a measure of "ideal community", or some such general concept.

It will be interesting to see if it is a reliable scale, for the concept of "ideal community" is itself an important one.

Table 1. Sample questionnaire of ideal community items.

Please indicate how strongly you agree or disagree with the items below using this code:

1	2	3	4	5
Strongly disagree	Disagree	Neutral	Agree	Strongly agree

1 2 3 4 5 1. Our community should have at least one pubic park monument to celebrate or promote international peace.

1 2 3 4 5 2. Any community that has a monument to war ought to have at least one monument to peace.

1 2 3 4 5 3. Citizens in our state should have the right to limit what sorts of movies or television programs are marketed in their community.

1 2 3 4 5 4. I disapprove of some types of movies that are shown in our local movie theaters, television programs or over the Internet.

1 2 3 4 5 5. The citizens of our community should be invited to contribute ideas about how to make our community better.

1 2 3 4 5 6. We should poll local citizens to get clear and reliable measures of features they want our community to have.

1 2 3 4 5 7. We should try to design our community to be sustainable for generations.

1 2 3 4 5 8. We should encourage government research on chemi-

cals in our blood that we inadvertently absorb from our environment and that could harm our health.

1 2 3 4 5 9. Government should regulate and control processes in the community that could or do expose honey bees and citizens to dangerous chemicals via foods, pesticides, gasoline or other products.

1 2 3 4 5 10. I would be willing to cooperate with a community-wide effort to reduce our use of all fossil fuels.

1 2 3 4 5 11. I would be willing to cooperate with rationing of gasoline and diesel fuel, and reduce my use by 10% per year.

1 2 3 4 5 12. I would be willing to change my yard design to eliminate grass so it doesn't have to be cut with a power mower.

1 2 3 4 5 13. I would be willing to limit my automobile use to just 3 days per week, scheduling my car trips as necessary.

1 2 3 4 5 14. I would like a section of my local newspaper to regularly report research on how to avoid ingesting foods and drinks that may contain unhealthy chemicals, and exposure to other dangerous chemicals.

1 2 3 4 5 15. If I have a home mortgage, I would prefer to have it with a local bank that keeps it at the bank instead of packaging it up and reselling it.

1 2 3 4 5 16. Government and our local state universities should do research to determine the "carrying capacity" of towns and counties in our state so we can plan for limits on population so we don't overwhelm our resources and so we can protect our farm and forest land for unending productive use.

1 2 3 4 5 17. The citizens of our community should vote on large local construction projects to assure that local compa-

nies and workers have jobs rather than having them contracted to outsiders.

1 2 3 4 5 18. Our community should adjust its imports to the community to help assure that all local citizens have jobs, as by producing locally as much as we can of what we use.

1 2 3 4 5 19. Our public high schools should provide training for students who are better suited for crafts and service jobs than for college and university courses.

1 2 3 4 5 20. I would support a thorough review of the Second Amendment of the national Constitution and a repeal or revision of it if deemed necessary to reduce gun violence among our citizens.

1 2 3 4 5 21. Politically, I think of myself as conservative.

1 2 3 4 5 22. Politically, I think of myself as liberal.

For practice, you can get forty persons to complete this questionnaire. Take the results to a local college or university and ask a research psychologist or sociologist to run the statistics, computing the mean and standard deviation for items 1-20. For an added insight, have them run Pearson product moment correlations between each item and the total score for all of the first 20 items. If they all correlate significantly with the total score, they form a reliable scale or measure.

If you can get 200 persons to take the questionnaire, including 40 strong liberals and strong conservatives, compute the mean score for both of these groups and compare them. Items 21 and 22 provide the measures of liberal and conservative political orientation. "Strong conservatives" will be those persons with scores of 4 or 5 on item 21. "Strong liberals" will be those with scores on item 22 of 4 or 5.

If you feel creative, do your own brain-storming and add more items to the questionnaire before you administer it and compute your statistics.

If you enjoy this process, you'll get a good taste of what it will be like to be part of a political party designed to promote the common good.

Chapter 30

Commencement

All God's creatures got a place in the choir
Some sing low and some sing higher
Some sing out loud on the telephone wire,
And some just clap their hands or paws or anything they got
now.

—Bill Staines

We have reached the end of our journey. But only the journey of design. For the design to take form, craftsmen and craftswomen will be needed.

My wife has repeatedly instructed me that for this project to take wing, an inspirational leader will be needed. By this, she means me. She thinks I'm a good public speaker, when I don't refer to too many numbers.

I am willing to help people create a new party, but for several reasons I am not the one to lead the charge. I am not by disposition or training an organization leader. And I think this party needs to germinate almost spontaneously in many places at once, not in only one place. Thus, many leaders in many communities must step forward. If the movement is highly centralized it will be easier to infiltrate and sabotage by those who find common good government threatening to their special interests.

I am willing to help, especially with creating questionnaires and related issues. But I may have limited opportunities to do so. I am 74 years old. During the past couple of years (2012-13) I have been diagnosed with and cured of large B-cell non-Hodgkin's lymphoma. While my oncologist presents a very optimistic prognosis for disease-free living for years to come, this brush with mortality has been a wake-up call. I have been working full-time for over 40 years since graduate school. There are national parks that my wife and I have never seen, bed and breakfasts that beckon and wall-eyed pike in Ontario that have my name on them.

Gene Sharp's book *From Dictatorship to Democracy*, translated into over 30 languages, has inspired and guided citizens in many nations to promote transitions from dictatorships to democratic forms of government in their nations. Gene is in his eighties and is not an activist. I hope my book will find a similarly vibrant audience without my direct involvement.

Some readers of this book will just talk to others about its ideas. Some will inspire others to read it and then have a meeting to exchange ideas. I hope that some will feel moved to start chapters of a new political party. Churches could sponsor chapters of the party, as could colleges and universities.

Current organizations, such as the Occupy movement, the League of Women Voters and even Rotary International, could conceivably morph into this new party.

Chapters of the new party will require many talents, including leadership, bookkeeping and accounting, secretarial services, research services, public speaking, legal counsel, committee work, and even arranging for meals, snacks and beverages. It will require meeting space, as in churches, grange halls or hotel conference rooms. It will require money, legal services, research on political issues and public service announcements, invocations and inspirational music and singing. There will be a place for virtually every citizen's talents and contributions.

Whatever your place in the choir, may the universal spirit of human goodness and kindness be with you all. And may you together make lovely political music, and be happy in your efforts.

When you get one of your party candidates elected to public office, have a party. It will truly then be "Party Time"!

One last urging: "Do democracy."

This is an admonition of Abbie Hoffman. Abbie was an American actor, writer and activist: "Democracy is not something you believe in or a place to hang your hat, but it's something you do. You participate. If you stop doing it, democracy crumbles."

In short, Abby believed that democracy is not something that people just have, it is something you do. If you don't do democratic government it can be replaced with other forms of government, such as oligarchy or dictatorship.

Oligarchy is rule by the few, typically the rich, the elite. The Occupy Movement's slogan, "We are the 99%", asserted that they represented majority public interests, not the elite, super-rich few. They wanted the oligarchic democracy of the United States revised to government promoting majority interests. You have seen in my research results of the Occupy Movement and other citizens that the majority of citizens, from both the left and right, endorse key goals of the Movement.

At meetings of psychology profession leaders, I have heard it said that if you aren't a discussant at the lunch table, you are lunch. If psychologists don't make a place for themselves in meetings where the interests of their profession are at stake, then their interests will take second place to those of other institutions, such as physicians, psychiatrists, insurance companies and governments.

So, if citizens in democracies are passive and uninvolved, their interests will be superseded by those of small, strongly self-interested, wealthy minorities, such as large corporations, the defense industry, commercial banks, tobacco companies, etc., etc.

So, I encourage you to do democracy, but not just any democracy. Don't just vote among special interest group candidates. Don't settle for special interest group democracy, oligarchic democracy.

Do common good democracy.

Start by discussing this book with a friend. If that goes well, add another friend. Build from there.

Good luck.

CHAPTER 31

EPILOGUE: COMMENCEMENT LESSONS AND DISCOVERIES

FIRST DISCIPLE

After completing this book manuscript and while waiting to hear from a local publishing agent, I received a call from a fellow who introduced himself as Chris Page. He'd been referred to me by a mutual friend, who is a member of my church and a peace activist.

Chris wanted to read my manuscript, as he was very interested in trying to fix national government. He is a semi-retired building contractor and had thought of running for political office. A consultant had suggested he write a book to make a name for himself in the field of politics, but Chris didn't think he had the skill for that.

I printed a copy of the manuscript for him. In a few days he had read it and wanted to get together to talk. He was very excited about the book. We met and soon he was explaining that he wanted to promote my model for a new party, starting by talking to others about it, including several close friends who were also well-versed in business, politics and related matters. These included a pastor and a retired business executive, Earl, who had run a large company in the aerospace industry for fifteen years after turning it around. Earl had also worked successfully as a book editor.

Soon thereafter Chris and I met and brain-stormed together. Chris had talked to leaders in the local Democratic and Republican parties and had plans to talk with Congressional Representative DeFazio's office. He had an appointment with Senator Ron

Wyden as well. He planned to drive across the country to the East Coast to a family wedding in a month and thought he could stop in at least three cities in each state along the way to spread the word about the political party model I proposed in the book. He wondered if I had any objections. I didn't.

He introduced me to his friend, Earl, who offered to edit the manuscript, having read it and thinking the model was very promising. He had ghost written about 20 books himself. He said the manuscript was interesting, clear and needed only a little editing of content and paring out of some material that he judged was peripheral to the main message. I agreed.

Earl also recommended self-publishing initially via a print-on-demand service. The strategy was to sell 5,000 copies in this mode, then approach a big commercial publisher. I followed his suggestions and located a local publishing agent, Patricia, who could engineer the print-on-demand services and coordinate other needed services.

Chris wanted to leave in two weeks. He knew some local folks who might provide him with travel funds. He had a friend in Denver who had lined him up for a visit with a personal friend, the Secretary of State in Colorado. Chris called the Pew Trust and arranged a meeting with them in Washington, D.C. He showed us the two-page spiel he was using to present the book model to listeners. It was clear and catchy. Earl and I made a few editorial contributions to improve it.

Patricia helped us design and print a few dozen paperback copies of a 50-page promotional piece for Chris to carry across the country on his road trip for interested persons at his presentations. It included the book table of contents and two sample chapters. She used an on-demand publisher back east to do the printing.

We discussed strategy. Chris wanted to know if I wanted him to concentrate on selling the book or encouraging people to start chapters of a new party. I said to play it by ear, just spread the word and see where it led. He said he had his own 501-c-3 corporation that might be used to start the party and would talk to his attorney about that.

Earl discussed the importance of looking for an opportunity to replicate some of my key studies on large, random samples of U.S. citizens, to meet the expectations of sophisticated scientists. I agreed and pointed out that if we could find a sample of citizens from around the country, they could simply go to my web site and complete a key questionnaire, specifically, Study #15.

Chris pointed out that all of the people he'd talked to so far seemed open-mined, and many expressed much interest. The Pew Trust was very interested, but only do "Big" projects. Chris thought this would qualify as "Big" in their eyes. Earl thought eventually someone would offer to fund a big replication study of the sort the Pew Trust could conduct. He thought that if my research findings were confirmed on a big sample of citizens that the project would "take off".

We joked about me appearing on Stephen Colbert, John Stewart or Bill Moyers' T.V. programs. I was cautiously optimistic, but certainly buoyed by this enthusiasm and did everything my schedule permitted to ride the wave of their interest and help. Soon Chris was on his way across the country.

He stopped along the way at the Vote Smart headquarters in Montana and visited with the Secretary of State of Colorado. He found some in his audience recommending, as Earl had, a replication of my key study findings to test their broader validity. He had second thoughts and returned home. Then there was a delay for several weeks, as one of Chris' elderly brothers, who had had a stroke some years earlier, needed help. Earl's elderly mother also needed Earl's help for a few weeks.

Before Chris' trip, he and I had met with the executive director of the local Democratic Party, Julie, and a local church pastor, to discuss the book ideas. I met again later with Julie. She was very interested in techniques for assessing candidates for office via rating scales, as I discuss in a chapter of the book, one that had been included in the promotional piece. She explained to my surprise that her Party does not sponsor or pick candidates for political office. Anyone can run for office, she said. All her Party can do is to endorse a candidate. She wanted tools for sizing up candidates to see which would most likely promote the common good if elected.

I asked her what she thought of the requests by folks Chris had talked to, the requests for more research data, as on a random sample. She thought this was an excuse to avoid accepting the implications of the book research. I offered to explore building a questionnaire specific to her Party's interest in assessing candidates from afar with a rating scale and asked her to meet with colleagues and brain-storm to develop a list of desirable characteristics or traits. She agreed.

Reflecting on her comments later, I realized that Julie's focus on assessing current candidates was actually peripheral to what my new party model points to. Especially regarding assessing candidates that are self-selected rather than Party-selected. But, I was willing to work with her, as she was generally quite interested in my book model.

I had another meeting with Chris to help him find a focus for activity. I realized his forte was promoting projects, more than creating a project, in this case a chapter of this new party. He kept referring to the need for much money to start a new party. This had been a concern of Julie's as well, as her Party has limited funds even for their current modest local operations.

I sensed that both Julie and Chris, each for their own reasons, were not ready to start a chapter of a new party and were perhaps coming up with their own excuses for not doing so. I told Chris that rather than spend a lot of further energy talking up the model in my book he should wait until we had it published in full and then sit down with others who have read it and brain-storm together about its implications and their ability and willingness to start a party chapter.

Church comments

Our new Congregational Church pastor and his wife held social meetings at their home, 15 persons at a time, to become familiar with members of the church and us with them. I chatted with his wife over coffee and cookies before the formal conversation began. She had read the promotional pamphlet and found it quite interesting. She said it was very dense, full of ideas, and that she would get more out of it if she could discuss it with others who had also read it. She thought it would be a great college text book, to be explored by students in class discussions, etc. She also suggested I contact NPR, National Public Radio, thinking they'd be very interested in it, as for an interview with me about the ideas and implications.

Her husband, the pastor, was open to my suggestion during the formal meeting about doing questionnaire research of church members to clarify what they want from a church experience to help the church, locally and nationally, address steadily waning memberships across all denominations in recent decades. He made a note for himself and suggested we talk more about that later. I found both his and his wife's responses to be quite encouraging.

I was also interested to hear from the dozen or so church members during our general meeting at the pastor's house. Many had come from disappointing experiences in other church denominations, either as children or adults. A rather universal thread in their answer to the pastor's question about what drew them to our particular church was a sense of "home", kindred spirits, persons seeking religious and spiritual answers. They also appreciate our church's support and a respect for independent thinking. They appreciate the de-emphasis on dogma and the warmth, caring and support they feel from our church members. The pastor's wife explained that she and he had also been drawn to our particular church because of this quality of human kindness. There was very little mention of either Jesus or God as central concepts during this meeting, and even the Bible was referred to more as a challenge to comprehend than a clear guide to spiritual and religious support.

I suggested that the concept of *universal spirit of human goodness and kindness*, perhaps touched on in the New Testament as the "Holy Spirit", was the concept that best captured the spirit of kindness and support that drew many of us to this particular congregation.

The pastor said that the Congregational Church he last led back in Connecticut was much more conservative and constrained than ours, perhaps captured most succinctly in the self-image of those Easterners as "God's frozen chosen."

REPLICATION STUDIES ON LARGE RANDOM SAMPLES

I had mixed feelings about the call from Earl and some of Chris' various contacts for replication of my studies on a large random sample of Americans. I knew it was a reasonable expectation, because I was generalizing from local samples. Until one has firm data on a representative sample of a whole population, it is appropriate to generalize only with caution.

While my samples had included University of Oregon students from around the world in one study, first generation Eastern Europeans in another and students and other citizens from New York, Kansas, Wisconsin and Florida in others, and while my findings were consistent with those by other researchers in as many as forty nations around the world, I still did not have data directly from a study of a random sample of U.S. citizens.

I told Chris that it would be relatively easy to do such a study.

Study #15 on my web site measures all the basic dimensions on which I had found the key data on liberals and conservatives; all we needed to do is get a random sample of, say, 1500 U.S. citizens to go to the web site and complete this questionnaire. It takes only about 20 minutes. But, we'd have to find a research organization that had a random sample of persons willing to do such a study and money to pay this organization and the persons who they'd have complete the questionnaire.

Chris and Earl had expressed confidence that we could find both the funding and a research organization that could do a random sample study. But I felt impatient and eager to get the book on the market. I made a few calls to organizations Chris thought might be willing to do the study, but they turned out to be dead ends. I bided my time, busy with other projects.

Then, my friend, Lew, from Oregon Research Institute sent me a reference to a study done by a professor using the General Social Survey data files for subjects (1). The traits were selected to reflect characteristics of persons by their Zodiac signs, as predicted by astrology. The study documented no meaningful differences on personality traits between groups of Americans of differing birth months. In effect, the study suggested that astrology is not scientifically valid.

This gave me an idea. I had been introduced to the General Social Survey (GSS) data files while attending the Stanford Summer Institute in Political Psychology in 2007. This was a three week intensive sponsored by the International Society of Political Psychology. Another student and I had used the GSS files to do a research project for class. The GSS is an interview survey of a random sample on U.S. citizens conducted every four years since 1972. It asks persons for information with hundreds of questions about all sorts of social and politically relevant issues. The data is stored in electronic files that any researcher can download and study, for free.

The General Social Survey research is supervised by staff at the University of Chicago and is highly respected as a research system. For example, by coincidence, my wife showed me an article in the New York Times by Arthur Brooks, president of the American Enterprise Institute, a public policy think tank in Washington, D.C. (2). This article, "A Formula for Happiness", summarizes findings from the GSS data and other sources that elucidate the origins of human happiness. Happiness, it concludes, is 40 percent due to genetic predisposition. In terms of politics, conservative women are the happiest. Liberal men are the least happy.

Brooks describes the GSS data as "the richest data available to social scientists" and "the scholarly gold standard for understanding social phenomena." If I could find GSS data that replicated my findings, I should satisfy critics' call for a large random sample. The American Enterprise Institute appears from the Wikipedia web site to be a clearly conservative organization. If their president, Arthur Brooks, respects GSS data, then even doubting conservatives might respect what this data source might show about variables paralleling my local research findings.

I upgraded my SPSS software and downloaded data for several different GSS surveys: 1987, 2008 and 2012. I was excited by what I found. The surveys include sensitive seven-point measures of both liberalism-conservatism and Democratic-Republican Party preference. They include data on religious beliefs, including several dimensions of religious fundamentalism, and attitudes about government spending for military, foreign aid and welfare programs. They even include several items measuring gender attitudes, such as the notion that women should confine themselves to family life and leave political issues and running the country up to men.

I ran statistics and was delighted to find essentially the same phenomena that I had seen in my studies of smaller, local samples of college and university students, church members, Occupy members, homeless persons, etc. Liberals and conservatives differed slightly but significantly on political trait measures when computed by correlation coefficients but were relatively close together as groups in terms of their average scores on these same traits. The data provided measures on military, welfare, environment and race issues, gender issues and even whether persons had pistols or revolvers in their homes.

Liberals tend to want less military spending and more spending for welfare and environmental protection programs. Conservatives tend to endorse fundamentalism, and military spending, own pistols or revolvers, expect women to be subservient to men and are less keen on government help for minority group citizens. But, both groups, strong liberals and strong conservatives, are relatively close together on all these dimensions, in terms of their average group scores.

These findings were based on random samples of over fifteen hundred citizens in each survey year. This addressed the critics' call for a national random sample replication of my studies. I wrote up my findings as a research paper and published it on my web site (3). And there was a bonus benefit from this research. I included in the paper additional information from the GSS data files about the proportion of the population that hold liberal and conservative worldviews, as presented in Table 1.

TABLE 1. PROPORTIONS OF LIBERALS, MODERATES AND CONSERVATIVES IN GSS SAMPLES.

	Number/Percent	Number/Percent	Number/Percent
GSS Sample date/size	"Strong" liberal	Moderates: most central, and some leaning slightly to liberal or conservative	"Strong" conservative
1987, N = 1679 total	281, 17%	1145, 68%	253, 15%

2008, N = 1933	309, 16%	1229, 64%	395, 20%
2012, N = 1872	325, 17%	1187, 63%	360, 19%

Fully two thirds of the population falls in the mid-range between those who think of themselves as strong liberals or strong conservatives. The "strong" categories include those who think of themselves as "Liberal" or "Extreme Liberal", or "Conservative" or "Extreme Conservative", respectively in the GGS surveys.

Only about a sixth of the population is in the strong liberal category and another sixth in the strong conservative camp. From what we see and hear in the newspapers, television and other media, you'd think most citizens are either liberal or conservative. However, only a third clearly are. The majority of citizens fall in between, seeing themselves as moderates, with some leaning a bit left and some a bit right but most feeling no clear pull either to the left or right. These are the citizens who the liberal and conservative groups try to sway to their camps during elections.

In terms of a political party that tries to unite liberals and conservatives, such as the Common Good Party I model in the present book, this data takes on special meaning. Presumably such a party would have members in the proportions presented above, 1/6 strong liberals, 1/6 strong conservatives and 2/3 moderates. If the party purports to promote government that is "of, by and for the people", then party polls should clearly honor the opinions of all party members. As a result, platform agenda items will reflect not so much the interests of liberals or conservatives per se but the interests of the moderate majority.

We can imagine this moderate majority saying to liberals and conservatives in the party: "You folks can give us your best arguments for how you think things should be done, but in the final analysis, it will be up to us moderates to vote in our polls and decide by our sheer majority numbers how things are to be. And we don't want any deception, lies or other misrepresentation of issues in your arguments; we'll be studying the issues ourselves too, so don't try to pull the wool over our eyes." In such a party, the majority will not be "silent" but will have the loudest voice of all.

Then, a couple of weeks later in January of 2014, I read in the newspaper of a talk that day at the local Downtown Athletic club, sponsored by the City Club of Eugene. It caught my interest and I was free to go to the lunch hour meeting. The presenters were Tom Bowerman of Policy Interactive and Adam Davis of DHL, polling companies in Eugene and Portland. They had done studies of large random samples of Oregonians recently, measuring their political attitudes. The majority of citizens, they found, wanted protection of our state environment and open land, development of public versus private transportation systems, a national health-care program and several other programs. During the Q and A I asked if they had measured liberal and conservative political orientation and if their data files were available for other researchers to study. The answer to both questions was "yes".

I met with Tom the following week and found him to be passionately interested in environmentalism and public polling, which he had learned by doing for the past seven years with the guidance of many experienced pollsters. Adam's company in Portland was a very experienced for-profit corporation, he explained. Tom sent me the data file in SPSS format and the codebook that explained each item of the questionnaire. The file was on almost 1200 Oregonians studied in 2013.

I analyzed the data and again found what I had seen in my prior studies: liberals and conservatives consistently differed on political attitudes in terms of correlation coefficients, but were relatively close together on most of these same attitudes in terms of mean group scores for strong liberals and strong conservatives.

The majority of citizens endorsed a primarily constructive political agenda, including a national health care program, protection of the environment, public transportation, improved K-12 and higher education, aid to low income citizens and energy conservation and efficiency programs. The data was interesting especially because it measured more specific government programs than I had measured or seen in the GSS surveys, including emergency and disaster preparations, school funding at different levels, public transportation programs, cost control programs for essential medical services and government spending to create jobs and rebuild infrastructure.

The questionnaire demonstrated how public opinion polling could measure not just general public attitudes but also specific public preferences on detailed policies and programs, giving elected officials a specific agenda for government.

I was able also to replicate the frequency data regarding the numbers of liberals and conservatives in the general population, finding about 1/6 strong liberals, 1/6 strong conservatives and 2/3 in between, virtually the same as for the national data in the General Social Surveys.

I wrote up my analysis and published it on my web site as Publication # 41 (4) and sent it to Tom. The same day he invited me to join him in a panel presentation of the study findings at the upcoming Environmental Law Conference at the University of Oregon later in February. He said it was the largest such conference in the country and would be attended by thousands of researchers, professors and students. He had planned to do it with Adam, but Adam had been called out of state on business. I accepted with pleasure. We made a lunch date to plan our presentation.

I shared these GSS and Oregon data analysis results with Chris, Earl and Julie and told my book publishing agent that it was full steam ahead. I told her I'd have the manuscript revised and references included in a few weeks, at which time we could go to press.

Acknowledgements

I AM VERY GRATEFUL FOR HELP FROM MANY PERSONS AND RE-search subjects in pursuing my research in political psychology and related topics over the past many years, especially from Professor David Leung, Lane Community College, Pastor Ted Berktold, several professors at the University of Oregon, Lew Goldberg of Oregon Research Institute, and Sam McFarland, professor of psychology at Western Kentucky University and past president of the International Society of Political Psychology. Students at Lane Community College and the University of Oregon, and inmates at teen and adult incarceration facilities in Oregon were also very helpful, as were students at public schools in an entire Oregon town, and from universities in New York and Florida. Especially generous with their time in completing questionnaires were members of several Eugene churches and even homeless persons in Occupy Eugene camps and food kitchens in Eugene.

I am particularly grateful to the International Society of Political Psychology, the Midwestern Political Science Association and the Stanford Summer Institute in Political Psychology for stimulating learning and sharing opportunities. I am grateful also to many editors and reviewers of journals and book manuscripts who have processed several of my research writeups. I am also very grateful to Patricia Marshall, Jennifer Revoal, Earl Strumpell and Chris Page for their help in book publishing, editing and promotional guidance and efforts.

I am especially grateful to Tom Bowerman for his permission to analyze Oregon polling data and to the General Social Survey for providing access to large random sample data files to replicate my findings on State and national populations.

Finally, I am deeply grateful to my wife, children and friends, as good listeners and commentators on my research findings and their implications.

DISCUSSION GUIDE

General Overview

Party Time! How You Can Create Common-Good Democracy Right Now allows the reader to explore the psychological traits that make up people's worldviews and explores how strong liberals and strong conservatives as groups are actually very close together in their desire for better government. This book offers significant hope that both groups can merge to promote a new form of democracy that serves not special interest groups but rather the common good. *Party Time!* summarizes research that leads to this prediction, details how local citizens can create a new kind of political party that works for us all, and thus offers a workable blueprint for a brighter future.

LEADING DISCUSSIONS

Leading discussions is both a skill and an art. There are many resources on how to lead good book discussions as well as how to facilitate group dialogue. Here are some sources to consider:

Iowa Center for the Book

http://www.iowacenterforthebook.org/discussion-groups

How to Facilitate Group Discussions

www.uhs.berkeley.edu/home/news/pdf/groupdiscussion.pdf

Section 1.
Psychological Traits That Underlie Politics

Chapter 1. Understanding Our Minds Explains Much About Politics

1. Columnist Kathleen Parker writes that government by representatives of the "moderate middle" would be better than government representing one or another extreme, right or left, conservative or liberal. You can see her full article at: https://www.washingtonpost.com/opinions/kathleen-parker-a-brave-new-centrist-world/2013/10/15/ea5f5bc6-35c9-11e3-be86-6aeaa439845b_story.html

2. Do you agree or disagree?

3. Dr. McConochie maintains that partisan politics is too prone to "gridlock" to effectively address big problems such as global warming, gun control and international wars. Do you agree? If not, why not?

Chapter 2. When Is an Opinion Not an Opinion?

1. Do you agree with the author that a reasonable definition of personal truth is those personal beliefs upon which we are willing to base our behavior? (p. 11). If so, why? If not, why not? Do you understand why the author differentiates personal truths from scientific truth? Is this important? Why? Why not?

2. Political parties in the United States do not have direct control of who runs for political office under their banners. (p. 13). Did you know this? Do you think they should have control over candidates that claim to be of their party? If so, why? If not, why not? Was the Republican Party in control of Donald Trump in his 2016 bid for the Presidency?

3. Dr. McConochie asserts that whether humans are basically competitive or cooperative is more a matter of personal opin-

ion than of scientific fact (p. 13-14). What is your view on this? How would you differentiate between personal opinions and scientific facts on this issue?

Chapter 3. The Killer Mind: Violence Proneness and Warmongering Endorsement

1. What psychological dimensions does the author discuss that might incline a person to be violent? Can you think of any additional psychological dimensions? (p. 20).

2. Does it surprise or worry you that some teenagers and some adults in the United States endorse each of the homicide endorsement items on page 21? Can you think of another such statement that might be a reliable measure of homicide endorsement in a questionnaire?

3. Similarly, does it surprise or concern you that some citizens endorse each of the statements in the 10-item Warmongering Endorsement scale? (p. 26). Do you know anyone personally whom you think might endorse these items?

4. Does the term "warmongering" itself bother you? Does it make you doubt the objectivity of the author? Would it be wiser for him to have used a different term or would that have whitewashed an unflattering human trait that needs to be clearly understood for what it is?

5. Are you surprised at how many traits warmongering endorsement correlates with? Do any of these correlations surprise you? Why do you suppose warmongering endorsement correlates with so many types of fear, and especially with fear in Americans of Muslims?

6. During the 2016 Presidential primaries Donald Trump was said to have attracted votes by persons who endorse authoritarianism, leadership characterized by very strong leader dictates that citizens are expected to follow without question. What does the correlation between warmongering endorse-

ment and authoritarianism in *Party Time!* (p. 31) suggest about the type of military activity that Trump as President might have been prone to promoting in the Middle East? Were the Big Five personality traits of low Agreeableness and low Emotional Stability evident in Trump's behavior during the primary debates?

Chapter 4. Terrorism Endorsement and Warmongering-Proneness

1. The Terrorism Endorsement scale (pages 36-37), which was developed using Americans, is statistically very reliable. Some Americans endorse each of these items, marking "Agree" or "Strongly Agree" on questionnaires. Persons with higher scores on this scale are truly different from persons with lower scores. Does this concern you? And what do we learn about persons with higher scores on this trait who also tend to endorse anarchy, defined as no government at all?

2. Do the scores for warmongering-proneness for various historical figures (p. 40) fit your understanding of how these persons behaved in real life? Would it be valuable for citizens to know the warmongering-proneness scores of candidates for political office before national Presidential elections? If so, who would you trust to do the ratings to get these scores? How could we minimize bias in the raters? If the average score on the scale for Obama by 6 conservative raters was close to the average scores for 6 liberal raters, 6 independent raters and 6 Canadian raters, what would that imply about the reliability of the scale?

Chapter 5. The Cozy Relationship between Religious Beliefs and Politics

1. Some citizens in the United States think that government and religion should be melded together, in spite of the Constitution provisions of separation of the two. Do you agree with melding religion and government or not? Discuss your opinions

with others. Do you think that the President should be sworn in with hand on Bible, pledging to serve "Under God"? Does this disrespect the interests of citizens who believe in a god other than the Christian God? Or of citizens who are atheists? Would you vote for an atheist for President? Must a President be religious? Christian? If so, why? What harm might there be in having an atheist for President? Or a Muslim? Or Jew?

2. Considering the questionnaire scale items presented in this chapter, do you think of yourself as primarily endorsing fundamentalist religious beliefs, kindly beliefs or neither? Are others close to you, such as family members, of the same religious orientation as you? If different, does the difference color your relationship with them? Do your religious beliefs color your political beliefs?

3. What do you make of the correlations between fundamentalism and warmongering-endorsement and endorsement of many fears? Why do you suppose these traits tend to cluster together statistically?

4. What do you think about the evidence for a second basic dimension of religious beliefs, "kindly religious beliefs"? Do you see reflections of this type of religious attitude in persons you know? In members of your faith?

5. Do you agree or disagree with the idea that U.S. Government officials should not say "God bless America" in public speeches? Discuss your opinions with others.

6. If religious beliefs are correlated with political ideology, how can this be constructively managed to avoid conflicts about what is taught in primary public school grades, and whether it is legal for gays to marry?.

Chapter 6. Activism, Protest and Hope: The Occupy Movement, Social Disenfranchisement, Oppression, Humiliation and Social and Political Activism

1. Does it surprise you that all segments of society, on average, endorse all of the Occupy questionnaire items as presented in this chapter? Does this mean that the Occupy movement did indeed speak for the majority of citizens?

2. What do you make of the relationship between endorsement of social disenfranchisement and endorsing anarchy, dictatorships and special interest group democracies? Why might persons who endorse the current form of democracy in the United States (that serves special interest groups) tend to feel vulnerable, helpless, treated unjustly, distrusting and superior?

3. Does it surprise you that persons who felt mistreated, oppressed or humiliated in childhood also tend to feel similarly toward authorities, governments and even religions in adulthood? Have your own childhood experiences colored your adult views of society, government and religion? If so, how?

4. What do you think of the notion of "promotional" versus "oppositional" forms of activism (pages 78-80)? Do you think of yourself as one or the other of these types of activist? Do you write letters to the editor of your local newspaper to express your views? Are letters to the editor a form of activism? Have you ever participated in a protest march? Are such marches promotional or oppositional? Is graffiti a form of activism? If so, what type, promotional or oppositional?

Chapter 7. Retirement Benefits: An Inadvertent Evil?

1. What do you think about the very high retirement benefits made available to some Oregon public employees? If you live in another state, what is the status of retirement benefit program for your state's employees? Is there enough money in the state retirement account to pay all the benefits mandated? What do you think about the fact that collectively the states of the United States have over 1 trillion dollars of public employee pension obligations for which the states have not set

aside sufficient funds to pay? How did such obligations outrun the money set aside? Or was the money lost in poor investments, such as those that were wiped out in the 2008 financial meltdown?

2. Discuss your reaction to the ordinary citizens acting so inhumanely in the Milgram and Zimbardo experiments (pages 89-91). Does it surprise you that many ordinary Germans were persuaded during the Nazi regime in the 1930s and 40s to commit atrocities against German Jews, all civilians in invaded neighboring countries and even against fellow non-Jewish Germans who opposed Hitler? Are all humans vulnerable to being misled in this manner? If so, how can nations guard against this tendency?

3. What do you think of the author's "proportional budgeting system" for managing public school budgets (pages 95-96)? What are its pros and cons?

Chapter 8. Foreign Policy, Human Rights and Executive Ethics

1. This chapter proposes that citizen opinions should be the main basis for *general* government program preferences. Should information, knowledge and facts be the basis for *specific* government program preferences? Do you think it is too much to expect citizens to be knowledgeable enough to vote on specific programs?

2. Would it be helpful to have citizens vote on foreign policy by completing the Foreign Policy Scale (page 101-102) in this chapter or scales like it? Should such scales be used to measure citizen preferred policies about waging war or about staying in or terminating wars initiated by the Congress or the President? If so, how should the poll results be used?

3. Do you think citizens should be polled to determine how strongly they endorse various human rights? Do you think citizen opinions would agree with those of religious leaders?

Educators? College and university philosophy professors? Members of Congress? The Supreme Court? Conservatives? Liberals? How should such citizen poll results be used?

4. Is it important to know the ethical beliefs of top corporate and political leaders and candidates for those positions? If so why? If so, how could citizens obtain reliable measures of those dimensions? By rating scales? If so, who should do the ratings? Would it be desirable for heads of banks that are too big to fail to be evaluated on ethical dimensions before they take such positions? Should they have to demonstrate certain ethical perspectives as a condition for leading such banks? Should candidates for the Senate, Supreme Court and Presidency also have to have certain ethical belief profiles? If so, what profiles and who should do the ratings? Would screening on leader ethics prevent the scandalous hoarding of public monies by political and industrial leaders around the world, as exposed on April 4, 2016 in the Mossack Fonseca off-shore money-laundering and tax evasion schemes?

5. If one half of one percent of adult citizens endorses in-group elitism and if one half of one percent of 1 million is 5000, how many of 150 million adult citizens in the United States are likely to endorse in-group elitism? Is that number enough to be of concern, knowing that this trait correlates positively with warmongering-endorsement, violence-proneness and authoritarianism?

Chapter 9. Government Type Preferences and Political Philosophy

1. Should we be concerned that the estimated 25% of citizens in the United States who endorse special interest group democracy also tend to endorse warmongering-endorsement and violence-proneness? Do you agree with the author that current U.S. government is a special interest group democracy? If so, would you rather that it be a common good democracy? Why? Why not?

2. Does it surprise you that U.S. citizens independently of government give as much as 166 billion dollars per year to charitable organizations? Do you agree that this is a reflection of the kindly religious beliefs orientation? Or could it include non-religious generosity and kindness? How could a questionnaire study answer these last two questions?

Chapter 10. Good Guys Versus Bad Guys

1. Consider the finding that 90% of community college students in one study endorse a "pro-government" cluster of traits (page 124). Some Republicans have said "the less government the better." What proportion of Republicans do you imagine are "anti-government"? Does it seem logical to you that persons who voice anti-government ideas could hold positions of elective office in the United States national government? Or does this seem an oxymoron? What does "oxymoron" mean? At what extreme does "anti-government" become traitorous, "a violation of allegiance to one's sovereign or state?"

2. The author has estimated from his studies that only about 1 percent of U.S. citizens are likely to endorse authoritarianism. Some persons opined that persons who endorsed Donald Trump for President in primary elections in 2016 tended to endorse authoritarianism. Is the endorsement of a candidate by one percent of the electorate significant when considering that person for the Presidency?

3. Does it make sense to you that evolution has resulted in humans of two general types, a majority who are primarily peace-loving and kind and a minority who are comfortable with warmongering? (p. 126 and following). If not by evolution, how else might we explain the presence of these two psychological trait clusters? What do you think of the finding that 5 percent of a class of over 200 University of Oregon students endorsed aggressive war, 70 percent defensive war and 25 percent no war participation? What would be the breakdown in your group, e.g. college or university students, church members, extended family members? What would the breakdown be at U.S. Military Academies? At religious seminary degree programs?

Chapter 11. Into the Political Fray

1. Does it interest you that the CIA has staff who develop psychological profiles on foreign leaders? Would you like to see psychological profiles that other nations develop on our leaders? Would it be valuable for U.S. citizens to know profiles on their candidates for elective office? If so, who could they rely on to create profiles that are objective and unbiased? A nonprofit organization specializing in such profiles? University professors? What value would such profiles have for voters? What desirable traits should government leaders have? What traits should they not have?

2. Do you see evidence of "mortality salience" in yourself or oth-

ers? (p. 133 and following.) Was this manifest in Nazi Germany? Did Hitler preach threat and fear to motivate Germans to rearm and aggress against Jews and neighboring nations? Do politicians running for President of the United States preach fear and threat to attract votes for themselves as "saviors" who can protect the nation from danger?

3. Discuss the results of twin studies (p. 136) that suggest political attitudes are 40 to 50% genetically grounded. Have you felt that your own political attitudes are to some extent deeply ingrained in you in a manner consistent with this?

Chapter 12. Jungle Politics: Biological and Evolutionary Origins of Conservative and Liberal Worldviews

1. Does the author's theory of an evolutionary origin of the conservative and liberal clusters of psychological traits make sense to you? If not, how would you explain these two clusters? Did they evolve to serve some other species-important function or functions? Were they creations of humans rather than of evolutionary forces? If so, how do you explain their presence world-wide?

2. Does the author's cluster of 10 basic dimensions of political discourse (p. 143 and following) cover all the important issues in politics? If not, what additional dimensions would you add? What important functions do your additions serve?

3. Conservatism correlates positively with disease phobia. Does this surprise you? Do you know conservatives who are disease phobic?

4. Which of the sample questionnaire items in Table 3 (pages 148 – 156) do you find most interesting? Why? Discuss this and listen to other people's choices. Do any of these run counter to your personal attitudes? For example, if you are conservative, do some of the conservative items seem alien to your political attitudes? If liberal, do some of the liberal items not ring true

for you? If they don't, the next chapter may explain why.

Chapter 13. The Psychological Anatomy of Liberal and Conservative Worldviews: The Secret to Making Harmonious Political Music

1. Should the media report accurate information about what the majority of citizens think and feel about political issues? Do the media instead tend to report the opinions of extreme liberals and extreme conservatives?

2. How important is it that much of the media, both newspapers, television news programs and news magazines are owned by just a few very large corporations controlled by relatively few citizens? Is this a recent development? In the interests of controlling costs and minimizing criticism of wealthy special interest groups, do media owners limit investigative reporting? Investigative reporting exposed the Watergate Hotel scandal of the Nixon administration burglary of democratic offices, the Catholic Church cover-up of for decades of child sexual abuse by priests, and dictatorship atrocities in many nations around the world. What are the pros and cons of such reporting? If corporations that own media outlets are engaging in corruption, will their investigative reporters be permitted to investigate and report such corruption? What risks might they run in doing so?

3. With the major media resources of our nation controlled by just a few corporations, how can the general citizen gain access to objective, in-depth news coverage of business and government doings that may jeopardize the welfare of the common good? Some citizens think this is one of the major issues of our time…our need for media that are independent enough from big corporations and from government to be able to investigate and report possible corruption in corporations and government. Do you agree? Discuss this with others. Keep in

mind that scores of journalists in other less democratic nations have been murdered for such investigative reporting.

Chapter 14. Are Worldviews Fixed or Flexible?

1. At a meeting of some of your friends, repeat the little study described on page 176, asking them how many grew up in families of all conservatives, all liberals or a mixture of the two. Do you get mostly "a mixture of the two"? Were your own blood relatives a mixture of the two, liberals and conservatives? Do you agree that most families are such a mixture? Does it make sense to you that this may reflect a genetic grounding of these two political worldviews? If not, why not?

2. The author concludes that biological and genetic data support the notion that political worldviews are largely a reflection of genetics (p. 180). Do you agree? The author offers his opinion that it is impractical to try to change either liberals or conservatives very much. Is this true or false in your experience? Can you imagine much hope for politics without changing one or the other, or both of these groups?

Chapter 15. Fear and Groupthink.

1. Does it surprise you that conservatism is associated with all sorts of fears? Can you see value in such fearfulness? Can you see a protective value?

2. Have you had personal experience with groupthink? Have you been in a group that became so insulated from other groups or individuals that it made foolish decisions? Have you made personal decisions based on too little information that turned out badly for you and wouldn't have if you had been more open-minded and careful?

3. Have you noticed candidates running for elective office lying in campaign speeches? Do conservatives do this more than liberals? Lying in court, which is perjury, is a crime. Why isn't lying in campaign speeches considered a form of perjury?

Who could we trust to serve as objective judges to detect campaign speech perjury? Or must we simply trust that private organizations and newscasters will provide such information?

4. Gerrymandering is the convoluted design of electoral districts to maximize the number of one's preferred political party seats in government. Why is this permitted? It is conniving? Would it be possible instead to create electoral districts objectively? Who could be trusted to do this?

Section III.
Creating a New Type of Political Party to Unite Conservatives and Liberals

Chapter 16. Party Time: Creating a New Type of Political Party:

Introduction and Overview

1. What is your first reaction to the idea of a new type of political party that bases its platform (agenda) on polls of the general public?

2. Do you think the majority of liberals and conservatives could work together in such a party? Why? Why not?

3. Are you attracted to the present Democratic or Republican parties? Do they invite you to participate in regular meetings in your community to have a meaningful role in grooming candidates for elective office? Would you like such a role?

4. Are you familiar with Rotary International, or other such organizations that provide services for the common good in communities, have regular meetings and attract community leaders as members to get things done?

Chapter 17. Specific Suggestions for Creating a Chapter of the Common Good Democratic Party: Basic Structure and Function

1. Are you familiar with Roberts Rules of Order? (For a quick

overview, see en.wikipedia.org/wiki/Robert's_Rules_of_Order).

2. How do these rules guide committee members in discussing issues, making decisions and taking constructive action to co-ordinate efforts to make things happen?

3. Complete the Sample Liberal Conservative Dimension questionnaire (Table 1B, pages 214-216). Does your score seem accurate? Does it place you on the liberal-conservative continuum where you have thought you would be? Does the exercise add to your self-understanding?

Chapter 18. Functions of the Polling and Research Committee

1. Would you be willing to complete a poll to help the political party of your choice define its agenda? Or should political party leaders decide the party's agenda?

2. What do you think of polls of party member opinions on political agenda issues? Would you like to be a member of a party that solicited your opinions to help it form its agenda? Do you feel qualified to make such decisions?

Chapter 19. Program, Mission and Ethics, Strategies and Networking Committees

1. Which of the committees presented in this chapter, if any, would you be interested in serving on if you were a member of this proposed party?

2. Do you think a political party of both liberals and conservatives could operate on the principle of cooperation or are humans too competitive about political opinions to work together constructively? Does the U.S. Congress demonstrate cooperation or competition more prominently?

3. If you were on the proposed Common Good Party networking committee, what other groups would you network with to strengthen the party chapter? How might such networking be helpful? Can you imagine this new party networking with lo-

cal chapters of the Democratic and Republican parties? If so, why? If not, why not?

Chapter 20. Selecting and Grooming Candidates for Elective Office

1. What do you think of a political party screening and grooming candidates for political office? Would this be better than the current absence of such practices in our system, which permit anyone to run for office, whether endorsed or not by a party the candidate claims to represent? What are the pros and cons of selecting and grooming candidates?

2. Does it seem reasonable to you to screen candidates for high political office on the Warmongering-Proneness scale? (pages 244 – 249) If so, why? If not, why not? If you were running for office would you mind being rated on this instrument by persons who know you well?

3. Do the scores on this scale for historical leaders (pages 249 -250) make sense to you? Consider rating a political leader with whom you feel quite familiar. Does the score you get place that leader on the continuum of leader scores in a position that you find reasonable? See if you can get a friend to rate a leader. Discuss your results.

Chapter 21. Constructive Leadership Traits

1. What do you think of the suggestions in this chapter for using many different techniques to screen candidates for leadership within party chapters and for elective office? Are they too complex? Are the too thorough? Do they require too much effort and expertise of a candidate selection and grooming committee? Is it necessary to be this thorough? What dangers does a political party run without such screening and grooming? Should just anyone be allowed to run for office under a party's banner? Were all the candidates running for President of the United States under the GOP banner in 2016 worthy of that office? Why did Mitt Romney speak out vigorously against

Donald Trump as a candidate in the middle of the race?

2. What do you think of assessing a Presidential candidate on warmongering-proneness? Would this be "over-kill"?

3. The term "warmongering" seems to upset some people. Should this trait be called something else? Or, should we call a spade a spade, use it, and expect candidates for high office to be willing to pass muster on this trait? Would it have been helpful to Europe to have had Hitler rated on this trait as he first sought political power in Germany? Are there political leaders in the world today that you would expect to have high scores on this dimension? Could we trust journalists or graduate students in political science classes to accurately rate political leaders and candidates for political or high military office? If so, how might this help to protect nations?

4. What do you think of rating leaders on "constructive leadership attitudes"? (pages 262 – 266) What do you expect this might add to assist citizens in casting votes for candidates? Does the scale for doing this seem comprehensive enough or are there dimensions that are important but not covered by the items in the scale? How could such dimensions be added to an improved scale? How could the scale be validated?

5. What do you think of the idea of assessing political candidates on the three dimensions of executive ethics: In-group elitism, messianic nationalism and common good concern? (pages 267 – 268) If you like this idea, how could rating scales be developed to assess candidates on these dimensions, assuming that we couldn't expect candidates themselves to be willing or able to provide unbiased responses on questionnaire measures? How could such rating scales be validated? Would avoiding candidates who are high on in-group elitism help to reduce the influence of wealthy special interest groups and money controlling government policies? Would it help reduce the threat of our nation engaging in warmongering? How

do the correlations in Table 2 (pages 268 – 270) inform your thinking on this issue?

Chapter 22. Preventing Corruption: System Sickness and Cures

1. Do you think it would be helpful to do extensive polling of citizens, insurance company personnel, physicians and others to come up with a design for a health care program for our nation? Might the design differ from the current one that was crafted by our government? If so, why? Were government decisions for our present system heavily influenced by health care providers? By insurance companies? By citizens? By physicians? Who had the most say? Who *should* have the most say in such decisions?

2. Can you think of other systems that might be "sick", in need of improvement? How about the job industry? The higher education industry? The population control "industry"? Are there too few good-paying jobs? Is higher education too expensive compared to 50 years ago? Is the world becoming overpopulated, considering that since 1940 it has tripled in size? Are world starvation, disease and warmongering activities a function of this rapid growth? Are current governments effectively addressing these three problem areas (jobs, education, over population)?

3. Is the increasing and steady rise in earth's temperature (global warming) a case of "system sickness"? If so, what fuels this rise (pun unintended)? Who profits from the sale of oil, natural gas and coal? Who benefits from the use of these fuels? If we are all benefitting in one way or another and are thus complicit in promoting this "system sickness", how can we develop the courage, political power and will power to cure it?

4. What are your feelings and thoughts about the author's research finding that human intelligence itself may be slowly waning as an apparent side-effect of world-wide air pollution?

If intelligence is indeed waning, from whatever cause, and at the rate suggested, do you have confidence that humans can prevent this mental decline and related inevitable collapse of civilization? What should be done? What can individual citizens, such as yourself, do to address this?

Chapter 23. Measuring What People Want From Government

1. Do you find helpful the statistics on how strongly citizens want various improvements in government services (Table 1, pages 286 - 289)? Should this sort of data be used to inform government policies, programs and priorities? Does your local city government do such polling to guide its decisions? How can you find out?

2. What do you think of the author's Proportional School Budgeting system? (pages 297 - 298) Do you think it is possible to use? Would teacher unions prevent its use? Would such prevention be appropriate in a democracy, or an expression of too much power in a special interest group?

3. What do you think of a code of ethics for a political party? Do the Democratic and Republican parties have codes of ethics? Do they have web sites? Are their codes of ethics on those sites?

4. Do you notice conflicts within yourself between your personal code of ethics, what is good for you as an individual, and your social code of ethics, what is desirable for you to do as a member of one or another social group?

5. Do you often think of yourself as a member of a town, city, college, sports team, the NRA, the Democratic party, your county, state, and/or nation?

6. Does your town have a code of ethics? If not, should it? If so, how could it be crafted, and by whom? What ethical principles might it espouse?

Chapter 24. Clues about Public Opinion across Political
Dimensions

1. If the religious fundamentalism trait is endorsed by only 6 per-
    cent of adult voters, should their desires for Christian teach-
    ings be allowed to determine public school curricula, e.g. the
    teaching of Creationism? Or, should majority attitudes deter-
    mine this issue?

2. Should the religious belief that a god/God has granted a given
    people the "right" to a given geographical territory, e.g. Isra-
    el to Jews, be honored simply because it is a religious belief?
    Should a religious belief that a god/God has told believers to
    kill non-believers be honored simply because it is a religious
    belief? Does the "common good" supersede religious beliefs?
    Are answers to these questions relative to the culture in which
    they are issues?

3. Do you agree with the author's suggestion that in the United
    States an incoming President should not be sworn in with
    hand on the Christian Bible and with an oath to serve under
    the Christian God? What are the issues involved in this mat-
    ter? How can such issues be best decided? Would it be reason-
    able to revise the ceremony depending on the religious faith of
    the incoming President? Even if she was a Muslim?

Chapter 25. More Citizen Attitudes: Social Group Belonging,
Gender Issues, Foreign Policy, Government Type Preference and
Economics

1. The author's Cultural Conservatism scale (page 322) corre-
    lates positively with conservatism and negatively with liberal-
    ism. Do the items in the scale seem typical of ideas expressed
    by conservative members of the U.S. Congress and candidates
    for political office?

2. Do the items in the Female Egalitarianism scale (page 326)
    seem consonant with Democratic Party policies and liberal at-

titudes, e.g. that women should have primary say in how many children they bear?

3. If only 8 percent of citizens endorse the Militaristic Philosophy Scale items (pages 326-328), how can the United States government maintain a rather constant military activity overseas for decades on end since World War II? Does this suggest that forces other than majority public opinion drive U.S. foreign policy? What might those forces be?

4. What are the implications of the percentage of citizens who endorse Power Politics Government (0%) and Common Good Government (88%) in the studies cited? (pages 330 – 332) What do the related statistics on these graphs tell you about liberalism and conservatism? What do they imply about whether the common good as defined by public opinion is driving U.S. government policy?

5. What do the related statistics for the two violence enabling and violence prevention scales (pages 335 – 338) suggest about whether U.S. civilian gun policy is determined by minority or majority group preferences?

Chapter 26. Social Group Relations, Leadership Type Preferences and Environmental Attitudes

1. The Power Oligarchy and Anti-Power Oligarchy scales (pages 341-343) have several items each. Which of these two scales do you tend to endorse? What if Congress were characterized predominantly by one or the other of these orientations? What might the implications be?

2. Donald Trump reportedly attracted support from persons who endorse authoritarianism. Do the items in the scale for this trait (page 344) seem consonant with how Trump campaigned and his campaign comments and behavior? Did he seem "authoritarian" in disposition? Do you see any dangers in authoritarian leadership? Advantages?

3. The environmentalism scale statistics reflect a strongly pro-environmentalism citizen orientation. (pages 346-348) Does U.S. government reflect such an orientation? If not, why not, given the very strong public endorsement of it? How can the public use information from such questionnaires to promote its desires?

Chapter 27. More Citizen Attitudes: Clues from Ten Additional Scales

1. Which of the 10 additional attitude scales catches your attention? (pages 350-358) Why? What does the scale imply about what the majority of citizens want from government? How can such scale statistics be used by citizens to promote their desires?

2. What does the 2% endorsement level for the Political Lying and Conniving scale (page 358) tell you about political campaign speeches? How would it guide you in preparing your own campaign speeches if you were running for elective office? If you opponent bad-mouthed you in the campaign, would you retaliate in kind or simply point out that the majority of citizens disapprove of bad-mouthing and that your opponent's tendency to do this seems to reflect either his/her ignorance of public opinion or indifference to it?

Chapter 28. Party Platform in a Nutshell

1. How does the hypothetical Common Good Party philosophy as summarized in this chapter sound to you? Does it appeal? If so, why? If not, why not? Can you think of issues that you would want that aren't addressed or included? Are there items that you would want omitted? Does the below 15-second "elevator speech" serve as an adequate thumbnail sketch of the party? "The Common Good Democracy party would base its agenda on good polls of the public and of party members, carefully groom its candidates for elective office and fund

their campaigns only from party member dues." If not, what is missing from it?

2. Do you know what the philosophies are of the Republican and Democratic parties in the U.S.? Are they clearly stated on their party web sites? (www.democrats.org, www.gop.com). Do they appeal to you? Are they too vague? Do they omit some important issues? Do they include principles of carefully polling citizen desires and incorporating the results in their philosophies? If not, why do you suppose they omit polling? Do they want authoritarian leadership to define party policy? If so, what dangers might that pose for the nation?

Chapter 29. Dreaming

1. What do you think of brainstorming to imagine an ideal community? Aeronautical engineers brainstorm to create new commercial airplanes. And they carefully solicit desires from potential customers to maximize the chances of designing excellent planes that customers will like and purchase. Should not communities and governments do likewise?

2. Review Sample Questionnaire of Ideal Community items on pages 381-383. Do a 40-minute exercise with a few other friends, classmates, relatives or others. Brainstorm together to create features of an ideal community. Don't criticize. Write down all ideas offered. If you like what you come up with, explore ways to share your plan with others, such as through a letter to the editor of your local newspaper, or to a city committee that focuses on community development. Follow where this leads you. You might end up on a city or county committee. Such committees tend to welcome constructive new members.

Chapter 30. Commencement

1. Has this book inspired you? Have you discussed its ideas with others? Are you inclined to act? Do you know others who

might be? Would you like to talk to them about issues raised in the book or that you have in response?

2. Would you like to have a "place in the choir" of politics? What role would you like to take?

Chapter 31. Epilogue: Commencement Lessons and Discoveries

1. Can you imagine a church denomination starting a chapter of the Common Good Democracy party? If so, how might that happen?

2. Did you find interesting the scientific approach to politics as pursued in this book? Did you know about the long history of the General Social Survey (GSS) that explores and measure public opinion every few years on scores of topics? (www.gss.norc.org) Did you know that the results of such surveys are available free for any researcher to explore, analyze and write and publish research papers on? Do the results of the author's analyses of Oregon and national survey data increase your confidence in his ideas and research findings on smaller, local samples?

3. Columnist Kathleen Parker in Chapter 1 hoped to empower the majority of citizens in the political "middle". Does it surprise you that this middle is twice as big as the two extremes, the "left" and the "right"? Do you think it would be better or worse for the middle to govern politics in a nation? Why? Why not?

4. Which of the actions below are you most inclined to take after reading this book? Discuss your choices with others who have also read it.

   A. Tell others to read it.

   B. Ask a friend or two to read it and then get together with them to discuss it.

   C. Encourage a local elected government official in my community to read it.

D. Write a letter to the editor of my newspaper, telling the community what I thought of the book. (See sample letter, next page.)
E. Go to Amazon and write a review of the book to help others decide whether to read it.
F. Encourage a book club that I'm in to read it.
G. Talk to others about starting a chapter of the Common Good Party.

Here's a sample letter to the editor for your consideration

The recent EgyptAir jetliner loss in the Mediterranean Sea smacks of continuing terrorism, highlighting the futility of our military efforts in the Middle East.

A local successful business owner migrated to the U.S. 30 years ago from his violent childhood homeland in the Middle East. He continues to lose relatives to that military mayhem, recently a cousin by shelling in Aleppo.

He cares deeply about the Middle East and studies it carefully. He believes the religious factions are so numerous and complex that resolution by either conventional or radical military means is impractical.

He believes the only solution is to follow India's example of simply outlawing any religious leader teachings of violence and killing as an expression of religion. Imams got the message in India and radical Muslim violence was prevented.

In the Middle East we've tried to impose resolution with the most powerful military in the world for a dozen years but without success. An informal definition of neurosis is repeating the same unsuccessful behaviors over and over, expecting a different outcome.

Building on our immigrant citizen's ideas, let's make membership in the U.N. very appealing. And require member nations to have constitutions that explicitly prohibit religious-based violence. Violation of this requirement would result in suspension of U.N. benefits until resolved.

Don't like this idea? Then come up with a better one. But don't persist in our militaristic Middle East foreign policy, expecting a different outcome.

That's proving to be as crazy as our violent misadventure in South Vietnam.

—William A. McConochie,
Eugene Register Guard

References

Chapter 1.

1. Parker, Kathleen, Most of us live quietly between the extremes, Register Guard, Eugene, OR, October 17, 2012.
2. Tetlock, P.E. (2005) Expert Political Judgment: How Good is it? How Can We Know? Princeton, Princeton University Press.
3. Eidelson, Roy J. & Eidelson, Judy I., Dangerous Ideas; Five Beliefs That Propel Groups Toward Conflict, American Psychologist, March 2003, Vol. 58, No. 3, 182-192.

Chapter 2.

1. McConochie, W., Government Service Preferences, Publication # 7, Publications Page, Politicalpsychologyresearch.com.

Chapter 3.

None.

Chapter 4.

1. McConochie, W., Political Psychology Research Instrument Manual, Publication #4, Publications Page, Politicalpsychologyresearch.com.

Chapter 5.

1. McConochie, W., Comparing a Two-Factor Theory of Religious Beliefs to a Four Factor Theory of Isms, Publication #35, Publications Page, Politicalpsychologyresearch.com.

Chapter 6.

1. McConochie, W., Publication # 7, Government Service Preferences, Politicalpsychologyresearch.com.

Chapter 7.

1. Register Guard, Eugene's Halls of *Not* Learning, Susan Palmer, Jan 29, 2012, pg. A1.

2. http://money.usnews.com/money/blogs/planning-to-re-tire/2009/09/04/the-biggest-...

3. Zimbardo, Philip, The Lucifer Effect, Understanding How Good People Turn Evil, Random House, New York, 2007.

4. Milgram, Stanley, Obedience to Authority, Perennial Classics, Harper Collins, New York, 2004.

5. Zimbardo, Philip, The Lucifer Effect, Understanding How Good People Turn Evil, pg. x, preface , Random House, New York, 2007.

6. Wall St. Journal, Jan 5, 2012.

Chapter 8.

1. McConochie, W., Publication #29, Publications Page, Politi-calpsychologyresearch.com

Chapter 9.

1. www.numberof.net/number-of-lobbyists-in-washington/ .

2. www.occasionalplanet.org/2011/01/24/military-mystery-how-many-bases-does-the-us-have-anyway.

3. http://nccsdataweb.urban.org;nccs/viPub/index.php, 2006.

Chapter 10.

1. Gilbert, Gustav, The Nuremberg Diary, Farrar, Straus and Company, New York, (1947).

Chapter 11.

1. Simonton, Dean K, Presidential I.Q., Openness, Intellectual Brilliance , and Leadership: Estimates and Correlations for 42 U.S. Chief Executives, *Political Psychology*, Vol 27. No. 4, 2006.

2. Jost, J. (2006). The End of the End of Idelogy. *American Psychologist*, October, Vol. 61, No. 7, 651-670.

3. Jost, J, Glaser, J., Kruglanski, A, & Sulloway, F. (2003), Political Conservatism as Motivated Social Cognition, *Psych. Bulletin*, Vol. 129, No. 3, p 339-75.

4. Jost, J, Nosek, B, & Gosling, S. (2008), Ideology: Its Resurgence in Social, Personality, and Political Psychology. *Perspectives on Psychological Science*, Vol. 3, No. 2, pp 126-136.

5. Jost, J, Federico, Federico, C., & Napier, J, Political Ideology: Its Structure, Functions, and Elective Affinities, *Annu. Rev. Psychol*, 2009, 60:307-37.

Chapter 12.

1. Thornhill, R., Fincher, C., Aran, D., (2009). Parasites, democratization and the liberalization of values across contemporary countries. *Biological Reviews*, 84, 113-131.

2. McConochie, W., Sixty-four Psychological Facets of Conservative and Liberal Worldviews, Politicalpsychologyresearch. com, Publications Page, Publication #30.

3. McConochie, W., Manual: Conservatism / Liberalism Study Questionnaire Scales, Politicalpsychologyresearch.com, Publications Page, Publication #33.

4. McConochie, W., What Liberals and Conservatives Really Think, Publication # 36, Politicalpsychologyresearh.com.

5. McConochie, W., Getting Beyond In-fighting, Publication #37, Politicalpsychologyresearch.com.

Chapter 13.

1. McConochie, W., What Liberals and Conservatives Really Think; Psychological Traits Differentiating Liberal from Conservative Worldviews. Replication study #1, Politicalpsychologyresearch.com, Publications Page, Publication #36.

2. Haidt, J, & Graham, J., When Morality Opposes Justice: Conservatives Have Moral Intuitions that Liberals May Not Recognize, *Social Justice Research*, 2007 DOI: 10.1007/s11211-007-0034-z.

Chapter 14.

1. Chris G. Sibley, Danny Osborne, John Duckitt, Personality and

Political Orientation: Meta-analysis and test of a Threat-Constraint Model, *J. of Research in Personality*, 46,(2012) 664-677).

2. Hatemi, P., Hibbing, J., Medland, S., Keller, M, Alford, J., Smith, K, Martin, N. and Eaves, L., Not by Twins Alone: Using the Extended Family Design to Investigate Genetic Influence on Political Beliefs, *American Journal of Political Science*, Vol 54, No. 3, July 2010, pp 798-814.

3. Hatemi, P, Funk, C. Medland, S., Maes, H. Silberg J., Martin N., and Eaves L., Genetic and Environmental Transmission of Political Attitudes Over a Life Time, *The Journal of Politics*, Vol. 71, No. 3, July 2009, Pp. 1141-1156.

4. Alford, J., Funk, C, and Hibbing J., Are Political Orientations Genetically Transmitted?, Faculty Publications: Political Science, University of Nebraska, Lincoln, 5-1-2005.

5. Kanai, R., Feilden, T, Firth, C and Rees, G., Political Orientations Are Correlated with Brain Structure in Young Adults, *Current Biology*, 21, 677-780, April 26, 2011.

6. Amodio, D, Jost, J., Master, S. and Yee, C., Neurocognitive correlates of liberalism and conservatism, *Nature Neuroscience*, Sep. 2007, Nature Publishing Group, http://www.nature.com/natureneuroscience.

Chapter 15.

1. http://pewresearch.org/assets/pdf/gun-control-2011.pdf.

2. Ricks, Thomas E., The Generals, Penguin Press, 2012.

3. Turse, Nick, Kill Anything That Moves: The Real American War in Vietnam, Holt Henry & Co., 2013.

4. *Science*, Vol. 339, 25 Jan 2013, p 373.

5. VanderBos, Gary R., APA Dictionary of Psychology, APA, Washington, D.C. , 2007.

Chapter 16.

1. Sharp, Gene, *From Dictatorship to Democracy*, Serpent's Tail in London, England (2012).

Chapter 17.

None.

Chapter 18.

1. Marinacci, Barbara and Krishnanmurthy, Ramesh; Linus Pauling on Peace, Rising Star Press, Los Altos, Ca., 1998, page 43.

Chapters 19-21.

None.

Chapter 22.

1. Register-Guard, Dec. 27, 2012, pg. A8.
2. Pamela L. Wible, MD, 3575 Donald St. #220, Eugene, Oregon 97405

Chapter 23.

None.

Chapter 24.

1. McConochie, W., Sixty-four Psychological Facets of Conservative and Liberal Worldviews, Politicalpsychologyresearch. com, Publications Page, Publication #30.
2. McConochie, W., Manual: Conservatism / Liberalism Study Questionnaire Scales, Politicalpsychologyresearch.com, Publications Page, Publication #33.

Chapter 25.

None.

Chapter 26.

1. Register Guard, A7, Feb. 20, 2112.
2.   McConochie, W., Authoritarian Endorsement Scale, Political-psychologyresearch.com, Publications Page, Publication #8.
3. Worldpublicopinion.org, Publics Around the World Call for

Greater Efforts to Address Climate Change, November 30, 2011

Chapters 27-28.

None.

Chapter 29.

1. The Register-Guard, A-1, Jan. 29, 2013 and *Scientific American*, Dec. 2, 2009.
2. www.lymphomahelp.org./SolventsIntro.pdf.
3. www.oeconline.org;resources/publications/factsheetarchive/benzenefactsheet.
4. WSJ, Sat.-Sun., Jan. 19-20, 2013, B1.
5. Keillor, Garrison, Lake Woebegone Days, Penguin Books, N.Y., 1986.

Chapter 30.

None.

Chapter 31.

1. General Social Survey, www3.norc.org/GSS+website/.
2. Brooks, Arthur, "A Formula for Happiness", New York Times, Dec. 13, 2013, Sunday Review, p. 1.
3. McConochie, W., Exploring Psychological Dimensions of Liberal and Conservative Worldviews in National General Social Survey Samples, Politicalpsychologyresearch.com, Publications Page, Publication #39.
4. McConochie, W., Replication of Studies of Liberal and Conservative Worldview Facets; Analysis of Random Sample Data on 1201 Oregonians' Political Opinions, Politicalpsychologyresearch.com, Publications Page, Publication #41.

Belligerent peaceniks, 77–78
Belongingness, 143, 161
Big Five Inventory (BFI) test, 124,
    258
Big Five personality traits
in candidates, 250, 256–258
childhood to adulthood, 81
conservatism, 131–137, 172
emotional stability, 32–33, 81, 95–96,
    122–123, 242–243, 256–258, 272,
    299, 406
executive ethics, 105–108, 268–272
extroversion, 79, 81, 122–123,
    242–243, 256, 258, 272
factor analysis, 121–125
ideal communities, 378–379
in job applicants, 242–243
promotional activism, 79
proportional budgeting systems,
    95–96, 101, 124, 299
special interest group democracy, 114
trait research, 136
warmongering, 32–33, 39, 248
See also Agreeableness; Conscien-
    tiousness; Openness
Bill of Rights, 48
Blagojevich, Rod, 41
Brooks, Arthur, 397
Bush, George W., 34, 39–41, 104, 118,
    130, 250
Business Activity Preference and
    Management tests, 258

C
Campaign financing, 12–13, 88, 109,
    200, 240, 268, 275
Candidates, for political office
authoritarianism, 39, 268–272
Big Five personality traits, 250,
    256–258
Common Good Party, 204, 207, 223,
    238–251, 290, 332–333
constructive leadership traits,
    252–261, **262–267**

degrading opponents, 64, 156, 351,
    358-359
executive ethics, 267–273
lying and conniving, 195, 358
polling, 204
power oligarchy, 153
selection and grooming, 12–13,
    238–243, 255
special interest groups, 255
warmongering, 34, 38–39, 42–43,
    244, 250–251
Census questionnaires, 67–68, 70
Charitable giving, 79, 119, 228, 268
Charters, 80, 103
Childhood abuse, 70–71
Childhood/adulthood trait consis-
    tencies, 71–73, 74–77, 81, 134,
    138, 180
Citizen authority, 144–145, 155,
    346–347
Citizen ethics, 300–303
Citizens United Supreme Court deci-
    sion, 113–114
Civilian violence management,
    144–145, 159, 161, 257, 331,
    338–341, 363
Civility promotion, 144, 153, 188
Claustrophobia, 31, 184
Climate change, 281, 283, 285–286,
    297, 300, 318, 340
Closed to help, 20, 22, 37
Colbert, Stephen, 4, 11
Collateral damage, 190–191
Committees, 210–221, 222–229,
    230–237
Common good concern, 86–87,
    89–92, 97–98, 106–108, 267–272
Common good democracy endorse-
    ment, 105, 119, 151, 268–272,
    332–333
Common Good Party
basic structure and function,
    210–221
candidates, 204, 207, 223, 238–251,

www.ingramcontent.com/pod-product-compliance
Lightning Source LLC
Chambersburg PA
CBHW051431250726
48655CB00001B/5